UNIT 32
PROFESSIONAL ETHICS

AAT Diploma Pathway

British Library Cataloguing-in-Publication Data

A catalogue record for this book is available from the British Library.

Published by
Kaplan Publishing UK
Unit 2, The Business Centre
Molly Millars Lane
Wokingham
Berkshire
RG41 2QZ

ISBN 978-1-84710-825-8

The text in this material and any others made available by any Kaplan Group company does not amount to advice on a particular matter and should not be taken as such. No reliance should be placed on the content as the basis for any investment or other decision or in connection with any advice given to third parties. Please consult your appropriate professional adviser as necessary. Kaplan Publishing Limited and all other Kaplan group companies expressly disclaim all liability to any person in respect of any losses or other claims, whether direct, indirect, incidental, consequential or otherwise arising in relation to the use of such materials.

Printed and bound in Great Britain.

We are grateful to the Association of Accounting Technicians for permission to reproduce past assessment materials. The solutions have been prepared by Kaplan Publishing.

CONTENTS

CONTENTS

WORKBOOK

PREFACE

STUDY TEXT

The study text is written in a practical and interactive style:
- key terms and concepts are clearly defined
- frequent practice activities throughout the chapters ensure that what you have learnt is regularly reinforced

WORKBOOK

The workbook comprises two main elements:

A question bank of key techniques to give additional practice and reinforce the work covered in each chapter. The questions are divided into their relevant chapters and students may either attempt these questions as they work through the study text, or leave some or all of these until they have completed the study text as a sort of final revision of what they have studied.

Practice simulations.

STANDARDS OF COMPETENCE

Unit commentary

The Professional Ethics unit requires the candidate to provide evidence of their ability to demonstrate the ethical duties and responsibilities necessary and the knowledge required to underpin ethical practice in this sector.

The unit has been developed using the existing AAT Guidelines on Professional Ethics (based upon principles approved by the International Federation of Accountants, IFAC). From this basis, the key components have been extracted and assimilated to reflect the most critical requirements for professional conduct and competence in this field.

The Professional Ethics unit is not designed to replicate the ethical requirements detailed by the professional sponsoring bodies of the AAT. However, it provides a sound basis for progression in application of ethics and related knowledge and understanding required of students at the higher level.

In addition to the specific learning outcomes for this unit, the ethics subject matter forms an ideal basis for developing the candidate's communication skills, at a level sufficient to provide a smoother progression for candidates from level 3 to level 4. The AAT National Archive Forum identified recently that candidates' communication skills were an area that could benefit from further enhancement to provide a smoother transition to level 4. This unit also provides an ideal forum to develop critical decision making skills.
The unit can be taken at either level 3 or level 4.

Elements contained within this unit are:

Element: 32.1
Apply general principles and procedures for ethical compliance expected within the accounting sector

Element: 32.2
Develop, maintain and apply ethics in employer / employee situations

Element: 32.3
Develop, maintain and apply ethics in public practice

Knowledge and Understanding

To perform this unit effectively you will need to know and understand:

		Chapter
1	The guidelines of your professional body, including professional liability and negligence	
2	A principle based approach to professional ethics.	
3	Legal considerations: UK or own country with particular consideration of:	Through out
·	The common types of fraud	
·	Ownership of records,	
·	Lien : retention of books and other documentation.	

Element 32.1 Apply general principles and procedures for ethical compliance expected within the accounting sector

Performance Criteria
In order to perform this element successfully you need to:

		Chapter
A	Identify and apply the fundamental principles of honesty and integrity.	1
B	Highlight situations within professional work that require objectivity and fairness, and where judgements and actions could compromise personal or organisational integrity and reputation.	1
C	Recognise the principles of effective Continuing Professional Development (CPD) to maintain professional and technical competence (to include sources of advice and information outside formal learning).	4
D	Recognise and explain why certain types of information should be regarded as confidential.	1,2,3
E	Identify circumstances when it would be appropriate to disclose confidential information.	1
F	Identify the key issues which ensure professional services are performed within the scope of professional ethics guidance.	1,2,3
G	Make critical decisions to identify appropriate ethical behaviour when interacting with others in a variety of circumstances.	1,2,3
H	Refer and seek advise from relevant sources for issues beyond own professional competence.	1,2,4
I	Describe the types of contractual obligations you would have in providing services to clients to include due care and carrying out assignments within a reasonable timescale.	1
J	Discuss, agree and resolve any ethical conflict.	1,2

Range Statement
Performance in this element relates to the following contexts:
Fundamental principles:

· Integrity

· Objectivity

· Professional and technical competence

KAPLAN PUBLISHING

- Due care
- Confidentiality
- Professional behaviour

Professional work situations:
- Provision of services as self-employed
- Preparation of financial statements for client or own organisation
- Performance of internal audit services
- Provision of financial management services
- Acceptance of gifts

Professional services:
- Taxation
- VAT calculations
- Financial management consultancy

Sources of information for CPD:
- The internet
- Professional journals
- Professional body network opportunities
- Organisational /company training updates

Confidential information & disclosure:
- Basic duties
- Usage
- Non disclosure and disclosure (when expressly authorised by client, or legal, regulatory or professional body)

Contractual:
- Nature of service/contract (to include performance and responsibilities by whom, for whom, by when, fees, due care, ownership and lien)

Organisational:
- Inland Revenue
- Customs and Excise
- Client organisations
- Employer
- Professional bodies

Communication and personal skills:
- Communication with peers, superiors, clients, external bodies and agencies, and including specifically skills of negotiation, critical decision making, discussion, letter and report writing

Element 32.2 Develop, maintain and apply ethics in employer / employee situations

Performance Criteria

In order to perform this element successfully you need to:

		Chapter
A	Describe the type of culture within organisations which supports and promotes high ethical values and helps resolve any conflict of loyalties.	5
B	Resolve conflicting loyalties where an employer may ask you to perform tasks which are illegal, unethical or against the rules or standards of the accounting profession.	5
C	Follow appropriate procedures where you believe an employer has or will commit an act which you believe to be illegal or unethical	5
D	Respond appropriately to requests to work outside the confines of your own professional experience and expertise.	5

Range Statement

Performance in this element relates to the following contexts:

Cultural values:

- Openness
- Trust
- Integrity
- Respect
- Empowerment
- Accountability

Procedures:

- Seek confidential independent or professional counselling and advice
- Keep accurate records of meetings/discussions,
- Persuade employer not to perpetrate action
- Advise client of ethical and legal considerations
- 'Enforced' resignation

Acts (illegal or unethical):

- Fraud
- Other illegal activity
- Falsification of records
- Supply of information or statements which are misleading, false, or deceptive
- Client influence
- Employer influence
- Actions of delegated staff

Performance in this element relates to professional conduct with: peers, employers, superiors and subordinates.

KAPLAN PUBLISHING

Element 32.3 Develop, maintain and apply ethics in public practice

		Chapter
A	Prepare appropriate letters of engagement and develop and implement a fair fees policy for your professional services.	6
B	Identify and explain how specific situations can undermine professional independence.	6
C	Prepare a policy to be followed for handling clients monies.	6
D	Maintain independence and objectivity and impartiality in a range of circumstances.	6
E	Make recommendations for a policy statement in relation to a client wishing to change accountant.	6
F	Identify scope of professional liability.	6
G	Prepare clear guidelines which should be followed to advertise your accounting services in a professional and ethical manner	6
H	Give advice to clients on retention of books, working papers and other documents.	6

Range Statement
Performance in this element relates to the following contexts:
Specific situations & professional independence:

- Simultaneous engagement in other related business
- Ownership or interest in client's companies
- Personal and family relationships
- Agency commission

Recommendations to policy on performing recurring work for a client:

- Which has or is being currently undertaken by another professional advisor, in relation to instructions by another advisor who is taking work over that you are currently performing for a client

Performance in this element can relate to the following contexts of Self Employment: Accounting Services Work assignments such as taxation, reporting, accounting services, and advertising of such services.

ETHICS – PRINCIPLES AND PROCEDURES

INTRODUCTION

This unit is broken down into three elements. The first element is essentially general in nature and is intended to set the scene for the standards of professional behaviour expected from an accounting technician. In this chapter we set out what is required of an individual to demonstrate a professional commitment to working within the fundamental acceptable principles of honesty, integrity, objectivity, professional and technical competence, due care, confidentiality and professional behaviour and within the overall scope of the latest AAT guidance on ethics.

CONTENTS

1 Business ethics
2 Fundamental principles
3 Professional work situations
4 Professional services

PERFORMANCE CRITERIA

- Identify and apply the fundamental principles of honesty and integrity (32.1 A)
- Highlight situations within professional work that require objectivity and fairness, and where judgements and actions could compromise personal or organisational integrity and reputation Performance criteria (32.1 B)
- Recognise and explain why certain types of information should be regarded as confidential (32.1 D)
- Identify circumstances when it would be appropriate to disclose confidential information (32.1 E)
- Identify the key issues which ensure professional services are performed within the scope of professional ethics guidance (32.1 F)
- Make critical decisions to identify appropriate ethical behaviour when interacting with others in a variety of circumstances. (32.1 G)
- Refer and seek advice from relevant sources for issues beyond own professional competence (32.1 H)
- Describe the types of contractual obligations you would have in providing services to clients to include due care and carrying out assignments within a reasonable timescale (32.1 I)
- Discuss, agree and resolve any ethical conflict (32.1 J)

1   Business ethics

1.1 Introduction

The word 'ethics' comes from the Greek word 'ethos' relating to the study of standards of right and wrong: that part of science and philosophy dealing with moral conduct, duty, and judgement. Ethics deals with voluntary actions taken by an individual with sufficient knowledge of the options available to him or her. It can be described as:

· the discipline dealing with what is good and bad and with moral duty and obligation
· a set of moral principles or values
· a theory or system of moral values and the principles of conduct governing an individual or a group
· a guiding philosophy, generally accepted standards of right and wrong.

1.2 Business ethics

Business ethics is not a separate area of interest in its own right. There is no separate 'business ethic' that puts it beyond the range of moral judgements. Business ethics is the application of ethical principles to the problems typically encountered in a business setting.

> **□ DEFINITION**
>
> Donaldson in Key Issues in Business Ethics, describes **business ethics** as 'the systematic study of moral matters pertaining to business, industry or related activities, institutions or practices and beliefs'.

Business ethics is concerned with the expectations of society, fair competition, advertising, social responsibilities and corporate behaviour (at home, as well as abroad), with how individuals interact with each other and with how organisations ought to relate to their external stakeholders and the community as a whole.

1.3 The 'stakeholder' approach

The 'stakeholder' approach suggests that corporate objectives, are, or ought to be, shaped and influenced by the collective pressures of those internal and external organisations or coalitions of people that have sufficient involvement or interest in the company's operational activities.

An organisation provides goods and services for the community and uses raw material and labour and also makes use of other facilities such as the laws, which protect it. No management can ignore the environment in which it operates and the success of organisations may depend to a large extent upon their public image. The attitude of the organisation to its employees forms part of this image.

The company is responsible to subscribers of capital, e.g. shareholders who allow their money to be used by a company, as they are entitled to a fair reward for the use of their capital and the risk involved. If such obligations are not honoured, future capital would be harder to obtain and unemployment may result.

Consumers have a right not to be exploited by an organisation that depends upon the community in many ways. Legislation, e.g. on resale price maintenance and monopolies, has shown that the government adopts the attitude that companies must act in the public interest. Management therefore cannot avoid the fact that its responsibility for industrial and commercial direction is mainly its responsibility to society.

Managers face ethical issues all the time. Examples are:
· dealing with direct and indirect demands for bribes and attempts at extortion
· situations of unfair competition
· expectations of social responsibility in relation to society and the environment
· demand for safety and compliance with legislative standards in relation to products and production
· marketing policies – should they avoid manufacturing products detrimental to health, e.g. cigarettes, weapons
· policies that imply social costs, e.g. pollution of rivers – the organisation reduces its costs by pumping waste into rivers and this involves social costs in clearing the rivers
· the relations which an organisation should have with political parties
· whether or not to export to particular countries.

Those who are interested in business ethics examine various kinds of business activities and ask, 'is the conduct ethically right or wrong?

1.4 Typical issues in business ethics

When values get twisted and careers go off the rails, the impact can be enormous. Ethics and ethical standards have thus become the focus of greater attention by organisations, especially in the realm of reputation management. Greater emphasis is now placed on accountability, ethics, codes of conduct and monitoring and reporting of violations.

Some typical issues addressed in business ethics include:
· accounting and financial standards, and 'creative accounting'
· advertising deception
· data and privacy
· bribery and kickbacks
· business intelligence and industrial espionage
· political contributions
· corporate governance, including hostile takeovers, fiduciary responsibility and shareholder rights issues
· corporate crime, including insider trading, price fixing and price discrimination

- competitive disinformation
- employee issues, such as rights, duties and professional conduct discrimination
- whistle blowing
- environmental issues and related social concerns
- marketing, sales and negotiation techniques
- product issues such as patent and copyright infringement, planned obsolescence, product liability and product defects.

1.5 Ethics at four levels

Ethical issues regarding business and public-sector organisations exist at four levels:
- macro level
- corporate level
- group level
- individual level.

(a) At the **macro level**, there are issues about the role of business in the national and international organisation of society. These are largely concerned with the relative virtues of different political/social systems, such as free enterprise, centrally planned economies, etc. There are also important issues of international relationships and the role of business on an international scale.

Ethical standards differ, particularly among nations and societies. This can cause great concern when managers are working in a foreign country. For example, in some countries it is normal to make payments to expedite business transactions – indeed, in many cases such payments to ensure the landing of a particular contract are considered a desirable and accept-able way of doing business – but this may be considered a bribe in other countries.

(b) At the **corporate level**, the issue is often referred to as corporate social responsibility and is focused on the ethical issues facing individual corporate entities (private and public sector) when formulating and implementing strategies.

(c) At the **group level** there are issues affecting particular professional and other groups within an organisation.

(d) At the **individual level**, the issue concerns the behaviour and actions of individuals within organisations.

1.6 Approaches to business ethics

There are two approaches to managing ethics; one is compliance-based and the other is integrity-based. They are both different in terms of objectives, activities, standards and ethos, as well as other areas.

- A **compliance-based approach** is designed to ensure that the organisation complies with the relevant law. Compliance means doing what one must do, because it ought to be done. It is reflected where the activities develop standards, train and communicate, handle reports of misconduct, investigate, enforce, oversee compliance and where the behavioural assumption is that people are solitary self-interested beings. Any violations are prevented, detected and punished.

·   An **integrity-based approach** enables legal and responsible conduct. It emphasises managerial responsibility for ethical behaviour, as well as a concern for the law. Integrity means wanting what ought to be done.

An integrity policy rests on the following principles:

·   application of the same ethical and professional principles in all dealings
·   respect for laws and regulations and advancement of a climate of transparency
·   creation of confidence relationships with clients, members of staff and shareholders
·   definition of a policy on the prevention of fraud or any other abuse of assets, systems, information or procedures
·   adopting an honest mode of conduct, in particular when dealing with information or financial transactions.

1.7 Ethical obligations

Each of us has our own set of values and beliefs that we have evolved over the course of our lives through our education, experiences and upbringing. We all have our own ideas of what is right and what is wrong and these ideas can vary between individuals and cultures.

There are five factors that affect ethical obligations.

(i)   **The law** – this defines the minimum ethical standards in a given area of practice. For example, deceptive advertising is illegal and violators of this law are liable to large fines, court action and/or loss of goodwill. Some unethical behaviour is often not considered illegal, such as head hunting employees from other companies, padding expense accounts, etc.

(ii) **Government regulations** – these are also fairly clear-cut outlining what is acceptable and what is not. These regulations set standards on issues such as unfair competition, unsafe products, etc. Failure to comply with these regulations could lead to criminal charges, or fines etc. Unfortunately, there are times when these regulations do not force ethical behaviour. In the U.S. cyclamates (artificial sweeteners) were banned because there was evidence that they were carcinogenic. Following the ban a major food manufacturer sold 300,000 cases of cyclamate sweetened food overseas. Similarly many banned food additives and pesticides etc are being sold overseas, mainly to third world countries.

(iii) **Industry and company ethical codes** – are codes that clearly state the ethical standard an employee should follow within his or her organisation. These standard practices are usually followed if they are written down and the rules enforced, however many companies have 'unwritten' codes of practice or if written down, have no method of enforcing these rules. Generally, written codes clarify the ethical issues but leave the resolution to the individual's conscience.

(iv) **Social pressures**

(v) **Tension between personal standards and the goals of the organisation** – we can refer back to the example involving the sale of banned substances

overseas. It is not illegal, but it may be against your personal values to sell these products to unsuspecting overseas clients. What would you do if this action were a direct order from a superior? Does this take away your responsibility? As with many ethical problems there are no easy answers.

1.8 Benefits of managing ethics in the workplace

Many people are used to reading or hearing of the moral benefits of attention to business ethics. However, there are other types of benefits, as well. The following list describes various types of benefits from managing ethics in the workplace.

Consideration of business ethics has substantially improved society. A matter of decades ago, children in our country worked 16-hour days. Workers' limbs were torn off and disabled workers were condemned to poverty and often to starvation. Trusts controlled some markets to the extent that prices were fixed and small businesses choked out. Price fixing crippled normal market forces. Employees were sacked based on personalities. Influence was applied through intimidation and harassment. Then society reacted and demanded that businesses place high value on fairness and equal rights. Government agencies were established. Unions were organised. Laws and regulations were established.

Ethics programmes cultivate strong teamwork and productivity. They align employee behaviour with top priority ethical values preferred by leaders of the organisation. Usually, an organisation finds surprising disparity between its preferred values and the values actually reflected by behaviour in the work-place. Ongoing attention and dialogue regarding values in the workplace builds openness, integrity and community – critical ingredients of strong teams in the workplace. Employees feel strong alignment between their values and those of the organisation. They react with strong motivation and performance.

Ethics programmes help ensure that policies are legal. It is far better to incur the cost of mechanisms to ensure ethical practices now than to incur costs of litigation later. A major intent of well-designed personnel policies is to ensure ethical treatment of employees, e.g. in matters of hiring, evaluating, disciplining, firing, etc.

Ethics programmes promote a strong public image. Attention to ethics is also good for public relations – admittedly, managing ethics should not be done primarily for reasons of public relations. But, frankly, the fact that an organisation regularly gives attention to its ethics can portray a strong positive to the public. People see those organisations as valuing people more than profit, as striving to operate with the utmost of integrity. Aligning behaviour with values is critical to effective marketing and public relations programmes.

2 Fundamental principles

2.1 Code of ethical conduct

A code is a statement of policies, principles or rules that guide behaviour. Codes of ethics do not only apply to organisations but should guide the behaviour of people in everyday life. Most of us operate with a more or less well defined set of ethical values, principles or rules of thumb that guide decision-making. They are seldom spelled out explicitly in a list but if you had to make a list, it would probably include:

· obey the law
· be fair
· avoid harming others
· prevent harm to others
· respect the right of others
· help those in need
· do not lie or cheat.

Codes of ethical conduct have existed for many years in a number of professions and organisations. Their purpose is to guide managers and members of professional institutes in their behaviour as they perform their tasks. Carefully drawn up codes can also reassure customers, suppliers and even competitors of the integrity of the organisation. Because of recent governmental and business scandals, there has been increased public interest in the existence and use of such ethical codes.

Codes of ethic are usually general statements that are abstract, and are prescriptions for what a person's values should be, rather than descriptions of what they actually are. They are typically statements of principle with which few would disagree.

However, simply stating a code of conduct (or ethics) is not enough. The organisation should appoint an ethics committee, consisting of internal and external directors, to institutionalise ethical behaviour. The duties of the committee must be to:

· hold regular meetings to discuss ethical issues;
· deal with 'grey' areas;
· communicate the code to all members of the organisation;
· check for possible violations of the code;
· enforce the code;
· reward compliance and punish violations;
· review and update the code.

2.2 Principle-based approach to professional ethics

As members of a profession, AAT members have a duty to observe the highest standard of conduct and integrity.

In order to achieve the objectives of the accountancy profession, the AAT guidelines on professional ethics set standards of conduct for professional accountants and state the fundamental principles that must be observed.

(a) **Integrity** – a professional accountant should be straightforward and honest in performing professional services.
(b) **Objectivity** – a professional accountant should be fair and should not allow prejudice or bias or the influence of others to override objectivity.

(c) **Professional and technical competence** – a professional accountant should refrain from undertaking or continuing assignments for which they are not competent to carry out unless advice and assistance is obtained to ensure that the assignment is carried out satisfactorily. All assignments should be undertaken with respect for legal and regulatory requirements.

(d) **Due care** – a professional accountant having accepted an assignment has an obligation to carry it out with due care and reasonable despatch having regard to the nature and scope of the assignment.

(e) **Confidentiality** – a professional accountant should respect the confidentiality of information acquired during the course of performing professional services. He or she should not use or disclose any such information without proper and specific authority or unless there is a legal or professional right or duty to disclose.

(f) **Professional behaviour** – a professional accountant should act in a manner consistent with the good reputation of the profession and refrain from any conduct that might bring discredit to it.

The fundamental principles have been used to develop a 'framework' or principle-based approach to professional ethics to make decisions based on principles rather than using a system of rules and regulations. It means making ethical decisions based on the fundamental principles outlined i.e., integrity, objectivity, professional and technical competence, due care, confidentiality and professional behaviour. Members are guided as to which threats they might encounter and which safeguards they might put in place to combat them. This analysis by way of threats and safeguards assists members in deciding the proper course of action.

A principle based approach needs to consider the process of enquiry and how judgement on an issue is reached. It means that you look at the objective that is to be achieved and focus on that objective. Alternatively, a rule-based approach means that you apply the rule exactly as stated regardless of the circumstances (i.e. literally).

The AAT Guidelines assume that unless a limitation is specifically stated the objectives and fundamental principles are equally valid for all members, whether they are in industry, commerce, the public sector, public practice or education.

2.3 Integrity

Principles, values, standards, morality, integrity, honesty, honour, mores, conscience and decency are words we think of when we think of ethics.

A professional accountant should be straightforward and honest in performing professional services. He or she should not be party to the falsification of any record or knowingly or recklessly supply any information or make any statement that is misleading, false or deceptive.

> **□ DEFINITION** □□□□
>
> **Integrity** implies not merely honesty but fair dealing and truthfulness. A member's advice and work must be uncorrupted by self-interest and not be influenced by the interests of other parties.

To maintain integrity, members have the following responsibilities:

Unethical and dishonest behaviour (and its legal consequences) creates powerful negative public relations within the profession, the wider community and the organisation itself. You should abide by the law and regulations in the area of your responsibility and remember that, as well as legal documents, letters and verbal agreements may constitute a binding arrangement. Promises may not be legally binding but repeatedly going back on them can destroy trust, break relationships and lose co-operation. At all times you should strive to be fair and socially responsible and respect cultural differences when dealing with overseas colleagues or contacts.

As a member of the accounting profession, you are expected to present financial information fully, honestly and professionally and so that it will be understood in its context.

Financial information should describe clearly the true nature of business transactions, assets and liabilities. It should classify and record entries in a timely and proper manner. Members should do everything that is within their powers to ensure that this is the case, and in particular that such information is in accordance with accepted accounting standards.

2.4 Objectivity

> **□ DEFINITION** □□□□
>
> **Objectivity** is a combination of impartiality, intellectual honesty and a freedom from conflicts of interest.

It is defined as 'the state of mind which has regard to all considerations relevant to the task in hand but no other. It is sometimes described as **independence of mind** – the state of mind that permits the provision of an opinion without being affected by influences that compromise professional judgement, allowing an individual to act with integrity and exercise objectivity and professional scepticism. **Independence of appearance** is the avoidance of facts and circumstances that are so significant that a reasonable and informed third party, having knowledge of all relevant information, would reasonably conclude that a firm's or a member's integrity, objectivity or professional scepticism had been compromised.

Objectivity is a distinguishing feature of the profession. Members have a responsibility to:
· Communicate information fairly and objectively.
· Disclose fully all-relevant information that could reasonably be expected to influence an intended user's understanding of the reports, comments, and recommendations presented.

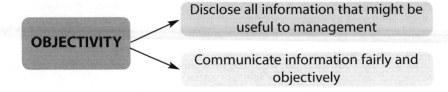

Whatever capacity members serve in, they should demonstrate their objectivity in varying circumstances. Those who are self-employed undertake professional services. Others as employees prepare financial statements, perform internal audit services and serve in financial management capacities in the accountancy profession, industry, commerce, public sector and education. Some may also educate and train those who aspire to admission to the AAT.

Threats to objectivity can be general in nature or relate to the specific circumstances of an engagement or appointment.

General categories of threats to objectivity include the following:
· **The self-interest threat** – a threat to a member's integrity or objectivity may stem from a financial or other self-interest conflict. This could arise, for example, from a direct or indirect interest in a client or from fear of losing an engagement or having his or her employment terminated or as a consequence of undue commercial pressure from within or outside the firm.
· **The self-review threat** – there will be a threat to objectivity if any product or judgement of the member or the firm needs to be challenged or re-evaluated by him or her subsequently.
· **The advocacy threat** – there is a threat to a member's objectivity if he or she becomes an advocate for or against the position taken by the client or employer in any adversarial proceedings or situation. The degree to which this presents a threat to objectivity will depend on the individual circumstances. The presentation of only one side of the case may be compatible with objectivity provided that it is accurate and truthful.
· **The familiarity or trust threat** – is a threat that the member may become influenced by his or her
   – knowledge of the issue
   – relationship with the client or employer
   – judgement of the qualities of the client or employer to the extent that he or she becomes too trusting.

· **The intimidation threat** – the possibility that the member may become intimidated by threat, by a dominating personality, or by other pressures, actual or feared, applied by the client or employer or by another.

Each of the categories of threat may arise in relation to the member's own person or in relation to a connected person e.g. a family member or partner or person who is close for some other reason, for instance by reason of a past or present association, obligation or indebtedness.

Where members decide to accept or continue an engagement in a situation where any significant threat to objectivity has been identified, they should be able to demonstrate that they have considered the availability and effectiveness of safeguards and have reasonably concluded that those safeguards will adequately preserve their objectivity.

2.5 Professional and technical competence

Professions such as accounting are generally highly organised; they have definitive minimum standards of admission; they regulate the activities of their members, in terms of both skilled practice and ethical conduct; they promote the advancement of knowledge and they encourage the formulation of standards.

In agreeing to provide professional services, a professional accountant implies that there is a level of competence necessary to perform those services and that his or her knowledge, skill and experience will be applied with reasonable care and diligence.

Professional accountants must therefore refrain from performing any services that they are not competent to carry out unless appropriate advice and assistance is obtained to ensure that the services are performed satisfactorily. Members have a responsibility to:
· Maintain an appropriate level of professional competence by ongoing development of their knowledge and skills.
· Maintain technical and ethical standards in areas relevant to their work through continuing professional development.
· Perform their professional duties in accordance with relevant laws, regulations, and technical standards.
· Prepare complete and clear reports and recommendations after appropriate analyses of relevant and reliable information.

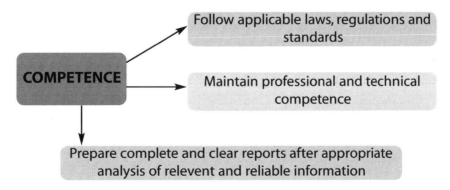

Professional competence may be divided into two separate phases:

1 Attainment of professional competence – this requires specific education, training, assessment or examination in professionally relevant subjects and, whether prescribed or not, a period of relevant work experience in finance or accountancy.

2 Maintenance of professional competence – this requires a continuing awareness and application of developments in the accountancy profession including relevant national and international pronouncements on accounting, auditing and other relevant regulations and statutory requirements. To achieve this, a programme of a minimum of 30 hours continuing professional development (CPD) is recommended each year.

Members should adopt review procedures that will ensure the quality of their professional work is consistent with national and international pronouncements that are issued from time to time.

2.6 Due care

> ☐ **DEFINITION** ☐☐☐☐
>
> The standard of **'due care'** is that level of diligence which a prudent and competent person would exercise under a given set of circumstances. It applies to an individual who professes to exercise a special skill and requires the individual to exercise that skill to a level commonly possessed by practitioners of that speciality.

Due professional care applies to the exercise of professional judgement in the conduct of work performed and implies that the professional approaches matters requiring professional judgement with proper diligence

2.7 Confidentiality

> ☐ **DEFINITION** ☐☐☐☐
>
> **Confidentiality** is the keeping of information, given 'in confidence' to particular parties, between these parties; not disclosing information to those not authorised to have access to it.

However, confidentiality is not only a matter of disclosure of information. It also requires that anyone acquiring information in the course of performing his or her work will not use that information for personal advantage or for the advantage of a third party.

Members should:

· be prudent in the use and protection of information acquired in the course of their duties. Please note that the duty of confidentiality continues even after the end of the relationship between the member and the employer or client.

· not use information for any personal gain or in any manner that would be contrary to the law or detrimental to the legitimate and ethical objectives of the organisation.

KAPLAN PUBLISHING

· inform subordinates as appropriate regarding the confidentiality of information acquired in the course of their work and monitor their activities to assure the maintenance of that confidentiality.

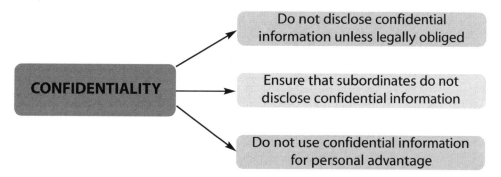

It is in the interest of the public and the profession that the profession's standards relating to confidentiality be defined and guidance given on the nature and extent of the duty of confidentiality and the circumstances in which disclosure of information acquired during the course of providing professional services shall be permitted or required. It should be recognised, however, that confidentiality of information is part of statute or common law and that detailed ethical requirements will depend on the law of the country in which services are performed, e.g., in the UK the contract of employment stipulates that all employees have a duty not to disclose confidential information. Personal details of employees are confidential under the Data Protection Act.

Examples of the points that should be considered in determining the extent to which confidential information may be disclosed are:
· when authorisation to disclose is given by the client or the employer, all the parties whose interests might be affected should be considered
· when the law specifically requires disclosure, it could lead to a member producing documents or giving evidence in the course of legal proceedings and disclosing to the appropriate public authorities infringements of the law. A particular example of the latter situation is in relation to money laundering.

Confidentiality and money laundering legislation
There are two pieces of anti-money laundering legislation:
· the Proceeds of Crime Act 2002
· the Money Laundering Regulations 2003.

Money laundering now includes possessing, or in any way dealing with, or concealing, the proceeds of any crime. It also involves similar activities relating to terrorist funds, which include funds that are likely to be used for terrorism, as well as the proceeds of terrorism.

The regulations apply to all companies whenever a business relationship is to be established, e.g. 'when an account is to be opened or a one-off transaction or series of linked transactions amounting to 15,000 Euros or more is to be carried out. An example of the types of business this will affect is car dealers and auctioneers who the regulations refer to as 'high value dealers'.

The 2003 Regulations mean that business have to:
- establish internal systems and procedures to prevent money laundering and report suspicious activity to the Serious Organised Crime Agency (SOCA)
- establish adequate customer identification procedures
- raise awareness through employee training to ensure the detection of suspicious activities
- ensure adequate record keeping.

▷ **ACTIVITY 1**   ▷ ▷ ▷ ▷

You visit a client who is a dealer in sports cars. He sells one of his cars to a customer for £16,000 and the customer offers to pay in cash.

Outline the rule-based approach and the principle-based approach in this case.

[Answer on p.22]

2.8   Professional behaviour

A profession is distinguished by certain characteristics including:
- mastery of a particular intellectual skill, acquired by training and education;
- adherence by its members to a common code of values and conduct established by its administrating body, including maintaining an outlook which is essentially objective; and
- acceptance of a duty to society as a whole (usually in return for restrictions in use of a title or in the granting of a qualification).

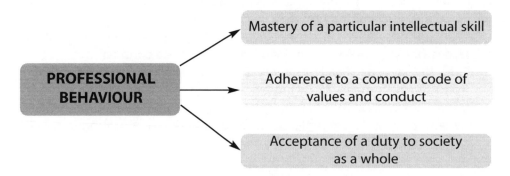

The objectives of the accountancy profession are to work to the highest standards of professionalism, to attain the highest levels of performance and generally to meet the public interest requirement. These objectives require four basic needs to be met:

(i)   **Credibility** – there is a need for credibility in information and information systems.

(ii) **Professionalism** – there is a need to be clearly identified by employers, clients and other interested parties as a professional person in the accountancy field.

(iii) **Quality of services** – assurance is needed that all services obtained from a professional accountant are carried out to the highest standards of performance.

(iv) **Confidence** – users of the services of professional accountants should be able to feel confident that there is a framework of professional ethics to govern the provision of services.

The most important privilege conferred on professionals is the right to a 'professional opinion.' Professionals can be distinguished from others in society by their right to form an opinion and to base their services and/or products on this opinion. Misuse of this privilege can result in serious harm, thus it is only granted to those who are able to show by education and experience the ability to properly exercise this right.

What is understood by the term 'professionalism' will depend on the context and culture of the organisation.

It should include:

Professional/client relationship:
- the client presumes his or her needs will be met without having to direct the process
- the professional decides which services are actually needed and provides them
- the professional is trusted not to exploit his or her authority for unreasonable profit or gain.

· **Professional courtesy** – this is a bare minimum requirement of all business communication.

· **Expertise** – professionalism implies a level of competence that justifies financial remuneration. Incompetence is bad PR. The professional will work out what range and standard of performance people are reasonably entitled to expect, and ensure that it can be achieved.

▷ ACTIVITY 2

When it comes to ethical principles, discussions often reveal that many employees think it is:

· acceptable to borrow money from the petty cash system if they have access (or their friends have access) and they are short of cash

· fine to browse the Internet or use the work telephone for unlimited numbers of personal calls

· quite appropriate to take a 'sickie' if they need a day off

· fun to invent a good story for being late or going early, and

· quite in order to use work materials and tools for personal use.

Which of the fundamental principles is being flouted in these examples?

[Answer on p. 22]

---

3 Professional work situations

Members serve in many different capacities and should demonstrate their objectivity in varying circumstances. Members in practice undertake professional services. Other members as employees prepare financial statements, perform internal audit services and serve in financial management capacities in the accountancy profession, industry, commerce, public sector and education. Members also educate and train those who aspire to admission to the AAT.

3.1 Responsibility to the public

A professional accountant's responsibility is not exclusively to satisfy the needs of an individual client or employer. A distinguishing mark of a profession is acceptance of its responsibility to the public. The accountancy profession's public consists of employers, creditors, clients, governments, employees, investors, the business and financial community and others who rely on its objectivity and integrity to maintain the orderly functioning of commerce. For example:

- financial managers serve in various financial management capacities in organisations and contribute to the efficient and effective use of the organisation's resources
- internal auditors provide assurance about a sound internal control system which enhances the reliability of the external financial information of the employer
- independent auditors help to maintain the integrity and efficiency of the financial statements presented to financial institutions in partial support for loans and to shareholders for obtaining capital
- tax experts help to establish confidence and efficiency in, and the fair application of, the tax system
- management consultants have a responsibility toward the public interest in advocating sound management decision-making.

This reliance imposes a public interest responsibility on the accountancy profession.

□ DEFINITION

The **public interest** is defined as the collective well being of the community of people and institutions the professional accountant serves.

Professional accountants can remain in this advantageous position only by continuing to provide these services at a level that demonstrates that public confidence is firmly founded. It is in the best interest of the accountancy profession to make known to users that the services it provides are executed at the highest level of performance and in accordance with ethical requirements set to ensure such performance.

3.2 Provision of services as self-employed

In addition to the fundamental principles above, professional accountants in public practice should be free of any interest which might be regarded, whatever its actual effect, as being incompatible with integrity, objectivity and independence.

Members of the AAT who provide accounting, taxation or related consultancy services on a self-employed basis in the UK must register on the scheme for self-employed members and comply with the Guidelines and Regulations for Self-employed members.

Unless appropriately authorised by a regulatory body established under statutory authority, members may not perform the following functions in the UK:

- external audit of UK limited companies
- external audit of other bodies that require the services of a registered auditor
- activities subject to the provisions of the Financial Services Act 1986. These include the undertaking of investment business and the provision of corporate finance advice to clients;
- insolvency practice in accordance with the provisions of the Insolvency Act 1986.

3.3 Contractual obligations in the preparation of financial statements

In compliance with applicable laws, and in accordance with accepted accounting standards, accountants have an obligation to make full, fair, accurate, timely and understandable disclosure when preparing financial records and statements, and when submitting or filing reports and documents to the regulatory authorities.

Under this contractual obligation, when members are performing their duties they must act in good faith, responsibly, with due care, competence and diligence, without misrepresenting material facts or allowing their independent judgement to be subordinated, in order to ensure that to the best of their knowledge the books, records, accounts and financial statements are maintained accurately and in reasonable detail. These should appropriately reflect the organisation's transactions, be honestly and accurately reflected in its publicly available reports and communications and conform to applicable legal requirements and systems of internal controls, including the organisation's disclosure policy.

3.4 Performance of internal audit services

☐ **DEFINITION** ☐☐☐

Internal auditing is an independent, objective assurance and consulting activity designed to add value and improve an organisation's operations. As we have already noted, internal auditors provide assurance about a sound internal control system, which enhances the reliability of the external financial information of the employer.

Whatever the nature of the professional services they provide, members may be exposed to situations that involve the possibility of pressures and threats being exerted on them. These pressures and threats may impair their objectivity, and hence their independence.

Objectivity is essential to the audit function. Therefore, accountants performing internal audit services should not develop and install procedures, prepare records, or engage in any other activity which they would normally review or assess and which could reasonably be construed to compromise their independence.

3.5 Provision of financial management services

Financial management and consulting services are advisory in nature, and are generally performed at the specific request of an engagement client. This type of service generally involves two parties:
· the person or group offering the advice – the accountant, and
· the person or group seeking and receiving the advice – the engagement client.

When performing consulting services the accountant should maintain objectivity and not assume management responsibility.

3.6 Acceptance of gifts

If a member, or his or her spouse or dependent children, accepts gifts, services, favours or hospitality from a client, work colleague or a person having or proposing to have a contractual relationship with the member's employer, objectivity may be threatened or appear to be threatened.

Accepting gifts raises issues associated with bribes. Very often when people are asked whether they would accept bribes they say no very firmly, but on reflection begin to wonder what is a bribe and what isn't. A bribe is something valuable given to persuade someone to do something that they would not do otherwise and whose acceptance is not to be disclosed. How does accepting a bottle of champagne from a client or supplier at Christmas fit with this, especially if this is the 'done thing'? You might argue that, as it probably would not affect how business is done with the supplier, the person can continue to act in the best interests of the organisation. A small gift merely oils relationships.

But if bigger gifts are involved there might well be a conflict between personal and organisational interests. Here the dilemma revolves around the size of a gift and the influence that is being sought. Some people believe that any sort of gift, even a small and public one, is a form of bribe, in that it tends to buy or corrupt.

▷ **ACTIVITY 3** ▷ ▷ ▷ ▷

Which of the fundamental principles of ethics is being threatened by the type of situation described in section 3.6 above?

[Answer on p. 22]

---

4 Professional services

4.1 Introduction

Accounting technicians work in all levels of finance from accounts clerks to financial controllers. They work in all industries and sectors, and in organisations large and small.

In a small organisation, accounting technicians may be the only trained finance staff employed. In a large organisation, they are a crucial part of a balanced team working alongside chartered accountants and administrative staff.

Some AAT members are regulated to provide accounting services on a self-employed basis. They provide cost-effective accountancy and taxation services, particularly to small and medium sized enterprises.

4.2 Direct and indirect taxation services

Accountants performing taxation services in the UK, Ireland and in other member states of the EU will be dealing with compliance and advice on Value Added Tax - an indirect tax and direct taxes based on income, gains, losses and profits. The administrative authorities and the legal basis for direct and indirect taxes differ substantially.

An accountant giving professional tax services is entitled to put forward the best position in favour of an employer, or a client, provided the service is rendered with professional competence, does not in any way impair integrity and objectivity, and is in the opinion of the accountant consistent with the law.

Doubt may be resolved in favour of the client or the employer if there is reasonable support for the position and provided legal obligations of full disclosure are satisfied. Neither should he or she hold out to an employer, or a client, the assurance that the tax return prepared and the tax advice offered are beyond challenge.

Instead, the accountant should ensure that the employer or the client are aware of the limitations attaching to tax advice and services so that they do not misinterpret an expression of opinion as an assertion of fact.

When an accountant undertakes or assists in the preparation of a tax return he or she should advise the employer or the client that the responsibility for the content of the return rests primarily with the employer or client. The accountant should take the necessary steps to ensure that the tax return is properly prepared on the basis of the information received.

Tax advice or opinions of material consequence given to an employer or to a client should be recorded, either in the form of a letter or in a memorandum for the files.

An accountant should not be associated with any return or communication in which there is reason to believe that it:
- contains a false or misleading statement
- contains statements or information furnished recklessly or without any real knowledge of whether they are true or false, or
- omits or obscures information required to be submitted and such omission or obscurity would mislead the revenue authorities.

In preparing a tax return, an accountant ordinarily may rely on information furnished by the employer or client provided that the information appears reasonable. Although the examination or review of documents or other evidence in support of the information is not required, the accountant should encourage, when appropriate, such supporting data to be provided.
In addition, the accountant:
- should make use of the employer's or client's returns for prior years whenever feasible
- is required to make reasonable inquiries when the information presented appears to be incorrect or incomplete

· is encouraged to make reference to the books and records of the business operations.

When an accountant learns of a material error or omission in a tax return of a prior year, with which he or she may or may not have been associated, or of the failure to file a required tax return, there is a responsibility to promptly advise the employer or the client of the error or omission and recommend that disclosure be made to the revenue authorities. Normally, the accountant is not obligated to inform the revenue authorities, nor may this be done without permission.

If the employer or the client does not correct the error the accountant:
· should inform the employer or the client that it is not possible to act for them in connection with that return or other related information submitted to the authorities, and
· should consider whether continued association with the employer or client in any capacity is consistent with professional responsibilities.

If the accountant concludes that a professional relationship with the employer or client can be continued, all reasonable steps should be taken to ensure that the error is not repeated in subsequent tax returns.

4.3 Financial management consultancy

Financial management encompasses all the activities within an organisation that are concerned with the use of resources and that have a financial impact. It can be defined as the system by which the financial aspects of an organisation are directed and controlled to support the delivery of its goals.

The financial management arrangements provide information that is used to:
· direct the activities of the organisation
· control the activities of the organisation
· report and discharge accountability
· utilise resources efficiently and effectively.

Financial management is a vital part of managing operations. It shows:
· how good financial management can help pro-tect an organisation against unexpected events and external risks
· how financial management contributes to giving an organisation a competitive edge over competitors
· the legal and moral obligations for good financial management.

The accountant's duties may include:
· structuring the accounts
· managing and accounting for core costs (overheads) – identifying direct and indirect costs, apportioning costs between projects
· building and using effective budgets – including project and organisational budgets; cash flow forecasts and funding grids; foreign currency and multi-year budgeting

· monitoring and controlling budgets – preparing and using budget comparison reports
· putting in place internal control mechanisms – using common sense precautions to safeguard the organisation's assets and protect staff
· managing cash flow
· reporting to clients – accessing the information that clients require to meet obligations
· performing shareholder value analysis
· using financial management to create strategies
· integrating ethical issues into financial planning. Some businesses often run according to strong ethical and moral values – most notably, perhaps, gender equality. Accountants may be required to examine how such values influence financial management and to organise projects to take these values into account.

▷ ACTIVITY 4

It has been argued that business corporations have only one responsibility, and that is to make as much money as possible. Other writers, more recently, contend that organisations have social responsibilities to their various stakeholders and that they should establish codes of conduct to ensure that such responsibilities are properly fulfilled.

To what extent is a corporate 'code of conduct' an adequate mechanism for ensuring that an organisation's employees behave ethically?

[Answer on p. 22]

5 Test your knowledge

1 Ethical issues regarding business and public-sector organisations exist at four levels. Briefly describe each level.

2 How does a compliance-based approach to business ethics differ from an integrity-based approach?

3 What does an integrity-based approach to ethics emphasise?

4 In order to achieve the objectives of the accountancy profession, the AAT guidelines on professional ethics set standards of conduct for professional accountants and state the fundamental principles that have to be observed. Outline the six principles covered in the guidelines.

5 What is sometimes described as 'independence of mind'?

6 What are the general categories of threats to objectivity?

7 What is understood by the professional/client relationship?

[Answers on p.23]

6 Summary

This introductory chapter has set the scene for further studies of management information. You should now know how management information differs from financial accounting information. You should also understand what is meant by cost centres, profit centres and investment centres and the basic type of classification of costs into materials, labour and expenses.

Answers to chapter activities & 'test your knowledge' questions

---

△ **ACTIVITY 1**   △ △ △ △

Using a rule-based approach, you report your client to SOCA.

A principle-based approach means you advise your client not to take the cash without verifying the identity of the customer under the Money Laundering Regulations. He refuses to take your advice, so you report him to SOCA.

△ **ACTIVITY 2**   △ △ △ △

The examples show how the principle of integrity can be flouted.

△ **ACTIVITY 3**   △ △ △ △

As well as integrity being threatened by this type of situation, it can also threaten or appear to threaten a person's objectivity. Gifts may be intended to influence the recipient or they could be interpreted by a reasonable person in full possession of the facts as likely to have that effect.

△ **ACTIVITY 4**   △ △ △ △

'Ethics' is a code of moral principles that people follow with respect to what is right or wrong. People that work for organisations bring their own values into work with them. Organisations contain a variety of ethical systems.

Personal e.g. deriving from a person's upbringing, religious or non-religious beliefs, political opinions and personality.

Professional e.g. medical ethics.

Organisation cultures e.g. 'customer first'.

KAPLAN PUBLISHING

Organisation systems. Ethics might be contained in a formal code, reinforced by the overall statement of values. A problem might be that ethics does not always save money and there is a real cost to ethical decisions. Also, the organisation has different duties to different stakeholders and there may be a problem when setting the priorities.

Some companies have a voluntary code of conduct. A code is a statement of policies, principles or rules that guide behaviour. Codes of ethics do not only apply to organisations but should guide the behaviour of people in everyday life. Most of us operate with a more or less well defined set of ethical values, principles or rules of thumb that guide decision-making.

For ethical codes to be effective, provisions must be made for their enforcement. Unethical managers should be held responsible for their actions. This means that privileges and benefits should be withdrawn and sanctions should be applied. Although the enforcement of ethical codes may not be easy, the mere existence of such codes can increase ethical behaviour by clarifying expectations. When integrated into the day-to-day operations of an organisation, such codes can help prevent damaging ethical lapses, while tapping into powerful human impulses for moral thought and action. Thus an ethical framework becomes no longer a burdensome constraint within which the organisation must operate, but the governing ethos.

Test your knowledge

1   Ethical issues regarding business and public-sector organisations exist at four levels:
   · At the macro level, there are issues about the role of business in the national and international organisation of society.
   · At the corporate level, the issue is often referred to as corporate social responsibility and is focused on the ethical issues facing individual corporate entities (private and public sector) when formulating and implementing strategies.
   · At the group level there are issues affecting particular professional and other groups within an organisation.
   · At the individual level, the issue concerns the behaviour and actions of individuals within organisation

2   A compliance-based approach to business ethics differs from an integrity-based approach.

   · A compliance-based approach is designed to ensure that the organisation complies with the relevant law. Compliance means doing what one must do, because it ought to be done. It is reflected where the activities develop standards, train and communicate, handle reports of misconduct, investigate, enforce, oversee compliance and where the behavioural assumption is that people are solitary self-interested beings. Any violations are prevented, detected and punished.

· An integrity-based approach enables legal and responsible conduct. It emphasises managerial responsibility for ethical behaviour, as well as a concern for the law. Integrity means wanting what ought to be done.

3 An integrity-based approach to ethics emphasise emphasises managerial responsibility for ethical behaviour, as well as a concern for the law.

4 The six fundamental principles that are covered in the guidelines are:
   (a) Integrity – a professional accountant should be straightforward and honest in performing professional services.
   (b) Objectivity – a professional accountant should be fair and should not allow prejudice or bias or the influence of others to override objectivity.
   (c) Professional and technical competence – a professional accountant should refrain from undertaking or continuing assignments for which they are not competent to carry out unless advice and assistance is obtained to ensure that the assignment is carried out satisfactorily. All assignments should be undertaken with respect for legal and regulatory requirements.
   (d) Due care – a professional accountant having accepted an assignment has an obligation to carry it out with due care and reasonable despatch having regard to the nature and scope of the assignment.
   (e) Confidentiality – a professional accountant should respect the confidentiality of information acquired during the course of performing professional services. He or she should not use or disclose any such information without proper and specific authority or unless there is a legal or professional right or duty to disclose.
   (f) Professional behaviour – a professional accountant should act in a manner consistent with the good reputation of the profession and refrain from any conduct that might bring discredit to it.

5 Objectivity is a combination of impartiality, intellectual honesty and a freedom from conflicts of interest. It is defined as 'the state of mind which has regard to all considerations relevant to the task in hand but no other. It is sometimes described as independence of mind – the state of mind that permits the provision of an opinion without being affected by influences that compromise professional judgement, allowing an individual to act with integrity and exercise objectivity and professional scepticism

6 The general categories of threats to objectivity are

   · The Self-Interest threat - a threat to a member's integrity or objectivity may stem from a financial or other self-interest conflict. This could arise, for example, from a direct or indirect interest in a client or from fear of losing an engagement or having his or her employment terminated or as a consequence of undue commercial pressure from within or outside the firm.
   · The Self-Review threat – there will be a threat to objectivity if any product or judgement of the member or the firm needs to be challenged or re-evaluated by him or her subsequently.

KAPLAN PUBLISHING

- The Advocacy threat – there is a threat to a member's objectivity if he or she becomes an advocate for or against the position taken by the client or employer in any adversarial proceedings or situation. The degree to which this presents a threat to objectivity will depend on the individual circumstances. The presentation of only one side of the case may be compatible with objectivity provided that it is accurate and truthful.
- The Familiarity or Trust threat – is a threat that the member may become influenced by his or her.
- The Intimidation threat – the possibility that the member may become intimidated by threat, by a dominating personality, or by other pressures, actual or feared, applied by the client or employer or by another.

7   The professional/client relationship:
- the client presumes his or her needs will be met without having to direct the process;
- the professional decides which services are actually needed and provides them;
- the professional is trusted not to exploit his or her authority for unreasonable profit or gain.

ETHICAL CONFLICT

INTRODUCTION

Ethics, in its broader sense, deals with human conduct in relation to what is morally good and bad, right and wrong. To determine whether a decision is good or bad, the decision-maker must compare his/her options with some standard of perfection. This standard of perfection is not a statement of static position but requires the decision-maker to assess the situation and the values of the parties affected by the decision. The decision-maker must then estimate the outcome of the decision and be responsible for its results. Two good questions to ask when faced with an ethical dilemma are, 'Will my actions be fair and just to all parties affected?' and 'Would I be pleased to have my closest friends learn of my actions?'

CONTENTS

1 Ethical dilemmas
2 Ethical analysis
3 Conflict resolution
4 AAT guidelines

PERFORMANCE CRITERIA

· Recognise and explain why certain types of information should be regarded as confidential (32.1 D)
· Identify the key issues which ensure professional services are performed within the scope of professional ethics guidance (32.1 F)
· Make critical decisions to identify appropriate ethical behaviour when interacting with others in a variety of circumstances (32.1 G)
· Refer and seek advice from relevant sources for issues beyond own professional competence (32.1 H)
· Discuss, agree and resolve any ethical conflict (32.1 J)

1   Ethical dilemmas

Ethical standards have changed tremendously in the last century. Ethical and moral values provide a foundation to society on how to function, live and work within the society. Determining the degree to which business has complied with established standards has presented a real problem. As seen through corporate corruptions such as Enron, without an ethical foundation, organisations collapse. The purpose of ethics in business is to direct individuals to abide by a code of conduct that help increase and maintain public confidence in their products and services.

1.1 Concepts

Ethical conflict arises when two ethical principles demand opposite results in the same situation. Solving ethical conflicts may require establishing a hierarchy or priority of ethical principles, or examining the situation through another ethical system. We know when we have a significant ethical conflict when there is presence of significant value conflicts among differing interests, real alternatives that are equally justifiable, and significant consequences for 'stakeholders' in the situation.

In every business decision we have to choose between alternatives. Sometimes the choice is clear; there is a right answer and a wrong answer. In many of these cases the choice is made difficult by what we call an ethical dilemma, where no matter which alternative we select, we will be subordinating one or more of our values.

Executives, managers, supervisors and employees routinely face ethical dilemmas. How they manage those dilemmas can have a significant impact on the success of the organisation.

□ DEFINITION

An **ethical dilemma** is an ethical problem in which the ethical choice involves ignoring a powerful non-ethical consideration.

Do the right thing, but lose your job, a friend or an opportunity for advancement. An ethical dilemma exists when it appears there is a conflict between a work-related decision and the law, your organisation's policies, the code of conduct or transparency (full disclosure of the situation).

There are four characteristics of an ethical dilemma. All four must be present to satisfy the definition that an ethical dilemma exists:
· There must be at least two courses of action from which a choice must be made as to the action to be taken.
· There must be significant consequences for taking either course of action.
· Each of the courses of action can be supported by one or more ethical principles.
· The ethical principles supporting the unchosen course of action will be compromised.

KAPLAN PUBLISHING

Perhaps too often, business ethics is portrayed as a matter of resolving conflicts in which one option appears to be the clear choice. For example, case studies are often presented in which an employee is faced with whether or not to lie, steal, cheat, abuse another, break terms of a contract, etc. However, ethical dilemmas faced by managers are often more real-to-life and highly complex with no clear guidelines.

A non-ethical consideration can be powerful and important enough to justify choosing it over the strict ethical action.

> ☐ **DEFINITION** ☐☐☐☐
>
> **Non-ethical considerations** are powerful human motivations that are not based on right or wrong, but on considerations of survival and well being.

They are important because they are often the powerful impediments to ethical conduct, and the cause of many conflicts of interest. Non-ethical considerations are many and diverse, and include:

· The need and desire for shelter, health, wealth, fame, security, self-esteem, reputation, power, professional advancement, comfort, love, sex, praise, credit, appreciation, affection, or satisfaction.
· The desire for the health, comfort, safety, welfare and happiness for one's family, loved ones, friends, colleagues, and co-workers. For example, a child receives a gift and has to write a thank you note to a relative. Suppose the gift was an old-fashioned shirt or blouse. The ethical dilemma is to tell a lie - thank you for the present, it was just what I wanted – or hurt a loved one's feelings. Either choice has us violating a basic value.
· The pursuit of vengeance or retribution.
· Hunger, lust, pain, ambition, prejudice, bias, hatred, laziness, fatigue, disgust, anger, fear.

1.2 Real life dilemmas

Real life dilemmas often present choices between equally unfavourable or dis-agreeable alternatives. Think about these business ethics scenarios that happen in organisations every day.

· An employee surfs the Internet shopping for personal items on company time.
· A customer (or client) asked for a product (or service) from us today. After telling him our price, he said he could not afford it. I know he could get it cheaper from a competitor. Should I tell him about the competitor – or let him go without getting what he needs?
· A plant manager decides to ship a product to a customer knowing the parts have a quality problem but realising the problem doesn't affect part function and the customer probably won't notice.
· Our company prides itself on its merit-based pay system. One of my employees has done a tremendous job all year, so he deserves strong recognition. However, he's already paid at the top of the salary range for his job grade and our company has too many people in the grade above him, so we can't promote him. What should I do?
· Our company prides itself on hiring minorities. One Asian candidate fully fits the job requirements for our open position. However, we are concerned

that our customers won't understand his limited command of the English language. What should I do?

· A salesperson marks parts as 'sold' in the company database thus depriving others of the ability to sell the parts, even though the sale is uncertain.

· A manager shares important company information with a competitor for his or her potential gain.

· A store misrepresents the quality or functionality of an advertised sale item.

· An employee takes office supplies home to stock his or her home office.

· A finance officer accounts questionably for purchases and expenditures.

· An accountant tells a supplier that their 'cheque is in the post' knowing that the cheque has not even been written.

· An organisation is intending to produce an electronic catalogue of products from which customers will make orders. It is both technically feasible and currently legal to include subliminal advertising into the catalogue software to promote 'special offers' and the like.

· My boss told me that one of my employees is among several others to be laid off soon, and that I'm not to tell my employee yet or he might tell the whole organisation which would soon be in an uproar. Meanwhile, I heard from my employee that he plans to buy a car for his daughter and a new carpet for his house. What should I do?

· My computer operator told me he'd noticed several personal letters printed from a computer that I was responsible to manage. While we had no specific policies then against personal use of company facilities, I was concerned. I approached the letter writer to discuss the situation. She told me she'd written the letters in her own time to practice using our word processor. What should I do?

· A fellow employee told me that he plans to quit the company in two months and start a new job which has been guaranteed to him. Meanwhile, my boss told me that he wasn't going to give me a new opportunity in our company because he was going to give it to my fellow employee now. What should I do?

You encounter these situations and others like them regularly if you spend any time in organisations. Are these 'bad people' or 'good people' making questionable ethical choices? Do they even consider whether the choices they are making are ethical? After all, the plant manager may think, the most important issue is to get the parts to the customer on time. Or, the employee rationalises, 'I give this employer lots of over-time and thinking time outside work hours so I deserve the time at work to surf the Web.'

▷ ACTIVITY 1 ▷▷▷▷

Select the most appropriate description of an ethical dilemma from the three options below:

A An ethical dilemma exists when one may gain personally from a work-related decision

B An ethical dilemma exists when a work-related decision could be in conflict with the law, the employer's policies or code of conduct, or when disclosure if the situation could cause embarrassment or concern.

C An ethical dilemma exists when a work-related decision potentially conflicts with one's moral values.

[Answer on p. 47]

1.3 Rationalising

Rationalising (or making excuses for) our behaviour usually means we are going in the wrong direction. When we try to convince ourselves or others that what we are doing is justified it usually means that we are experiencing an ethical dilemma. Presented below are five common rationalisations:

· **Everyone else is doing it** – this is a justification children often use with their parents – all my friends are doing it, so it's okay for me as well. In truth, we are each responsible for our own ethical behaviour, and it does not matter what any one else is doing. If you find you are in a situation where everyone else is shading the truth or bending the rules, you may need to find a new situation. It is not an excuse to act in an unprincipled way.

· **If I don't do it someone else will** – this handy excuse may be most commonly employed when there are many people willing to do something unethical. For example, the head of a large business asks a salesman to do something unethical (e.g. contract to sell a product to a customer and then substitute goods of a lesser quality for the original product). An unprincipled salesman rationalises that if he says 'no', there are plenty of other salespeople who will say 'yes'. Plus, they will have the benefit of pleasing the boss. It is important to remember that doing the right thing is not always easy but it is, nonetheless, the right thing.

· **It's not against the law** – there are many actions that are not strictly illegal, but that violate the spirit of the law. Consider the salespeople who 'pad out' their expenses claims. They know they are trying to get away with something that is ethically questionable.

· **It really doesn't hurt anyone** – this justification is often used when someone is stretching the truth. For example, a speaker at a conference makes his presentation more powerful by adding personal anecdotes that he claims are true, but that are really exaggerations.

· **No-one will ever know** – rationalisation assumes that unprincipled actions are acceptable as long as they remain secret (no one saw me copying some software that a friend wanted, so it's okay). It also suggests that others – family members, employers and colleagues – are responsible for regulating our behaviour. In fact, the responsibility to behave ethically resides within each individual, and it is up to each of us to make sound choices, whether or not any one else knows.

1.4 Representative work force – managing diversity

Great companies are admired for their products, services, people and integrity. Most large companies are strongly committed to upholding ethical standards and promoting diversity and inclusion.

An organisation's work force is representative when it reflects or exceeds the demographic composition of the external work force.

Diversity can be defined as 'all the ways in which we are different and similar along an infinite number of lines.' It refers to a broad range of characteristics including: gender, age, race, disability, cultural background, sexual orientation, education, religious belief, class and family responsibilities. From the employer's point of view, an organisation's work force is representative when it reflects or exceeds the demographic composition of the external work force. A representative work force reflects or exceeds the current proportions of women, visible minorities and persons with disabilities in each occupation as are known to be available in the external work force and from which the employer may reasonably be expected to draw from.

It is a good indication that an employer is not limiting access to the skills and talents of workers by discriminating on the basis of sex, race, colour or disability. A non-representative work force signals the need for evaluation and action, so that whatever is blocking or discouraging certain groups from employment and advancement may be corrected

1.5 Harassment policy

> ☐ **DEFINITION**   ☐☐☐☐
>
> **Harassment** can be defined as the persecution or intimidation of a person or group, motivated by prejudice or direct discrimination.

People may be harassed because of their race, colour, religion, sex, sexuality, illness or disablement. The aim of a harassment policy is to draw a clear distinction between acts of harassment and other incidents such as nuisance, vandalism or other disputes.

Harassment can take many forms of threatening or aggressive action – both verbal and physical, involving attacks on property as well as on people. Incidents of harassment include offensive graffiti, abusive language and behaviour, violence towards people of all ages and damage to homes or possessions.

All employees have a right to work in an environment that is free of unlawful discrimination and harassment. Any form of discrimination or harassment, including sexual harassment, whether based on race, sex, colour, religion, national origin, age or disability is unacceptable.

Employees who are found to have engaged in unlawful discrimination or harassment, or to have contributed to the creation of an offensive or hostile work environment, should be subject to disciplinary action, which may include termination of employment. In addition, employees who engage in unlawful discrimination or harassment may be subject to prosecution and civil or criminal penalties.

1.6 Insider trading policy

On the basis of inside information, it is against the law to buy or sell shares or pass on, tip or disclose material, nonpublic information to others outside the company including family and friends. While working for your company, you may learn important and confidential information, called 'inside information' about your company, or about one of your company's suppliers, customers or business partners, which could affect the company's share price.

KAPLAN PUBLISHING

Examples of information that may be considered material, non-public information in some circumstances are:

- a substantial contract award or termination that has not been publicly disclosed
- the gain or loss of a significant customer that has not been publicly disclosed
- undisclosed negotiations and agreements regarding mergers, concessions, joint ventures, divestments, etc.
- undisclosed financial results or changes in earnings projections
- undisclosed management changes
- information that is considered confidential.

Even when material information has been publicly disclosed, each insider must continue to refrain from buying or selling the shares in question until the beginning of the third business day after the information has been publicly released to allow the markets time to absorb the information.

1.7 Integrity of records and public disclosure policy

All company data, records and reports must be accurate, truthful and prepared in a proper manner. These include everyday documents such as expense reports, accounting entries, cost estimates, contract proposals and other presentations to management, customers and the public. It is essential that those who rely on these records and reports – managers, creditors, customers, auditors and other decision makers – have truthful and accurate information. The integrity of the company's accounting, technical, personnel, financial and other records is based on their validity, accuracy and completeness.

Anyone preparing the type of information described above must be diligent in assuring its integrity and anyone representing or certifying the accuracy of such information should make an inquiry or review adequate enough to establish a good faith belief in the accuracy of the information. Custodians of the company's data, records and reports must be sure that such information is released, whether internally or outside the company, only if adequately protected and then only for authorised purposes.

Employees involved in the preparation and submission of the periodic reports and other documents with various regulatory authorities reports must ensure that the information presented is full, fair, accurate, timely and understandable.

A retention policy sets down for how long different types of information are retained.

All employees must make themselves aware of retention guidelines prior to the disposal, or destruction of any company records or files. This is necessary because of laws and regulations that require retention of certain records for various periods of time, particularly in the tax, personnel, health and safety, environment, contract and corporate structure areas.

have access to sensitive information about clients, we may also have access to confidential financial and personnel records of the organisations we work with. Learning to keep confidences – to keep information private – is a skill and it must be practiced daily.

Honesty is the only policy – if you or your family will benefit financially from engaging other people in activities, disclose that information. Never use your relationships with others for economic or personal gain. If you have financial or personal interests that could affect decision-making, disclose that information or excuse yourself from participation in voting or discussion of any issues that could pose a conflict of interest.

Above all else, be honest. When people shade the truth or tell half-truths they jeopardise their reputations for integrity, and jeopardise the work they are committed to doing. If, in the course of our work, we are asked to do something that is dishonest, or that puts us in a compromising position, we should always express concern. If we behave in a straightforward and truthful manner we cannot go wrong.

Be transparent in your communication – give honest, clear, and objective information to others. Disclose any limitations that are imposed on you about sharing information. Recommend alternate sources for information gathering.

Take responsibility for yourself in the workplace – before you go to work for an organisation, talk to your potential employer about the difficulties that might accompany the job. Be sure to determine:

· what information can and cannot be disclosed to clients of the organisation
· what level of advocacy you can engage in without fear of repercussions, and
· what kinds of accommodations can and cannot be made for your special circumstances (e.g. health care and other needs).

Once you have been recruited, learn the organisation's policies, procedures, and rules of the workplace.

It is your responsibility as an employee to learn as much as possible about the workplace. A number of issues can be discussed more honestly and forthrightly before you sign on as an employee. Think about the kinds of things that will be important for you to fulfill your role.

· What is the best way to bring your concerns to someone's attention?
· Who should you talk with if an ethical dilemma or problem presents itself?
· Is there enough flexibility within the organisation and your job responsibilities to accommodate your or your child's health needs?

Be open and honest with your questions. Each person will have a different list of questions and concerns. It is important to identify and address the issues that may affect your individual performance and your ability to succeed in the workplace. In large measure, your effectiveness may depend on this kind of up-front conversation.

KAPLAN PUBLISHING

Interested parties – other parties, besides those directly mentioned in the case, may have a stake in the protagonist's decision. You might think of interested parties in progressively larger groupings, from the person facing the ethical problem, to the person(s) immediately affected (such as that person's subordinate, to the people in the relevant organisation (the company or university), to the community and society in general. Consider the reasonable expectations (rights) of each interested party. Frequently, consideration of the interested parties will bring more issues to mind.

Consequences – for each action considered, there are often several possible outcomes. The challenge in identifying consequences is not to identify every remote consequence, but to identify those that have a good probability of occurring, or those that would have very serious consequences even if the probability of occurrence is not particularly high. For example, the possibility that someone might die due to the release of a small amount of a toxic substance during an experimental procedure may be relatively remote, but the consequences would be so devastating that the potential benefit may not even be worth a remote risk.

When considering consequences, be sure to consider, in turn, each of the interested parties and the probable consequences of the proposed action on those parties. When considering consequences to the protagonist, keep in mind that consequences may be multifaceted. On the one hand, he or she might get caught in an unethical act and face a loss of reputation, or other serious negative consequences. On the other hand, he or she may get away with an unethical act and get a reward or promotion more easily and quickly than if he or she had acted ethically. But whether or not the act is detected, engaging in actions we believe are wrong undermines our sense of integrity. The effects of an action on a person's character may appear to be minor in the short run, but often have a cumulative and debilitating effect on one's self confidence, self esteem, and habits. Each time we reap the benefits of questionable acts and successful avoidance of the negative consequences, we enhance the probability that these acts will be repeated.

Obligations – for each case, consider primarily the obligations of the protagonist toward the various interested parties. It is sometimes tempting to dismiss the obligation of the protagonist when some other person fails to live up to his/her moral obligation, but this kind of reasoning often amounts to nothing more than a rationalisation – an excuse to do whatever one wanted to do in the first place – without real regard to the moral questions at hand.

2.3 Ethical questions

According to Kenneth Blanchard and Norman Vincent Peale, authors of The Power of Ethical Management, there are three questions you should ask yourself whenever you are faced with an ethical dilemma.

· Is it legal? In other words, will you be violating any criminal laws, civil laws or company policies by engaging in this activity?
· Is it balanced? Is it fair to all parties concerned both in the short-term as well as the long-term? Is this a win-win situation for those directly as well as indirectly involved?

· Is it right? Most of us know the difference between right and wrong, but when push comes to shove, how does this decision make you feel about yourself? Are you proud of yourself for making this decision? Would you like others to know you made the decision you did?

The three issues are:
1 Transparency – do I mind others knowing what I have decided?
2 Affect – who does my decision affect or hurt?
3 Fairness – would my decision be considered fair by those affected?

2.4 Ethical decision-making

Another ethical analysis goes through the process of identifying the problem, identifying uncertainties and exploring alternatives and values.

Identify problem – there are many reasons why ethical dilemmas are sometimes difficult to recognise. Sometimes a person fails to identify all of the stakeholders for a problem or all of the conflicts of interest among stakeholders. People may also be confused or have differences of opinion about what constitutes an ethical dilemma. For example, some people might argue that a 'small' violation of someone else's interests is unimportant and, therefore, cannot be an ethical dilemma. Others may argue that the magnitude of violation is unimportant. Cultural pressure within organisations or societies can lead to biased thinking, which in turn discourages investigation of potential ethical issues. Sometimes self-interest causes people to be blind to the effects of their actions on others or makes them unwilling to reconsider the values they use as they make decisions.

Identify uncertainties – it is frequently difficult to identify how one alternative versus another will affect others and society. It may also be difficult to identify which values are most important in a given setting. For example, managers may be faced with an ethical dilemma over the extent of employee layoffs during an economic downturn. Managers may need to weigh a value of loyalty and commitment to employees against a value of generating higher profits for shareholders. In addition, it is uncertain how to go about improving personal and organisational ethics. Improvement requires identification of better ways to do one or more of the following: identify ethical dilemmas, explore alternatives, or clarify and apply ethical values. No one way exists to achieve improvement in these areas.

Explore alternatives and values – the AAT Ethical Standards are not explicitly designed to help you recognise ethical dilemmas. However, the standards include descriptions of ethical conduct (e.g. 'Members have a responsibility to communicate information fairly and objectively'). One way to identify an ethical dilemma is to compare a potential course of action against these standards for ethical conduct. The AAT's standards also describe a process for the resolution of ethical conflict, which can provide guidance for objectively exploring alternatives and choosing a course of action.

KAPLAN PUBLISHING

2.5 Reaching the right decision

When facing a conflict of values, the following step-by-step approach to decision-making can lead to wise actions in resolving a dilemma. It encourages people to be explicit about their values, and intentional in their approach to resolving ethical conflicts.

Know your principles – regularly reaffirm your values and beliefs. Talk about them with your family, your friends, and people you work with.

Identify the problem – when a dilemma arises, be explicit about your concern. What is it about the situation that is troubling? Identify the issues and potential conflicts.

Propose alternative solutions – think about the ways you might solve the problem. Be creative and brainstorm a variety of approaches that you could use.

Test each alternative against your principles – once you have a list of possible solutions reflect on how each one 'feels'. Identify the solutions that are consistent with your values and beliefs. Eliminate those that are not.

Talk to a trustworthy individual – seek out a person whose judgement you value. Ask them to be a sounding board as you talk through your options. Listen carefully to their feedback.

Choose an alternative – decide on an option for action. Can you live with it? If not, try other solutions from your list until you feel comfortable with your decision. Be sure your choice reflects your principles.

Commit yourself to your decision – when you decide on your course of action, move ahead. But accept that you could make a mistake. These kinds of decisions are difficult and require repeated and ongoing effort. The goal of this process is to make the best choice you can with the information you have, not to make perfect choices. Learn from your failures and your successes.

Above all, be true to yourself – know your values, and be guided in all things by your own conscience. If you encounter situations that threaten your personal moral code, act in ways that are consistent with your own principles.

Respect yourself and respect others – do not stretch yourself too thin. Define and maintain your boundaries. Look for the best in others; listen to their opinions and perspectives.

Keep confidences – share confidential information only when necessary to prevent injury or death. Take care when telling stories about other people that neither the details nor the context of the story identify that person. Ask permission from your own family and friends before sharing information about them.

Maintaining confidentiality is an essential requirement of accountancy work. All of us are exposed to a great deal of sensitive information. Not only do we have access to sensitive information about clients, we may also have access to confidential financial and personnel records of the organisations we work with. Learning to keep confidences – to keep information private – is a skill and it must be practiced daily.

Honesty is the only policy – if you or your family will benefit financially from engaging other people in activities, disclose that information. Never use your relationships with others for economic or personal gain. If you have financial or personal interests that could affect decision-making, disclose that information or excuse yourself from participation in voting or discussion of any issues that could pose a conflict of interest.

Above all else, be honest. When people shade the truth or tell half-truths they jeopardise their reputations for integrity, and jeopardise the work they are committed to doing. If, in the course of our work, we are asked to do something that is dishonest, or that puts us in a compromising position, we should always express concern. If we behave in a straightforward and truthful manner we cannot go wrong.

Be transparent in your communication – give honest, clear, and objective information to others. Disclose any limitations that are imposed on you about sharing information. Recommend alternate sources for information gathering.

Take responsibility for yourself in the workplace – before you go to work for an organisation, talk to your potential employer about the difficulties that might accompany the job. Be sure to determine:
· what information can and cannot be disclosed to clients of the organisation
· what level of advocacy you can engage in without fear of repercussions, and
· what kinds of accommodations can and cannot be made for your special circumstances (e.g. health care and other needs).

Once you have been recruited, learn the organisation's policies, procedures, and rules of the workplace.

It is your responsibility as an employee to learn as much as possible about the workplace. A number of issues can be discussed more honestly and forthrightly before you sign on as an employee. Think about the kinds of things that will be important for you to fulfill your role.

· What is the best way to bring your concerns to someone's attention?
· Who should you talk with if an ethical dilemma or problem presents itself?
· Is there enough flexibility within the organisation and your job responsibilities to accommodate your or your child's health needs?

Be open and honest with your questions. Each person will have a different list of questions and concerns. It is important to identify and address the issues that may affect your individual performance and your ability to succeed in the workplace. In large measure, your effectiveness may depend on this kind of up-front conversation.

Once you become an employee, request a thorough orientation. This is especially important if you have never before held a job. Ask for your organisation's performance guide and if there is an ethics policy. Also request a copy of the personnel manual that sets forth the rights and responsibilities of employees. These manuals are very explicit about what is acceptable in the workplace. Request that someone go through them with you. People who have been in the workforce for many years forget how complex the rules and behavioural expectations can be. Or they may just assume that new employees know. It is up to you to take the responsibility to ask for information and training.

Be impeccable in your conduct – maintain the highest standards of professional and personal behaviour. Aspire to be your best self and pursue that goal with grace and optimism.

When in doubt, admit it – be truthful about your own skills and abilities. Take responsibility for informing others when you need additional support and training.

Most of us have had the experience of pretending we know something that we do not. Usually we do this when we do not want to draw attention to ourselves. Unfortunately little fibs or exaggerations can get people in real trouble. When we do not understand what is being said or done, or what is being asked of us we must admit it. And we must ask for help.

3 Conflict resolution

3.1 Resolution of ethical conflict

From time to time AAT members may encounter situations that give rise to ethical conflicts. Such conflicts may arise in a wide variety of ways, ranging from the relatively trivial dilemma to the extreme case of fraud and similar illegal activities. An honest difference of opinion between a member and another person is not itself an ethical issue but if members are instructed or encouraged to engage in any activity that is unlawful they are entitled and required to decline. For example, members should not be party to the falsification of any record or knowingly or recklessly supply any information or make any statement that is misleading, false or deceptive.

If the member would feel uncomfortable defending an action in open court or to the press then it is likely that such a course of action should be avoided on ethical grounds.

In resolving ethical conflicts the member should consider seeking counselling and advice on a confidential basis with an independent legal adviser and/or the Ethics Advice line (see www.aat.org.uk). It is important to keep a written record of all meetings and discussions that take place in seeking to resolve an ethical conflict.

There are many methods to resolve ethical dilemmas. However, most people agree that organisations should develop and document a procedure for dealing with ethical dilemmas as they arise. Ideally, they should be resolved by a group within the organisation, e.g. an ethics committee comprised of top leaders/managers and/or members of the board. Some have staff members on the committee, as well.

Methods to address and resolve ethical dilemmas include many ethical principles, checklists, a ten-step method and the application of the organisation's code of conduct.

3.2 Policies for ethical conduct

It may be left to you to decide which among many ethical principles you will follow, and how you will prioritise them. Some ethical principles with deep roots in many cultures that have survived throughout recorded history might be useful as a guide.

The Golden Rule – do unto others as you would have them do unto you. Putting yourself into the situation of others, and thinking of yourself as the object of the decision, can help you think about 'fairness' in decision-making.

Kant's Categorical Imperative is a principle that states that if an action is not right for everyone to take it is not right for anyone. Ask yourself, 'If everyone did this, could the organisation, or society, survive?'

Descartes' rule of change – if an action cannot be taken repeatedly, then it is not right to be taken at any time This is the slippery-slope rule: An action may bring about a small change now that is acceptable, but if repeated would bring unacceptable changes in the long run.

Policies for ethical conduct include:

The Utilitarian Principle – take the action that achieves the higher or greater value (the Utilitarian Principle). This rule assumes you can prioritise values in a rank order and understand the consequences of various courses of action

Risk Aversion Principle – take the action that produces the least harm, or the least potential cost. Some actions have extremely high failure costs of very low probability e.g. building a nuclear generating facility in an urban area, others have extremely high failure costs of moderate probability e.g. speeding and automobile accidents. Avoid these high failure cost actions, with greater attention obviously to high failure cost potential of moderate to high probability.

No free lunch rule – assume that someone else owns virtually all the tangible and intangible objects unless there is a specific declaration otherwise. If something created by someone else is useful to you, it has value and you should assume the creator wants compensation for this work.

3.3 Policies for ethical conduct

Doug Wallace and Jon Pekel, suggest the following checklist:

Relevant information test – have I/we obtained as much information as possible to make an informed decision and action plan for this situation?

Involvement test – have I/we involved all who have a right to have input and/or to be involved in making this decision and action plan?

Consequential test – have I/we anticipated and attempted to accommodate for the consequences of this decision and action plan on any who are significantly affected by it?

Fairness test – if I/we were assigned to take the place of any one of the stakeholders in this situation, would I/we perceive this decision and action plan to be essentially fair, given all of the circumstances?

Enduring values test – does this decision and action plan uphold my/our priority enduring values that are relevant to this situation?

Universality test – would I/we want this decision and action plan to become a universal law applicable to all similar situations, even to myself/ourselves?

Light-of-day test – how would I/we feel and be regarded by others (working associates, family, etc.) if the details of this decision and action plan were disclosed for all to know?

3.4 Ten-step method

Another method of resolving a dilemma is Wallace and Pekel's ten-step method.

1 What are the known facts in the situation?
2 Who are the key stakeholders, what do they value and what are their desired outcomes?
3 What are the underlying drivers causing the situation?
4 In priority order what ethical principles or operating values do you think should be upheld in this situation?
5 Who should have input to, or be involved in, making this decision?
6 List any alternative and action plans that would:
    (a) prevent or minimise harm to stakeholders
    (b) Id the priority values for this situation
    (c) good solution to the situation.
7 Build a worse case scenario for your preferred alternative to see how it affects the stakeholders. Rethink and revise your preferred alternative if necessary.
8 Add a preventative ethics component to your action plan that deals with the underlying drivers causing the situation.
9 Evaluate your chosen decision and action plan.
10 Decide and build an action plan, and implement and monitor it.

3.5 Ethical codes

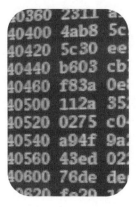

Your organisation's code of conduct is designed to help you recognise and resolve ethical dilemmas. It is a set of standards designed to:

· promote honest, ethical conduct
· ensure compliance with relevant laws and regulations
· encourage quick reporting to your employer of potential code violations
· make sure that everyone understands their obligations – managers, employees and others who are involved in the organisation.

Developing a code of business ethics will not stop unethical behaviour, but it will give people something to think about, a measurement against which to assess their behaviour. Organisations can develop a written code of business ethics that guides the decision-making and actions of all of their stakeholders. Their reputation and track record for ethical behaviour and integrity are vital for establishing the trust that is the basis for all successful relationships they sustain including those with their customers, employees, community and shareholders. When faced with significant ethical issues, you should follow the established policies of your organisation bearing on the resolution of such conflict.

If these policies do not resolve the ethical conflict, you should consider the following courses of action.

· Discuss such problems with the immediate superior except when it appears that the superior is involved, in which case the problem should be presented initially to the next higher managerial level. If a satisfactory resolution cannot be achieved when the problem is initially presented, submit the issues to the next higher managerial level. If the immediate superior is the chief executive officer, or equivalent, the acceptable reviewing authority may be a group such as the audit committee, executive committee, board of directors, board of trustees, or owners. Contact with levels above the immediate superior should be initiated only with the superior's knowledge, assuming the superior is not involved.
· Clarify relevant ethical issues by confidential discussion with an objective advisor to obtain a better understanding of possible courses of action. Consult your own solicitor as to legal obligations and rights concerning the ethical conflict.
· If the ethical conflict still exits after exhausting all levels of internal review, there may be no other recourse on significant matters than to resign from the organisation and to submit an informative memorandum to an appropriate representative of the organisation. After resignation, depending on the nature of the ethical conflict, it may also be appropriate to notify other parties.

Unfortunately, there are two problems associated with the use of ethical codes.

Firstly, their generality, which makes the translation of abstract concepts into guides for action difficult. Often individual managers have to make their own interpretation of the codes, which can result in different managers acting differently. Other managers may decide that the codes are too vague to be helpful, and disregard them.

Secondly, senior management may not actively support them, which can result in management feeling pressurised to compromise ethical standards to achieve organisational goals.

> ## ▷ ACTIVITY 2 ▷ ▷ ▷ ▷

Knowing the Code of Business Conduct will cause you to recognise all ethical dilemmas and resolve them. True or false?

[Answer on p. 47]

3.6 Cross border activities

When considering the application of ethical requirements in cross border activities a number of situations may arise.

A member qualifying in one country may reside in another country or may be temporarily visiting that country to perform professional services. In all circumstances, the member should carry out professional services in accordance with the relevant technical standards and ethical requirements. In all other respects, however, the member should be guided by the ethical requirements set out below.

When a member performs services in a country other than the home country and differences on specific matters exist between the ethical requirements of the two countries the following provisions should be applied:

· When the ethical requirements of the country in which the services are being performed are less strict than the AAT's ethical guidance then the ethical guidance of the Institute should be applied.

· When the ethical requirements of the country in which services are being performed are stricter than the AAT's ethical guidance, then the ethical requirements in the country where services are being performed should be applied.

· When the ethical requirements of the home country are mandatory for services performed outside that country and are stricter than set out in (a) and (b) above, then the ethical requirements of the home country should be applied.

> ## ▷ ACTIVITY 3 ▷ ▷ ▷ ▷

How would you apply ethical considerations to the following dilemmas?

· A rival company creates the legally permitted maximum of toxic waste. Your company has a range of expensive systems that keep waste to much lower levels. Not using these would reduce costs, and there is increasing pressure from industry analysts to increase the return on investment.

· A young, talented and ambitious team leader wants you to dismiss a member of his team, who is much older than the rest and does not really fit in. However, the worker in question has worked at the company a long time with a good record of service.

· You are forced to make redundancies in a department. The Human Resources manager has said, off the record, that it must not seem that gender or ethnicity is an issue, so you must make it look fair. However, this would require you to keep some weaker individuals, and lose some good ones.

[Answer on p. 47]

4 AAT guidelines

The AAT's Professional Standards Section has compiled a series of guidelines to help you through the ethical dilemmas you may face during your professional life. These apply to all AAT members (including student, affiliate, full and fellow members) and often to potential members.

4.1 Money laundering

The AAT Guidance on money laundering legislation explains the impact on our membership of the 2004 Money Laundering Regulations, along with the Proceeds of Crime Act (POCA) and Terrorism Act.

4.2 Guidelines on professional ethics

The Guidelines on professional ethics set out the standards of professional behaviour expected of all AAT members. The accountancy profession as a whole demands a high level of professional ethics and it is essential that members maintain these widely accepted standards.

Briefly, you are expected to:
· adopt an ethical approach to work, employers and clients
· acknowledge your professional duty to society as a whole
· maintain an objective outlook
· provide professional, high standards of service, conduct and performance at all times.

It is important to remember that the guidelines are more than a set of rules that you must abide by. They protect you and your reputation as well as that of your clients, employers and members of the public.
These Guidelines are designed to be consulted whenever you are faced with an ethical difficulty but of course they cannot cover every eventuality.

4.3 The ethics of whistleblowing

Thousands of workers witness wrongdoing at work. Most remain silent. They decide that it is not their concern; that nothing they can do would improve things, or they cannot afford problems at work.

Other workers choose to speak out. They 'blow the whistle' on unethical and illegal conduct in the workplace.

> ☐ **DEFINITION**   ☐☐☐☐
>
> **Whistleblowing** means disclosing information that a worker believes is evidence of illegality, gross waste, gross mismanagement, abuse of power, or substantial and specific danger to the public health and safety.

KAPLAN PUBLISHING

Whistleblower actions may save lives, money, or the environment. However, instead of praise for the public service of 'committing the truth' whistleblowers are often targeted for retaliation, harassment, intimidation, demotion, dismissal and blacklisting.

Here is a simple illustration: a civil engineer believes that a certain building practice is unsafe and reports this to their employer. The employer does not act on the report so the engineer takes it to their professional body. This body also does not act to the satisfaction of the engineer so they then decide to take their report to the media. The employer dismisses the engineer for gross misconduct in breaching confidentiality.

Whistleblowing thus has three essential elements:
·   the perception by someone within an organisation that something is morally amiss within that organisation
·   the communication of that perception to parties outside the organisation
·   the perception by at least some of those in authority in that organisation that such a communication ought not to have been made.

The Ethics of Whistleblowing highlights the matters that you should consider before you blow the whistle. It takes a realistic look at the effectiveness of the protection provided by the Public Interest Disclosure Act 1998.

Generally, as an employee, you owe a duty of loyalty to your employer as well as to the accountancy profession. However, there may be times where there is a conflict between the two. For example, your manager may ask you to 'cook the books' to reduce the company's VAT liability. Although this is clearly wrong and you should not be involved in doing this, how do you resolve such a problem? The AAT's Guidelines on Professional Ethics state that you should initially raise the issue with your immediate superior

Therefore, in this particular scenario, you would need to speak to your manager and advise him or her that you have concerns about doing this and cannot be involved in such an activity. If there is still a disagreement about a significant ethical issue with your manager, the Guidelines suggest that you should then raise the matter with higher levels of management or non-executive directors. Finally, if there is a material issue and you have exhausted all other avenues, you may wish to consider resigning – however, it is strongly recommended that you obtain legal advice before doing so.

Although you do have the option to remain silent about malpractice within your organisation, you may decide to take the bolder step of whistleblowing. Where you have blown the whistle but decided not to resign, in certain circumstances you may be protected from dismissal by the Public Interest Disclosure Act 1998 (PIDA) where you disclose otherwise confidential information. The Act (which has also been referred to as 'the Whistleblowers' Charter') gives protection where you have made a 'qualifying disclosure' (i.e. disclosure of information which you reasonably believe shows that a criminal offence, breach of a legal obligation, miscarriage of justice, breach of health and safety legislation or environmental damage has occurred, is occurring or is likely to occur).

You need to show that you made the disclosure in good faith, reasonably believed that the information disclosed was true and that you would otherwise be victimised or the evidence concealed or destroyed; or that the concern has already been raised with the employer/external prescribed regulator (i.e. a body prescribed under PIDA such as Customs and Excise).

4.4 Guidelines on criminal convictions

The Guidelines on Criminal Convictions outlines the AAT's policy concerning members and prospective members who have criminal convictions. All persons applying to join the AAT's courses and existing members must declare any criminal conviction that is not spent under The Rehabilitation of Offenders Act 1974. However, a criminal conviction is not necessarily a bar to joining or progressing within the accountancy profession with the help of the AAT.

4.5 Guidelines on personal insolvency

The Guidelines on Personal Insolvency outline the AAT's policy concerning members and prospective members who are or have been bankrupt or engaged in an Individual Voluntary Arrangement or any other formal arrangement with creditors. Insolvency need not be a bar to enhancing your career with the help of the AAT.

5 Test your knowledge

1 What are the four characteristics of an ethical dilemma?

2 Briefly explain what you understand by 'non-ethical' considerations.

3 Describe five common rationalisations.

4 When material information has been publicly disclosed, each insider must continue to refrain from buying or selling the shares in question until the beginning of the third business day after the information has been publicly released. Why is this?

5 What is the Golden Rule?

6 What are the three questions you should ask yourself whenever you are faced with an ethical dilemma?

7 Outline the three essential elements of whistleblowing.

[Answers on p. 48]

7 Whistleblowing has three essential elements:
- the perception by someone within an organisation that something is morally amiss within that organisation
- the communication of that perception to parties outside the organisation
- the perception by at least some of those in authority in that organisation that such a communication ought not to have been made.

KAPLAN PUBLISHING

COMMUNICATIONS AND INTERPERSONAL SKILLS

INTRODUCTION

In addition to the specific learning outcomes for this unit, the ethics subject matter forms an ideal basis for developing your communication skills at a level sufficient to provide a smoother progression from level 3 to level 4. This chapter provides an ideal forum to develop communication and personal skills with peers, superiors, clients, external bodies and agencies and including specifically skills of negotiation, critical decision-making, discussion, letter and report writing.

CONTENTS

1 Relationships at work
2 Interpersonal skills
3 Communication skills
4 Communication types
5 E-communications and information security
6 Confidential information

PERFORMANCE CRITERIA

· Recognise and explain why certain types of information should be regarded as confidential (32.1 D)
· Identify the key issues which ensure professional services are performed within the scope of professional ethics guidance (32.1 F)
· Make critical decisions to identify appropriate ethical behaviour when interacting with others in a variety of circumstances (32.1 G)

1 Relationships at work

1.1 Introduction

There are different ways of looking at this topic. We can start with the structural types of roles and relationships that show how power, authority and influence are built into the organisation. Working relationships can also be considered in terms of their contractual, ethical and legal effect. Overlaid on the structural factors, there are interpersonal relationships, which include team working, interdepartmental relations and networking. As with all relationships, there are people we do not get along with and situations that arise when there is a clash of interests and this means that we may have to handle disagreements and conflict.

1.2 Structural relationships

The formal structure, communications and procedures of the organisation are based on authority, responsibility and functional relationships

Accountants and accountancy is about communication. But communication is not just sending messages or emails, or indeed producing management reports or final accounts. It is about understanding the nature of the communication process, especially for the management of people. If people do not communicate then the accountants work can never succeed.

Central to the communication process is a fundamental element of management – understanding organisational structure. Everyone knows what an organisation chart is; every accounting practice, factory, shop and office proudly displays such a chart. But what message is it intended to convey?

The organisation chart describes in diagrammatic form the structure of the organisation. It is the skeleton upon which every other activity depends. More importantly, it is the framework that explains the communication pattern, process and the linking mechanisms between the roles. It illustrates to everyone who communicates with whom, how the control system works, who is in control, who has authority and above all, who is responsible. It explains how the organisation is co-ordinated and how individual departments relate. It describes:

· Directions of responsibility – the chart indicates the direct relationship between a group and its immediate supervisor and subordinates.
· Relationships between various sections within a department.

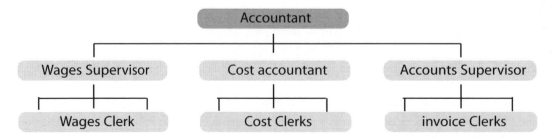

Peer relationships - there are people you work with and who share similar goals to you. Your plans and schedules need to dovetail with those of other individuals and teams with whom your work is linked.

An important skill in working with others is being able to identify what your role should be in relation to them and behaviour expected of you in this role. It will help you avoid inappropriate behaviour such as over-familiarity or insubordination.

In most organisations this role and the responsibilities involved in the role will be determined by the job description. Every employee should have a detailed job description. Only then can one fully appreciate one's own role and responsibilities.

Job descriptions – will provide the following information:

- **Identification of the job** – this includes the job title, the department/organisation structure and the number of people doing the job.
- **Purpose of the job** – identifying its objectives in relationship to overall objectives.
- **Position in the organisation** – many firms refer to existing organisation charts.
- **Duties** – the principal duties to be performed, with emphasis on key tasks, and limits to the job-holder's authority. When listing of all the tasks involved it is preferable to use an active verb to precede each duty e.g. types letters to clients; lists totals of debtors.
- **Responsibilities** – a statement outlining the responsibilities for the resources e.g. staff, money and machinery.
- **Physical conditions** – including details of noisy, dirty, dangerous conditions as well as pleasant office conditions, hours of work, overtime and unsocial hours, etc.
- **Social conditions** – the type of group the employee will be concerned with.
- **Grade and salary/wage range and fringe benefits** – details of the rates for the grade, plus fringe benefits such as luncheon vouchers, pension schemes, company car, etc.
- **Promotion prospects** – to whom the job reports and at what level, with possible indications about future succession, prospects of promotion or transfer.
- **Key difficulties** – no job description is complete without a full identification of the key difficulties likely to be encountered by the job-holder.

Example – you are a sales ledger clerk with certain responsibilities for a number of customer accounts. You have made an appointment with the sales ledger manager to discuss the credit limits of seven of your current customers. During the course of the meeting your manager makes it quite clear that the subject of credit limits is the sole responsibility of another member of the staff. They are quite clearly outside of your own responsibilities.

The result of not knowing your own role and responsibilities has meant wasted time for both yourself and your manager.

1.3 Organisation manual or handbook

An office manual is a useful document for drawing together and keeping up-to-date all relevant information for the guidance of staff about:

- the background and structure of the organisation – this could be a paragraph on the history and location of the organisation and an organisation chart
- the organisations products, services and customers
- rules and regulations
- conditions of employment – facilities for staff, pay structure, hours, holidays and notice etc.
- standards and procedures for health and safety
- procedures for grievance, discipline and salary review
- policy on trade union membership.

1.4 Relevant staff

If you wish to discuss a work related matter then an initial problem is who is the appropriate or relevant member of staff to discuss this matter with. This will usually depend on the roles and responsibilities of other members of staff, which you may not know in detail. However the options are usually as follows:

- **Line managers** – these are managers who manage various areas or departments of a business, for example the production manager, sales manager, marketing manager, finance manager, etc. If the matter to be discussed appears to be important or personal then the appropriate line manager will probably be the person to approach.
- **Immediate colleagues** – if the matter to be discussed is regarding, perhaps, advice as to how to approach a routine task then a colleague with more experience than yourself might be the appropriate person. It is worth bearing in mind that a great deal can be learnt from colleagues with greater experience than oneself.
- **Other members of staff with related work activities** – in many instances knowledge and understanding of a particular matter will be shared by a number of members of staff throughout the organisation, even though they are in different departments or activity areas. These could be the appropriate people to discuss matters with in certain circumstances.

1.5 Methods of establishing constructive working relationships

To establish constructive working relationships with other individuals the following points must be taken into consideration:

- Not all employees will have the same aptitudes, learning or experience as you. This does not mean they are better or worse than you at their job but these elements should be taken into consideration when dealing with that individual.
- Some employees will be highly motivated while others will be hardly motivated at all. In the work environment it is likely that students will deal with individuals with a wide range of motivation levels. Again this aspect must be taken into consideration when dealing with an individual.

- The employees that you have to work with will have a wide range of personalities. Some of these personalities will be akin to your own, but others will not. Wherever possible you should attempt to ignore any personality conflicts that might occur.
- We should acknowledge that we are all human and will get it wrong from time to time; when we get it wrong we should try to recognise this ourselves, apologise and put it right next time. By striving to work through problems and potential problems together, we can understand pressures and deadlines and support each other. We should understand that if there are problems that we cannot resolve between ourselves we ask for help from appropriate sources. Ideally, mutual agreement on referring unsolved matters to others should be reached.
- We all have a duty to share knowledge and expertise as appropriate and should aim to share sufficient knowledge of each other's work to cover priorities of colleagues' work in unforeseen circumstances.

There are a variety of ways of establishing constructive working relationships, for example:
- trying to help colleagues whenever possible
- providing information requested by the deadline specified
- bringing any potential issue/problem to the attention of your manager/supervisor at the earliest possible opportunity
- not taking part in arguments
- refraining from 'office gossip'
- trying to find a compromise where you cannot do everything required of you or cannot meet a deadline.

It is often easier to work with people when you know what is expected of you and how you fit into the organisation. In this way it is more likely that you and the people you work with will have the same expectations and for example make the same assumptions about who is responsible for 'what' work.

It is important not just to establish constructive working relationships within the organisation but also outside. A variety of relationships exist, such as;
- **Suppliers** – it is important that suppliers understand what exactly is required and when. Payment and delivery terms need to be clearly defined.
- **HM Revenue and Customs/External Auditors** – ensuring that all relevant information is provided, in the required format, at the appropriate time will assist with developing an effective relationship.

1.6 Contractual, ethical and legal relationships

Under your contract of employment there are various implied obligations. The payment of wages is sometimes described as the employer's primary duty – in that a failure to pay will be regarded as breach of a fundamental term of the contract, entitling you to leave immediately. There are also laws and regulations covering how your employer should treat you in health and safety issues, disciplinary situations and dismissal, redundancy and grievance procedures.

From your point of view as an employee, there is an underlying duty of faithful service implied into every contract of service. This duty may be expressed, in general, as follows:
- to use all reasonable steps to advance your employer's business within the sphere of your employment

· not to do anything which might injure your employer's business.

You also have specific responsibilities under the health and safety legislation to work in such a way as to avoid injury to yourself and others.

Working relationships should be conducted in a spirit of mutual respect. You should endeavour to attain good working relationships and systems of communication that enhance services to customers and clients at all times.

You should not allow your relationships with colleagues to be prejudiced by your own personal views about a colleague's lifestyle, gender, age, disability, race, sexual orientation, beliefs or culture. It is unacceptable and unethical to discriminate against colleagues on any of these grounds.

Actual legislation covers the following areas:

· **Sex discrimination** – this ensures that there should be no discrimination on the grounds of sex or marital status.

· **Race discrimination** – this ensures that there should be no discrimination on the grounds of colour, nationality, ethnic origin or race.

· **Disability Discrimination Act 1995** – provides for disabled people not to be discriminated against in a variety of circumstances including employment.

· **Equal pay** – the Act covers all conditions and terms of employment and not just pay. It aims to ensure that where men and women are employed in like work or work of an equivalent nature, they will receive the same terms and conditions of employment.

· **Rehabilitation of offenders** – it is unlawful for a person with an expired conviction to be refused or dismissed from employment because of that conviction.

1.7 Identifying working relationships

Who do you need to develop working relationships with? You can answer this question by drawing a **Role Map** of your relationships with other people.

· Who do you report to?
· Who reports to you?
· Who do you provide a service to inside the organisation?
· Who do you provide a service to outside the organisation?
· Who provides a service to you inside the organisation?
· Who provides a service to you outside the organisation?

A Role Map identifies those individuals you deal with on a regular basis, such as your team members. But you also have dealings with people outside your team, for example other team leaders and your manager. You may also have dealings with people outside your organisation, like customers or suppliers. Customer service plays an important role in any job. There are many different kinds of customers. External customers are the organisation's clients – they buy goods or services. External customers usually have a choice about where they do business. That is why it is important to know these customers well and give good customer service.

In many ways, relationships with suppliers are the same as those with customers and colleagues. The relationship requires:

· the projection of a positive image of yourself and your organisation
· cultivation through regular contact and communication
· courtesy as a minimum condition for its maintenance

- co-operation in achieving the aims of both parties
- integrity and reliability to build trust.

As business relationships, however, they raise a number of other issues.

- They involve dealings with other business organisations that have their own aims and objectives, which may or may not be in harmony with yours.
- They involve dealings with representatives of other business organisations, who have a dual responsibility to you (as their client) and (primarily) to their employers.
- They are governed by legal terms and constraints, expressed in contracts.
- They are subject to commercial and competitive pressures: if one party is not satisfied, they can break the relationship.

Even if your job does not involve dealing with the public, you still have customers. Your team members and your manager are your customers too. These 'on-the-job' customers are called **internal customers** – they are located within your work environment.

When customers are dissatisfied they will complain. With internal customers this can lead to conflict, poor communication, no decision-making and ineffective work. External customers may take their business elsewhere.

All organisations depend on people to get things done. They provide a service or a product to the organisation's customers. If people cannot work together then they are unlikely to be effective in their jobs. Effective means that they produce goods or services to the standard required and without wasting resources. Effective teams and team members satisfy their internal and external customers' requirements.

2 Interpersonal skills

2.1 Introduction

> **□ DEFINITION**   □□□□
>
> **Interpersonal skills** can sometimes be called interactive, face-to-face or social skills used in establishing and maintaining relationships between people.

If you can answer yes to any of these questions, it indicates your power is based on interpersonal skills.

- Do you have a sense of relationship – rapport – with other people?
- Are you an active listener? Do you make sure you have understood the other person's point of view? Do you make it clear to them that you understand and empathise?
- Do you avoid being either passive or aggressive in formal or informal discussions with others in the organisation?
- Can you persuade or influence another person?
- Are you aware that people admire you in some respects, and do others copy you?
- Do people want to be with you at informal meetings?

2.2 Steps to improve your personal skills

Being able to manage your relationships at work, so that they have the effect you want, is a prerequisite of optimum performance. Key interpersonal skills are the building blocks of relationships. They include

Self-management – when we think of people skills, we usually think of them in relation to other people, rather than how we handle ourselves, and yet most of us realise that we are better or worse at relating to people depending on our 'mood' or attitude. The reason for the 'mood' is the way we are choosing to react to a particular situation; we can learn to choose consciously, and use a mood to our advantage in any situation.

Building rapport – the word 'rapport' comes from the French word that means carrying something back; rapport is about actively making sure that we have some shared message that we both send and receive. We can build rapport by being aware of the non-verbal messages we communicate. If we make eye contact, use a friendly tone of voice, turn towards them, look relaxed and smile, we create the impression of being someone easy to deal with.

Giving attention – paying attention is not the same as listening, and if we want to develop good people skills, we need to learn to pay close attention to people. When someone is really paying attention we feel not just that they have listened, but that they have understood where we are coming from and what we really mean.

Recognising and working with differences – most of us have not been brought up to value other people for their difference, often we have to learnt to judge others because of it. By finding out how others are different from us, we gain very useful information to help us to deal with them more effectively. We can find out about other people's approaches or perspectives by asking 'what' and 'how' questions; e.g. How did you do that? What prompted you to handle it in that way? How is that important for you? If you were left to your own devices, how would you deal with this? Once you have found out what really matters to the other person, you can make your communication with them much more effective.

Conveying your message clearly – if we want to be sure our message is received correctly, it is important that we are sure what our message is! You may wish to tell people about new working practices, but additionally, your tone of voice, body language, choice of words will tell them what sort of person you are, what you feel about your overt message, how you operate in the world and what you think and feel about your listeners. Being clear in our

KAPLAN PUBLISHING

own minds what our message is, and what we want the listener to do or feel as a result helps to ensure that the right message is conveyed.

Using feedback – this is a term that describes a loop of action and reaction. The most common feedback we receive is that which is given unconsciously, it is the immediate response or reaction to what we have done or said. If you are not sure of someone's reaction, asking them is the simplest way of finding out, but we need to guide the feedback, as most people are not good at giving useful information about their reactions and will tend to rationalise or justify their responses.

Working in a team – good team skills include respect for each other's viewpoints, sharing information, mutual support, and presenting a coherent front.

Dealing with conflict – when you strongly disagree with someone, it is hard to maintain a good working relationship, as we tend to equate the disagreement with the person. It is important in dealing with conflict to step back and assess the situation objectively. Identify the reason for the conflict (misunderstanding, different approaches, different interests?) and where possible find common ground. Changing the language of discussion can improve the situation; notice the difference in feeling these pairs of comments produce:

You make me angry	I am angry about X
You're wrong	I don't agree with what you are saying
You don't understand	I haven't made myself clear

2.3 Negotiation

> **□ DEFINITION**   □□□□
>
> **Negotiation** is an activity that seeks to reach agreement between two or more starting positions.

It attempts to resolve and accommodate differing interests by moving towards an end point that is acceptable to both sides - a 'win-win' situation. A 'win-lose' situation culminates where one group has achieved its objectives at the clear expense of the other. This solution tends to cause dissatisfaction and the situation could deteriorate into a 'lose-lose' position where the benefits originally gained by the winner are continuously eroded by resistance and a lack of commitment.

Negotiation skills help you to resolve situations where what you want conflicts with what someone else wants. The aim of negotiation is to explore the situation to find a solution that is acceptable to both parties.

The skills of a negotiator can be summarised under three main headings:

· Interpersonal skills – the use of good communicating techniques, the use of power and influence, and the ability to impress a personal style on the tactics of negotiation.

· Analytical skills – the ability to analyse information, diagnose problems, to plan and set objectives, and the exercise of good judgement in interpreting results.
· Technical skills – attention to detail and thorough case preparation.

Everyone negotiates – almost every day – and certain principles seem to be present which anyone can learn.

Ask questions – before stating a position or making proposals, it is very helpful to inquire about the other side's interests and concerns. This will help you understand what is important to the other side and may provide new ideas for mutual benefit. By asking clarifying questions you can really understand the other's concerns in this negotiation and this will help determine their approach to negotiations: win-lose or win-win. You can then make more realistic proposals.

'Win-win' negotiations involve understanding each other's interests and finding solutions that will benefit both parties. The goal is to co-operate and seek solutions so both parties can walk away winners. If you come to the table thinking only one person can win (win-lose), there won't be an effort to co-operate or problem solve. By the same token, if you come to the table expecting to lose (lose-win), you play the martyr and resentment builds.

Respect – when the other side feels that you respect him or her, it reduces defensiveness and increases the sharing of useful information – which can lead to an agreement. When people feel disrespect, they become more rigid and likely to hide information you need.

Trust – people tend to be more generous toward those they like and trust. An attitude of friendliness and openness generally is more persuasive than an attitude of deception and manipulation. Being honest about the information you provide and showing interest in the other side's concerns can help.

In most situations a negotiation strategy is not an easy option but it is one that has much more of a positive outcome than an imposed solution. The first step is to get the parties to trust you. Next, you can try to find as much common ground as there is between the parties and encourage them to arrive at a middle ground. If neither party get what they want then you have a lose-lose situation. This is a very common situation where compromise comes in. Unfortunately, compromises result in needs not being satisfied. You are aiming for a win-win situation, where both parties get as close as possible to what they really want. This situation is not always possible but working towards it can achieve mutual respect, co-operation, enhanced communication and more creative problem solving. You need to start by identifying what both parties really want – as opposed to what they think they want. The parties also need to explain what they want it for and what will happen if they do not get it. This procedure is a severe test of a person's interpersonal skills, but it could bring about the best solution.

Negotiating styles that can be used are competing, collaborating, compromising, accommodating, and avoiding.

KAPLAN PUBLISHING

Competing – 'hard bargaining' or 'might makes right' Pursuing personal concerns at the expense of the other party. Competing can mean 'standing up for your rights' defending a position that you believe is correct or simply trying to win.

Where you do not expect to deal with people ever again and you do not need their goodwill, then it may be appropriate to 'play hardball', seeking to win a negotiation while the other person loses out. Many people go through this when they buy or sell a house – this is why house buying can be such a confrontational and difficult experience. Similarly, where there is a great deal at stake in a negotiation (for example, in large sales negotiations), then it may be appropriate to prepare in detail and use a certain amount of subtle games-manship to gain advantage.

Collaborating – 'sharing tasks and responsibilities' or 'two heads are better than one'. Working with someone by exploring your disagreement, generating alternatives, and finding a solution that mutually satisfies the concerns of both parties. In an ideal situation, you will find that the other person wants what you are prepared to trade, and that you are prepared to give what the other person wants.

· **Compromising** – seeking a middle ground by 'splitting the difference', the solution that satisfies both parties.
· **Accommodating** – 'soft bargaining' or 'killing your enemy with kindness' Yielding to another person's point of view – paying attention to their concerns and neglecting your own.
· **Avoiding** – 'leave well enough alone' Not addressing the conflict, either by withdrawing from the situation or postponing the issues.

Preparing for a successful negotiation

Depending on the scale of the disagreement, a level of preparation may be appropriate for conducting a successful negotiation.

For small disagreements, excessive preparation can be counter-productive because it takes time that is better used elsewhere. It can also be seen as manipulative because just as it strengthens your position, it can weaken the other person's.

If a major disagreement needs to be resolved, then it can be worth preparing thoroughly. Think through the following points before you start negotiating:

Goals: what do you want to get out of the negotiation? What do you expect the other person to want?

Trades: What do you and the other person have that you can trade? What do you each have that the other might want? What might you each be prepared to give away?

Alternatives: if you don't reach agreement with the other person, what alter-natives do you have? Are these good or bad? How much does it matter if you do not reach agreement? Does failure to reach an agreement cut you out of future opportunities? What alternatives might the other person have?

Relationships: what is the history of the relationship? Could or should this history impact the negotiation? Will there be any hidden issues that may influence the negotiation? How will you handle these?

'Expected outcomes': what outcome will people be expecting from this negotiation? What has the outcome been in the past, and what precedents have been set?

The consequences: what are the consequences for you of winning or losing this negotiation? What are the consequences for the other person?

Power: who has what power in the relationship? Who controls resources? Who stands to lose the most if agreement isn't reached? What power does the other person have to deliver what you hope for?

Possible solutions: based on all of the considerations, what possible compromises might there be?

If this is not the case and one person must give way, then it is fair for this person to try to negotiate some form of compensation for doing so – the scale of this compensation will often depend on the many of the factors we discussed above. Ultimately, both sides should feel comfortable with the final solution if the agreement is to be considered win-win.

▷ ACTIVITY 1

You are a manager of quite a large accounts department. You have three deputies and the rule is that only one of them can be away on holiday or attend a course at a time. All three approach you in March asking for the same two weeks off in June. Tom, who is the most senior of the three, wants to do a sponsored bike ride in Cuba. Dick wants to take his family to Las Vegas for his brother's wedding. Harry has been accepted on a special course that will enhance his promotional prospects.

Each of them hears about the other's applications and they have a furious row and now only talk to each other about work-related matters.

Outline five different ways of dealing with this situation.

[Answer on p. 83]

2.4 Problem solving

Problem solving and decision taking are virtually part of the same process. Most decisions are made to solve (or forestall impending) problems and most problems have a number of possible solutions. A decision has to be taken on which solution to adopt. A typical problem solving sequence has been defined as containing seven principal steps:

1 perceiving some need or problem
2 gathering relevant facts and identifying the real problem
3 looking for new information and analysing the wider picture
4 proposing alternative ideas for a solution
5 calculating and choosing a final solution which seems the most viable

6   implementing the solution

7   verifying and checking that the solution is satisfactory over a period of time.

One of the most powerful and yet simplest methods for getting at a problem is to gather all the facts and then ask the questions, for example, 'what is currently achieved, proposed or needed?'

2.5 Critical decision-making

Critical decision-making is the purposeful, systematic, balanced collection and evaluation of facts and circumstances used to determine a course of action consistent with one's role or purpose.

Decision-making is central to both planning and control. Decisions are based on facts and judgement. Because problems vary in nature (short term/long-term, easy/complex, quantifiable/qualitative, etc.) so too does the task of decision-making.

Variables affecting how we make decisions include the following.
·   the conditions under which decisions are made e.g. certainty, uncertainty or total uncertainty – relying on past experience
·   the style of decision making
·   the type of decision maker
·   the type of decision.

There are two distinct types of decision that can be arrived at when solving a problem – routine and non-routine.

1   Routine decisions are ones that are made frequently eg, re-ordering goods out of stock, granting discounts to certain customers. For most of these types of decision there are laid-down written rules and procedures to follow. But the more challenging problems are those, which are not covered by existing rules and procedures.

2   Non-routine decisions require you to go through the process of problem solving:
    –   What is the problem?
    –   What are the possible alternatives?
    –   Which alternative is the best as far as can be ascertained?

Herbert Simon in his research of administrative behaviour saw the decision-making process as having four parts:
(i)   perception of a decision need – the intelligence phase
(ii)   formulation of alternative courses of action
(iii)   evaluation of the alternatives
(iv)   choice of one or more alternatives for implementation.

To which can be added a fifth – **feedback**, to indicate why the decision proved to be the right – or the wrong one.

In an ideal world, people behave rationally and before making a decision they would:

· ask all the right questions
· obtain all necessary information
· discuss the problem with all the interested parties
· weigh all the factors carefully and accurately.

Rational decision-making is based on optimal choice.

The main stages in the decision making process are as follows:

· Identify an opportunity to exploit (proactive) or identify a way to solve a problem (reactive).
· Conduct a search to establish alternative courses of action.
· Gather information about each alternative.
· Undertake an analysis of advantages and disadvantages of each alternative.
· Rank alternatives in order of preference.
· Initiate action to implement decision.
· Monitor feedback to ensure response is as expected.
· Review outcome and add new knowledge to mental store.

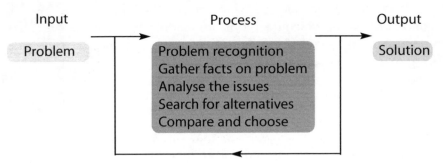

2.6 Discussion skills

Face-to-face discussions may be used where people need to exchange/ give/obtain information quickly, and or obtain documents. This form of communication is appropriate when working relationships need to be developed or negotiation/persuasion has to take place.

The reasons for joining in a group discussion are that it:

· helps you to understand a subject more deeply
· improves your ability to think critically
· helps in solving a particular problem
· helps the **group** to make a particular decision
· gives you the chance to hear other peoples' ideas
· increases your confidence in speaking
· can change your attitudes.

Asking questions and joining in discussions are important communication skills for students. If you find it difficult to speak or ask questions in tutorials, try the following strategies.

Observe – attend as many seminars and tutorials as possible and notice what other students do. Ask yourself:

·   How do other students make critical comments?
·   How do they ask questions?
·   How do they disagree with or support arguments?
·   What special phrases do they use to show politeness even when they are voicing disagreement?
·   How do they signal to interrupt, ask a question or make a point?

Practice – start practising your discussion skills in an informal setting or with a small group. Start with asking questions of fellow students. Ask them about the course material. Ask for their opinions. Ask for information or ask for help.

Participate – take every opportunity to take part in social/informal discussions as well as more structured/formal discussions. Start by making small contributions to tutorial discussions; prepare a question to ask, or agree with another speaker's remarks. Remember that a discussion is not an argument. Learn to disagree politely. Think about your contribution before you speak. How best can you answer the question/contribute to the topic?

Leading a discussion – you may be in a seminar group that requires you to lead a group discussion, or lead a discussion after an oral presentation. You can demonstrate leadership by:

·   introducing yourself and the members of the group
·   stating the purpose of the discussion
·   inviting quiet group members to speak
·   being objective
·   summarising the discussion.

Chairing a group discussion – when chairing a discussion group you must communicate in a positive way to assist the speakers in accomplishing their objective. The leadership skills you can use to influence other people positively and help your group achieve its purpose include:

1   introducing the topic and purpose of the discussion

2   acting as gatekeepers – encouraging more-or-less equal participation among group members by stopping dominators and making openings for less aggressive members by directly asking for their opinions or making a general request for input

3   occasionally compiling what has been said and restating it to the group in summary form – following a summary with a question to check for agreement

4   thanking group members for their contribution

5   being objective in summarising the group's discussion and achievements and stating the decision that seems to have been made

6   checking whether the team agrees with the summary.

3 Communication skills

3.1 The need for communication

Communication is the basis of our relationships with other people. It is the means whereby people in an organisation exchange information regarding the operations of the enterprise. It is the interchange of ideas, facts and emotions by two or more persons. To be effective, the manager needs information to carry out management functions and activities. All organisations have formal, acknowledged, and often specified communication channels. There will be lists of people who are to attend briefings or meetings, and distribution lists for minutes of meetings or memos. There will be procedures for telling people of decisions or changes, and for circulating information received from outside the organisation.

The goals of any organisation can only be pursued in the context of a complex series of relationships with external bodies.

To communicate effectively with the customers, various interest groups and the community at large, organisations should have an integrated communications strategy. Many companies seek to achieve this by working to a stakeholder model. One major bank, for example, produces an annual communications plan to take account of relationships with customers, regulatory bodies, political parties, suppliers, media, the community, education and training establishments, trade federations and other banking institutions. Targets are set in respect of each group, with a regular assessment of goals followed by implementation of appropriate actions.

3.2 Communication process

Communication is the process of passing information and understanding from one person to another. The communication process involves six basic elements: sender (encoder), message, channel, receiver (decoder), noise, and feedback. You can improve your communication skills by becoming aware of these elements and how they contribute to successful communication. Communication can break down at any one of these elements. The process of communication can be modelled as shown in the following diagram.

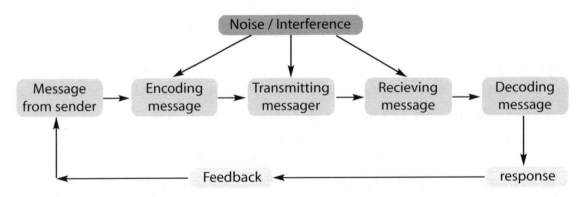

As a sender, the manager should define the purpose of the message, construct each message with the receiver in mind, select the best medium, time each transmission thoughtfully, and seek feedback. Whether written or spoken, words are used to create pictures and stories (scenarios), and are used to create involvement.

Within the communication process it is also important to note the problem of 'noise' or interference. Anything in the environment that impedes the transmission of the message is significant. Noise can arise from many sources, e.g. factors as diverse as loud machinery, status differentials between sender and receiver, distractions of pressure at work or emotional upsets. The effective communicator must ensure that noise does not interfere with successful transmission of the message.

As illustrated in the above diagram, it is feedback that makes communication a two-way process rather than a series of send-receive events. Feedback is a vital and often neglected aspect of the process, which indicates to the sender whether or not his message has been successfully received, understood and interpreted. Failure to seek or offer feedback, or ignoring feedback offered, is one of the major problems in communication.

Feedback takes various forms. In a conversation it can be immediate (e.g. the changed expression on a person's face). In business it might be delayed.

Just as feedback is a crucial part of the internal communication process, it is a vital issue in relation to external communications. Businesses must actively seek feedback in order to keep appraised of feelings, intentions and actions of the groups of stakeholders described above. For example, regular meetings with suppliers are essential.

3.3 Communication skills

Effective communication skills are vital requirements for accounting technicians. The overriding purpose of an accounting system is to communicate with other people in the organisation - to give information, to signal instructions, to control and to confirm information or estimates previously given. Good communication helps to advance the aims of the organisation. Failure to impart the right information to the right person at the right time in the right manner is one of the major causes of inefficiency.

Accountants need to demonstrate interpersonal skills and have the ability to communicate with peers, clients, developers, external bodies, contractors, agencies, suppliers and all levels of management in order to accurately disseminate information on projects, products, and services. In choosing the right type of communication for accounting information the following factors would be closely considered.

- **Urgency of information** – normally one would expect accounting information to be written but occasionally a speedy reply to an urgent request is given verbally, with written confirmation following soon afterwards.

- **Accuracy and detail of information** – the vast majority of people assume that any accounting information is correct to many decimal places. However, to achieve such accuracy costs both time and money, which in many cases is unnecessary and unjustified. Many accountants work to the maxim – 'better to be about right quickly, rather than precisely wrong too late' – particularly when preparing and presenting control information. Also, in many cases, too much detail can obscure the overall impact of the information – and it is up to the accountant to avoid this 'data-clog'.

- **Requirements of the recipient** – in too many cases the way in which information is to be presented is left solely to the accountant. It is up to the accountant to present a report in the recipient's terms, avoiding accountancy jargon and explaining any inescapable technical terms. For formal accounting reports, presentation has to be based on SSAPs, accounting convention and statutory requirements. However for control statements, the manager may prefer to act upon certain key ratios, or analyses based upon his own perceptions. In such cases, the service provided by the accounting department could be greatly improved by consultations with the manager concerned.

- **Confidentiality** – as much accountancy information is of a confidential nature it is important that this is allowed for in determining the method of communication.

- **Facilities required** (and available) – as stated above the presentation of accounting information can be both expensive and time consuming. Therefore, in determining what information can be made available, and in what detail, it is important that the equipment and staff required are investigated and that the benefit of the information provided is value for money.

- **Impression to be made** – obviously any communication from the accounting department must appear to be professional and instil confidence in the recipient. The quality of the paper used for any written communication must be carefully considered to create the right impression eg, quality paper for annual report, whilst routine internal reports may be prepared on less prestigious paper or possibly computer printouts.

4 Communication types

4.1 Written communication – letters

Written methods of communication of all sorts – letters, memos, bulletins, files, circulars – are the norm in many companies. They do have the advantage that being in permanent or hard copy form they are less open to misinterpretation. With meetings, for instance, formal minutes may be taken, circulated and agreed to as the definitive written evidence of the meeting. Written methods of communication can be very flexibly used. When trying to reach a number of workers in one place, notice boards are often used, typically to announce meetings, job vacancies, health and safety notices, details of company social events and similar matters which are not of crucial significance.

Letters and memoranda can cover a vast array of matters. The content is therefore likely to vary greatly. Some may be purely written in content, whereas others may involve some numerical information, perhaps in tabular or graphical form.

4.2 Business letters

Business letters are used as ways of communicating between companies. They may be used to request information, send information, sell products or for dozens of other reasons. Either way, business letters must look professional. A letter from your company is often the first impression that a potential client or buyer receives about your business. You want that first impression to be a good one and the way to do that is to format your business letters correctly and professionally.

Each basic part of a business letter is listed below with a complete explanation of its purpose. An example letter is provided as a reference at the end of this article.

- **Heading** – this is the address of the sender. Most businesses have a letterhead with this information already imprinted. If you do not have a pre-printed letterhead, you can create one on your computer that looks very professional. You should include the name of the company, the address, telephone and fax numbers and e-mail address. You may also choose to include your company's logo. If you are not using a letterhead, you should enclose a return address, this is simply the address of the letter's sender.

- **Date line** – the month should be written out in full, followed by the date and the year, also written out in full. Example: 1 January 2005. If you are using a company letterhead, the date line should be typed three lines below the heading. If you are using a return address, type the date line directly below the return address, leaving no spaces.

- **Inside address** – this is the name and address of the person or business that you are sending the letter to. The person the letter is addressed to is also called the addressee. Type the inside address five lines under the date line. The inside address should contain the same information that will be used on the envelope.

- **Salutation** – this is the letter's greeting. It should be typed two lines underneath the inside address. Include the addressee's name and courtesy title along with the greeting. Example: Dear Mr. Piper.

- **Body of letter** – this is where you discuss the purpose of the letter. The body begins two lines below the salutation. Usually the body paragraphs should be single spaced with two spaces between each paragraph. If the letter is very short, you may use double spaces between the sentences to give a balanced look to the letter.

- **Complimentary close** – this close is a courtesy signal at the end of each letter. It should be typed two lines below the body of the letter. Keep your complimentary close professional. Never close a business letter with Love, Your Friend or any other personal notation. Some good, professional choices are Sincerely, Cordially, Regards and Respectfully.

- **Writer's name and title** – the writer's name should be typed on the fourth line following the complimentary close. The writer's title should be on the line directly below the name. The space in between the complimentary close and the typed name is to be used for the writer' signature.

Letter styles

There are two basic styles in which to write a business letters. They are the block format and the modified block format with indented paragraphs.

In the block format, all parts of the letter are started at the left margin. The body of the letter is single spaced, with one line left between each paragraph. The paragraphs are not indented.

The modified block with indented paragraphs is very similar to the block format. The difference is that each paragraph is indented five spaces.

Example block business letter

123 Any Street
Anywhere, AB12CD
1 January 2005

Dear Mr Piper

This is where you will begin the first paragraph of your business letter. Do not indent any spaces in a block format. Start each line at the left margin. When you are ready, you may go on to your second paragraph.

This is where you will begin your second paragraph of your business letter. Just as in the first paragraph, you will not indent the paragraph. You should leave one line between the two paragraphs. After you have finished writing your letter, you are almost done.
Sincerely,

Chris Turner
Letter writer

Types of business letter

The main types of business letter that you might be required to send, or be involved in, are as follows:

· **Enquiry letter** – if information is required from a source external to the organisation the most appropriate way of gaining it might be by writing a letter to the appropriate source. This would be a letter enquiring about the particular information that was necessary. In such an enquiry letter it would be important that the precise details of the information required were made clear. In order to facilitate the provision of the information it might also be necessary to state why the information is required and for what purpose it would be used.

· **Information letter** – a letter that provides information to a customer, for example, is likely to be one of the most frequent types of letter that you might be involved in preparing. If information is to be given in a letter then the following factors should be considered:

   – the introductory paragraph should explain who required the information and any background regarding where this information has come from

   – the main body of the letter would include logically sequenced paragraphs showing the essential arguments or message of the information

   – a final concluding paragraph summarising the main points of the information and dealing with any further action required by the recipient of the letter.

· **Confirmation letter** – this is generally a letter in reply to an enquiry letter from someone outside the organisation eg, a letter confirming the price, availability or other details of products of the organisation.

· **Acknowledgement of receipt** – in some circumstances it is not possible to reply immediately to a letter that has been received. However one would not wish the sender of the letter to feel that their letter had been ignored or that it was not being dealt with promptly. If there is likely to be a delay before a reply can be sent to a letter, for example because information needs to be gathered in order to reply, then it is polite to send an acknowledgement letter. If possible some indication should be given of when a responding letter will be sent.

· **Letter of complaint** – in some instances it may be necessary to send a letter complaining about a product or service that has been received. Such a letter should state clearly the following points:

   – any background information necessary to fully comprehend the complaint

   – precise details of the goods or services being complained about

   – details of the actual fault or poor service giving rise to your complaint and a general description of the adverse consequences that resulted from this

   – your expectations of how this problem should be rectified.

· **Letter dealing with complaint** – if it is necessary to write a letter to a customer who has complained about the product or services of the organisation then it will be necessary to exercise a certain amount of tact and diplomacy. The general points to consider are as follows:

   – Apology – if the organisation is at fault in any way then a brief but sincere apology will be necessary.

- Explanation – it will also be necessary to explain the reason for the faulty goods or poor service, however it is not necessary to attach blame to an individual or a particular group of individuals.
- Action required – it will then be necessary to negotiate and agree with the customer any form of action that is required to compensate for the faulty goods or services.
  - **Standard letter** – this is an identical letter sent out to a large number of people. For each of the letters only the recipient's name and address, the greeting and any detail such as the amount of any balance outstanding, are to be filled in for each individual recipient of the letter.
  - **Covering letter** – this is usually a standard letter that is sent out with other material. The purpose of a covering letter is normally to explain the other material enclosed within the letter. For example if details of a new product are sent out to long-standing customers then a covering letter from the marketing manager might be included to explain details about availability, delivery dates etc. of this product. A further example might be when an organisation sends out a quotation for a job. The quotation might be on a standard form but a covering letter is included from the production manager explaining perhaps details as to how the total figure has been calculated.
- **Circular letter** – the main point to bear in mind when drafting a circular is that the same letter or memo is to be sent to a large number of people who may have differing degrees of knowledge, understanding, business sense etc. It is therefore important that a circular is drafted in such a way that it will be comprehensible to all parties due to receive it.
- **Engagement letter** – a clear and concise letter of engagement is part of the practitioner's duty of care to the client. The letter should aim to identify to the client:
  - the work to be done and the scope of that work
  - the respective responsibilities of the client and the practitioner in relation to the work and
  - the basis upon which fees will be charged.

We will be discussing this type of letter further in a later chapter.

> **▷ ACTIVITY 2** ▷ ▷ ▷ ▷
>
> Give a few more examples of the type of confirmation letter you may be required to send.
>
> [Answer on p. 83]

4.3 Written communication – reports

Written communication is important since it allows us to communicate our thoughts very precisely over distance and through time. Writing creates a permanent record that can be stored, filed, cross-referenced, duplicated, etc. Text can be read selectively if the reader is already familiar, or not concerned, with parts of the text. Lengthy reports will often contain an executive summary, which people will read before making a decision on whether the report is relevant to them and thus, requires further reading. For example, the Managing Director may only wish to read the conclusions and recommendations for action, whereas others might wish to acquaint themselves with all the details of how and why the investigation was undertaken.

A report is usually a formal clearly structured document, often a lengthy summary of an investigation of a problem culminating in a conclusion and recommendation. The clear structure allows specific parts of that information to be easily located by the reader. Reports range from verbal explanations through to many-paged complex documents.

The object of the report is communication. The reason for writing the report may be to:

· **Inform or define the problem** – by simply gathering the information and packaging it into a report.
· **Analyse** – by analysing the information and presenting that analysis in a report.
· **Evaluate** – by evaluating the information so that the reader can make a decision as a direct result of reading the report.
· **Recommend** – the report writer might be charged with the task of making a reasoned recommendation for a specific alternative or for a future course of action.
· **Describe** – the writer might have been asked to investigate how a specific job of work was progressing and to produce a report noting his or her observations.

A report can take on a variety of different forms:

· **Formal or informal reports** – a report to the board of a company analysing the potential profitability for a new product might be in the form of a large formal document incorporating large amounts of detail such as marketing information and competitor product detail. However, a report to a manager explaining how an employee dealt with a problem customer yesterday may well be a simple memorandum on a single sheet of paper.

· **Routine and special reports** – routine reports may be produced on a regular basis, for example, weekly sales reports and annual labour turnover and, because they are often statistical in nature, may require diagrammatic, tabulated or graphical data. Other reports may be one-off or special reports and commissioned on an ad-hoc basis, for example, the effect of computerisation or the level of employee wage rates.
· **Reports for an individual or a group** – the report might be commissioned by an individual such as the sales manager (effectiveness of advertising report) or requested by the board of directors (balance sheet and profit and loss accounts).
· **Internal or external** – most reports are for use within the organisation but there may be situations where a report for an outside organisation is required.
· **Confidential** – these are usually of a more formal nature, following a formal layout and must be clearly labelled as confidential.

4.4 Report writing – principles

Once the outline of a report has been sketched in the planning stage, the report will need to be written in detail. When writing any type of report it is worth bearing in mind a few style points:

Layout of the report – information is not only conveyed by the contents but also by its design and presentation. The overall impression is important.

Size of the report – diagrammatic, tabulated or graphical illustrations might make the data clearer and emphasise key facts and figures but will obviously add to the bulk of the report. Care should be taken not to waste managers' time by making a report overly long.

Logic of argument – the report should be clearly structured into sections under relevant headings so that the main topic of the report is clearly set out, developed and explained, and the subsequent conclusions fully supported.

Writing style – a formal report is written in the third person e.g. 'it should now be clear that' instead of 'you will be able to see that'. Simple reports in memo, letter or report format concerning day-to-day problems tend to be from and to people who address each other informally. The writing style tends to be more personal, using I, you and we.

Language – a report should communicate as quickly, as easily and as precisely as language will permit. There are different styles of writing used in different circumstances. 'C U 2nite at 8 at pub' is acceptable when texting friends or 'We are having a fab time, booze cheap, hotel out of this world and fantastic scenery' may be just right for a postcard home your sister but a formal business report should follow certain guidelines:

- Write in third person (do not use I, me, or we).
- Use standard English and grammar ('is not' not isn't, 'for example' not 'e.g.', 'thriving' not 'buzzing').
- Avoid abbreviations (if used they should be written in full the first time and the abbreviation shown in brackets), slang, jargon (as described in the Penguin dictionary of troublesome words, may be defined as 'the practice of never calling a spade a spade when you might instead call it a manual earth-restructuring implement'), acronyms, foreign phrases and colloquialisms (a Scot may use 'wee' in speech but should use 'little' in writing).
- Prefer the active to the passive voice (more important for informal reports) e.g., 'a receipt was issued by the shopkeeper' (passive) should be written 'the shopkeeper issued a receipt'.
- Start a new page for every part of the report.
- Number the sections and paragraphs.
- Shorter sentences can improve clarity.
- Use words economically e.g. 'in short supply' can be replaced by 'scarce'.
- Avoid clichés ('explore any avenue'), ambiguity (For sale – bull dog. Eats anything. Very fond of children) and split infinitives (I want to fully understand you).
- Choose the right word – some words are simpler than others. Plan, growth, limit and objective are easier than blueprint, escalation, ceiling and target.
- Replace longer words with shorter. Can you think of short words for perception, initiate and utilise? It might be easier to use view, start or use.

Objectivity – Even if the report is to inform rather than to reach any conclusions it is important that it appears to be written from an objective point of view i.e. is unbiased and impartial. Any emotive or loaded wording should be avoided at all costs.

It is very important to appreciate to whom the report is being addressed to and to understand their outlook and background. For example, an accountant must take care to explain technical terms to people outside the finance function. If you are writing to people higher up in the organisation, or outside it, the style you adopt in your language will tend to be more formal than it would otherwise be for, say, a close colleague or a subordinate.

Knowing what to leave out of a report is as important as knowing what to put in. You must consider the user of the report and ask yourself the following questions:

·   Who is the user?
·   How much background information does the user have?
·   Why did the user commission the report?
·   How much technical or business knowledge does the user have?
·   What does the user wish to get out of the report?

▷ ACTIVITY 3   ▷ ▷ ▷ ▷

Our language is cluttered with phrases that are best replaced by shorter expressions. Try to replace the following with one word.

·   In the near future
·   Along the lines of
·   In short supply
·   At this moment in time
·   Prior to
·   In very few cases
·   With regard to / in connection with
·   A number of

[Answer on p. 83]

4.5 General structure of a report

All reports, whether short or long, formal or informal, need the basic structure of beginning, middle and end.

The **beginning** should determine what the report is about and the relevance for the reader.

The **middle** should contain the main analysis and the detailed arguments supporting your conclusions, recommendations or proposed action.

The **end** should tell the reader what will happen or what you want them to do and include conclusions and recommendations.

Structure is very important. The report will be used for reference so readers need to be able to find the information they need quickly and easily. Formal written reports usually contain the basic sections listed below, though there are slight variations.

Title page:
Addressee or circulation list – the person or persons receiving the report should be identified. At this stage it would be worth stating clearly if the report is to be treated as confidential.

Date – the date of issue of the report should be stated.

Title – this should give a good idea of the subject of the report, without being too long. It should be easy to find in a filing system.

Name of author(s)

Author's position and department

Name and address of organisation

Contents page – many reports will be quite extensive and will include not only the main report but also appendices. This page should contain a list of headings and sub-headings, tables/figures, appendices, etc, and their corresponding page numbers.

Executive summary – the major uses of this are to:
· help readers decide whether to read the whole report
· enable readers to see the key points
· focus attention on the aim of the report.

An executive summary gives the reader a general overview/summary of the whole report without them having to read the entire document. It should be able to stand alone as a separate document if required. The executive summary needs to be written last, because it summarises the information contained in the whole report. As a rough guide it should be about 10% of the length of the report and should only contain material found in the main report.

This section usually includes:
· the *background* to the report
· the *purpose* of the report, i.e. an explanation of why the report was required
· the scope and *limits* of the investigation including brief details of the general procedure, i.e. *what* was investigated, and *how* the investigation was conducted
· the *important findings* or results of the investigation, and the *conclusions* which you drew from the results, i.e. an explanation of *what outcomes* the investigation provided
· *recommendations* for action, if required, i.e. suggestions for what future action needs to be taken.

Terms of reference – usually terms of reference need to state clearly and specifically the permitted and/or possible extent to which an investigation may reach.

Methodology – what research methods were used when preparing the report.

Introduction
The purpose of the Introduction is to orientate your reader to the whole document, and to give your report a context. You can do this by including:

- a clear statement of purpose – why this topic is being investigated
- background to the report – why the report was requested and by whom
- scope and limits of the report – what issues are covered in it, what issues are not covered and why
- the methods of investigation – how you investigated this topic

Main body of the report – here you describe what you found out from your investigation, and analyse what those findings mean. Each section and sub-section should have informative headings. The sections include:
- A fuller statement of the problem.
- How it was investigated and what was discovered – there is usually a para-graph that explains or identifies the methods of investigation or research used. When other sources of information have been used in writing the report, they can be acknowledged here.
- The results or findings.
- An analysis, discussion and interpretation of the results.
- You may find the following suggestions helpful in writing this part of the report:
- Adapt you preliminary plan if necessary to organise your ideas under head-ings and sub-headings.
- Be clear about what points you want to make to report your findings. Put what you consider to be the most important points first, followed by those of lesser importance. Support each of these points with relevant evidence, elaboration or explanation.
- Add any diagrams (e.g. graphs, tables, figures, etc) to support and present your material visually. Each diagram must have a title, and be numbered consecutively.

Conclusion and recommendations

The purpose of the conclusion is to restate in a shortened form the most significant points from your investigation and analysis and to make a general statement about the significance of these. This prepares the reader for any recommendations you go on to make. Note that no new information should be included in this section.

The purpose of the recommendations section is to make suggestions about the action(s) or future direction(s) that should be taken as a result of your conclusions. These should be written in order of priority.
Note that in some reports, the recommendations are presented as part of the conclusion. This allows any recommended action to follow directly on from the conclusion that it leads from.

Appendices – are used to present detailed information (numerical, graphical or tabular) that supports the arguments, findings or conclusions of the report and which is of interest but either too technical or too peripheral for most readers of the report. They may also include documentation (letters) or computer programs for facts presented in the report. The contents of the appendices will be referred to in the main body of the report.

References – must contain a list of books or articles that have been consulted, if the report has required it. When referring to information from these sources in the body of the report, they must be acknowledged by means of a referencing

system. The list of references needs the following details:
· Books: Author, Title, Publisher, Edition (unless 1st), Place of publication, Date, Chapter, and page number if relevant.
· Journals: Author, Title, Journal, Volume, Number, date and page number if relevant.

5 E-communications and information security

5.1 Using the electronic information facilities

This section addresses the important issue of your use as an employee of the organisation's electronic information facilities, which includes the computers and other electronic devices, as well as the electronic services such as e-mail (including instant messaging), message boards, chat rooms, voice mail, Internet access, and word processing.

You should use the highest level of care and professionalism in preparing any communications through the use of electronic facilities, such as e-mail or voice mail. Remember that electronic communications create a record of conduct that is more like traditional written communications than purely oral conversations, and that electronic communications may be required to be disclosed as part of legal proceedings.

When you send an e-mail, you may be called upon to explain it years later in the context of a litigation or investigation so do not write e-mails carelessly. Be professional and say only what you mean because deleting e-mails will rarely eliminate the problem. Not only are deleted items often recoverable, any attempt to delete or destroy documents, including e-mails, that are the subject of a request for production from the government or a private litigant is absolutely prohibited and may subject you and the Company to civil and criminal penalties.

The organisation's electronic information facilities should not to be used in a way that is disruptive or offensive to others. You must not:
· transfer, post, or communicate sexually explicit information and images
· send fraudulent, harassing or obscene communications
· make untrue or disparaging comments of co-workers or customers
· send unsolicited bulk e-mail
· send e-mail that appears to come from another person, or
· engage in any other conduct that is contrary to the organisation's policies or detrimental to their public image.

5.2 No privacy

Because e-mail, voice mail and other electronic information resources are used for company business and are the property of the company, you cannot expect that your e-mail and voice mail communications or any other electronically stored information will remain private.

Most organisations will reserve the right to monitor use of e-mail and voice mail communications or any other electronically stored information in order to ensure compliance with their policies and legal requirements. Even when employees leave the organisation, management will be given access to their e-mail, voice mail, and other electronically stored information.

5.3 Non-business use

From time to time, employees may need to send a personal e-mail while on the job from a business screen name or e-mail address. As noted above, however, these communications are not private and may be discovered in a legal proceeding or governmental investigation. In addition, of course, your use of these facilities should not interfere with your work.

If you make personal use of e-mail or other interactive services (such as chat services or bulletin boards), you should make it clear that you are not communicating in an official capacity. In fact, you should not communicate to the public (such as in a chat room or bulletin board) in an official capacity without proper authorisation. For personal matters, it is better to use a personal, rather than business, screen name or e-mail address.

6   Confidential information

6.1 Safeguarding confidential information

In certain limited circumstances you may become aware of confidential information that needs to be passed to the appropriate staff member.

This means that it should not be discussed in any circumstances other than with the person for whom the information was meant. The information should not therefore be discussed in passing with colleagues, managers or in social situations. Confidentiality should always be maintained where considered necessary. Your organisation's affairs and those of its clients are confidential and should not be disclosed to others unless the circumstances are appropriate.

If you are leaving a confidential message for someone who is not available it should be written down, and placed in a sealed envelope, marked 'Private and Confidential Addressee Only'. In particular:

·   You should consider, as appropriate, marking communications with 'confidential' or 'proprietary information' or 'do not re-transmit', since e-mails can be easily re-transmitted to multiple recipients.
·   You should follow the practice of deleting e-mail and voice mail messages in accordance with applicable document retention guidelines.
·   When transmitting extremely sensitive information, there may be risks associated with the use of e-mail. Cell phones and other portable devices using radio technology should not be used for transmitting confidential or propriety information unless the connection is encrypted.
·   Electronic communications must not include any statements that may imply contractual obligations, unless you have followed all the normal steps for reviewing hard-copy contractual documents.

6.2 Organisational procedures

It is each individual's responsibility to ensure that they are fully aware of the organisation's rules and procedures regarding confidential information. It is equally important that an individual follows them strictly.

For example if the organisation's policy is that documents marked as 'confidential' are kept under lock and key then it is important that such documents are stored in a locked storage cabinet or desk each night. This is reasonably easy to remember to do. It is perhaps harder to remember to keep the information locked away whenever the individual is not using it and is not in their office or at their workstation. Such information should not, under any circumstances, be left unattended on a desk.

When confidential information is considered, individuals should be aware that they are only likely to be able to access confidential information if they have been allocated a particular password. If an individual is given a password in order to access confidential information then under no circumstances should they tell anybody else what their password is.

Disclosure of information could damage the organisation if it fell foul of the data protection legislation and caused embarrassing publicity or helped a competitor by allowing sensitive information to be accessed by outsiders or non-related employees.

6.3 Safeguarding the systems

The organisation's electronic information facilities, including all computer and telecommunications networks, are critical to their daily operations. Everyone shares responsibility for its security. In particular:

- You should protect the system from computer viruses. For example, use caution in downloading files, and never download from an unknown source. Also, you must be careful not to hyperlink from e-mail sent to you from an unknown source.
- You should co-operate with the organisation's efforts to control and protect access to their information systems, such as through the use of IDs and passwords.
- Some employees may be provided with remote access as needed to perform work. This creates a risk of unauthorised access to systems. The organisation could be jeopardised if an unauthorised user gains access to the network and steals source code, product plans, or other proprietary information. Anyone accessing systems remotely must protect sensitive corporate data by following specified security measures.
- Unless properly authorised, you should not attempt to test, or attempt to compromise, the system security measures put in place for computers and communications systems, such as through hacking, password cracking, file decryption, or copying software.

6.4 Protecting intellectual property

Examples of intellectual property include logos, trademarks, copyrights, patents, software, and inventions. You should exercise the highest level of integrity and care in managing or accessing information that is available to you. Copyright and trademark laws, as well as contracts, may prohibit the duplication or distribution of others' intellectual property (such as articles, pictures, musical recordings, etc.). You may not use the organisation's facilities to reproduce or distribute others' intellectual property without their authorisation, or beyond the extent otherwise permitted by a license or the law. However, it is normally quite acceptable for an individual to copy a few pages of the work of another person in small amounts either for personal or business usage – even where they may have signalled their copyright by the international symbol of ©.

Unless you intend to copy an entire book or reproduce a copyright article for the entire organisation, it is unlikely that any copyright law would be infringed.

7 Test your knowledge

1   Organisation charts are used to give an impression of the structure of the organisation. Identify three of the following that are represented in diagrammatic form on the chart
(a)   the units (departments) into which the organisation is divided and how they relate to each other
(b)   the structure of authority, responsibility and delegation in the organisation
(c)   the number of employees at each level
(d)   the salary structure
(e)   the formal communication and reporting channels of the organisation.

2   You have just started a new job in an office. Where would you find details of the organisation's rules and regulations?

3   Under your contract of employment there are various implied obligations. From your point of view as an employee, what are your duties?

4   What are internal customers?

5   When negotiating what sort of an end point is acceptable to both sides?

6   Outline the four parts of Simon's decision-making process.

7   List the six basic elements of the communication process.

[Answers on p.84]

8   Summary

In this chapter we began by looking at the formal structure, communications and procedures of an organisation and how they are based on authority, responsibility and functional relationships because you need to know what areas you have authority over and how far that authority extends – who you report to and who reports to you.

Being able to manage your relationships at work, so that they have the effect you want, is a prerequisite of optimum performance. Key interpersonal skills are the building blocks of relationships and we looked at the three specified in the performance range statement of the syllabus – negotiation, discussion and decision-making. A decision implies a choice between alternatives and we discussed how alternatives can be generated, the optimum selected, and how feedback can improve subsequent decisions.

Accountants are used to dealing with figures, but they must also learn to express themselves clearly in words. This is important not only for the passing of examinations, but also in professional work. Over the course of their working life, accountants will write many e-mails, memos and letters and should be well prepared for the degree of precision and organisation required in report writing, but may need practice to improve their written style. We outlined the general structure of a formal report that can be used as a template throughout an accountant's career.

When preparing any communications through the use of electronic facilities, such as e-mail or voice mail, you should use the highest level of care and professionalism, respecting the confidentiality of any information acquired.

Answers to chapter activities & 'test your knowledge' questions

△ ACTIVITY 1 △△△△

As the manager you could deal with the situation in the following ways.

1 Call them all together and explain they must sort the matter out themselves, but if they fail to do so, you will sort the matter out for them by exercising your right to determine the holiday rota, and that no one will be allowed to go that fortnight anyway. If you go for this option, you are choosing the power route. This is fine if jobs are scarce, but highly risky. If you win, they all lose!

2 Call them all together and tell them they must sort the matter out themselves. By choosing this option and letting them sort it out themselves you are avoiding the situation.

3 Talk the matter over with each of them separately to discuss the facts with them. Make a decision as to whose need is the most pressing, get them all together and announce your decision. This option is an attempt at a compromise, although not allowing very much input from them.

4 Tell them individually not to be silly, and suggest they take an afternoon off and talk the matter over with their families/friends/training officer. This solution of patting them on the head and telling them to talk to others is trying to defuse the situation.

5 Discuss all the problems the situation raises with each fully, and if the matter still cannot be sorted out, go to the training officer and see if there is an alternative course; and the Chief Officer to see if on this occasion two deputies can be allowed on holiday at the same time. Bring them all back to hear the outcome. . Only this option begins to address the problems. Even though there is no knowing there will be a successful outcome you are trying to resolve all the conflicting needs.

△ ACTIVITY 2 △△△△

Other examples of confirmation letters might include the following:
· A letter confirming a customer or supplier's balance with the organisation.
· A letter confirming the date of a meeting with a customer.
· A letter confirming contract details to a customer.
· A letter confirming employment details to a potential employee.
· A letter confirming service details to a customer.

△ ACTIVITY 3 △△△△

In the near future – soon
Along the lines of – like
In short supply – scarce
At this moment in time – now
Prior to – before
In very few cases – seldom
With regard to / in connection with – about
A number of – several

Test your knowledge

1   Answer a, b and e

The organisation chart is a traditional way of setting out the way the organisation is divided into separate departments, functions, areas or products. It shows the formal relationship that exists between positions and the structure of authority, responsibility and delegation in the organisation. The formal relationship also sets out the communication and reporting channels. The chart only shows positions within the organisation and not the names, salaries or numbers of employees at each level.

2   An office manual or the organisation handbook is a useful document for drawing together and keeping up-to-date all relevant information for the guidance of staff about:
   ·   the background and structure of the organisation – this could be a paragraph on the history and location of the organisation and an organisation chart
   ·   the organisations products, services and customers
   ·   rules and regulations
   ·   conditions of employment – facilities for staff, pay structure, hours, holidays and notice, etc.
   ·   standards and procedures for health and safety
   ·   procedures for grievance, discipline and salary review
   ·   policy on trade union membership.

3   Under your contract of employment there are various implied obligations. From your point of view as an employee, there is an underlying duty of faithful service implied into every contract of service. This duty may be expressed, in general, as follows:

   ·   to use all reasonable steps to advance your employer's business within the sphere of your employment
   ·   not to do anything which might injure your employer's business.

You also have specific responsibilities under the health and safety legislation to work in such a way as to avoid injury to yourself and others.

4   Even if your job does not involve dealing with the public, you still have customers. Your team members and your manager are your customers too. These 'on-the-job' customers are called internal customers – they are located within your work environment.

When customers are dissatisfied they will complain. With internal customers this can lead to conflict, poor communication, no decision-making and ineffective work. External customers may take their business elsewhere.

5   Negotiation is an activity that seeks to reach agreement between two or more starting positions. It attempts to resolve and accommodate differing interests by moving towards an end point that is acceptable to both sides

– a 'win-win' situation. A 'win-lose' situation culminates where one group has achieved its objectives at the clear expense of the other. This solution tends to cause dissatisfaction and the situation could deteriorate into a 'lose-lose' position where the benefits originally gained by the winner are continuously eroded by resistance and a lack of commitment.

6   Simon saw the decision-making process as having four parts:
    (i)   Perception of a decision need - the intelligence phase.
    (ii) Formulation of alternative courses of action.
    (iii) Evaluation of the alternatives.
    (iv) Choice of one or more alternatives for implementation.

7   The communication process involves six basic elements: sender (encoder), message, channel, receiver (decoder), noise, and feedback.

CONTINUING PROFESSIONAL DEVELOPMENT

INTRODUCTION

Lifelong learning should be the concern of all employees in the organisation and, despite its title, it is arguable that the concept of continuing professional development (CPD) should not be seen as applying only to professionals or managers. Clearly, however, CPD does have particular significance for management development and career planning.

The view of the accounting profession is that the ongoing development of knowledge, judgement and expertise is essential in today's business environment.

All members owe it to themselves, and their fellow members, to ensure that they are professionally up-to-date so that the reputation of their qualification is safeguarded. In so doing, they will be able to provide quality service to their clients, employers and the business community as a whole.

CONTENTS

PERFORMANCE CRITERIA
- Recognise the principles of effective Continuing Professional Development (CPD) to maintain professional and technical competence (to include sources of advice and information outside formal learning) (32.1 C).
- Refer and seek advice from relevant sources for issues beyond own professional competence (32.1 H).

1 Continuing Professional Development (CPD)

1.1 Introduction

You should note that the Fundamental Principles of the Code of Ethics outlined in Chapter 1 highlight the need for members to maintain high standards of competence and to carry out work in accordance with the appropriate technical and professional standards throughout their professional careers. It is recognised that the best and most efficient way for members to maintain and improve their skills is through a planned programme of continuing professional education. This implies that individuals accept responsibility for their own development by drawing on a combination of self-education and using well-established and credible providers of training and education. When planned, this should assist members to accept new roles and responsibilities, and to adapt to changing situations such as new technology, policies, diverse client needs and external changes.

It is not suggested that Continuing Professional Development (CPD) on its own provides assurance to society at large that all members will provide every professional service with high quality. Doing so involves more than maintaining and updating technical and general knowledge; it involves applying that knowledge with professional judgement. Nevertheless, it is certain that members who are not up-to-date with current technical and general knowledge relating to their work cannot provide professional services competently.

1.2 What is CPD?

> **☐ DEFINITION** ☐☐☐☐
>
> **Continuing Professional Development** (CPD) can be defined as 'the continuous maintenance, development and enhancement of the professional and personal knowledge, skills and ability, often termed competence, which members of certain professions require throughout their working lives'.

Continuing because learning never ceases, regardless of age or seniority.

Professional because it is focused on personal competence in a professional role.

Development because its goal is to improve personal performance and enhance career progression and is much wider than just formal training courses.

It is an approach or process, which should be a normal part of how you plan and manage your whole working life. Put simply, a life-long learning approach to planning, managing and getting the most from your own development. Learning and development becomes planned, rather than accidental.

CPD is just the regular learning we all need to do to stay competent and develop new skills so we are effective and successful throughout our chosen careers.

KAPLAN PUBLISHING

There are two strands to CPD:

(i) update CPD, which ensures professional competence and prevents technical obsolescence within the member's field of work

(ii) developmental CPD, which provides new knowledge, broadens skills and opens up new career opportunities.

In any one year, you could be undertaking one or both strands. The term 'professional' is deemed to include both personal and technical competences.

1.3 What counts as CPD?

CPD is not just going on formal training courses or something you always have to take time away from your work for. It does not include learning activities that are unrelated to your work, or career development or activities where you do not learn anything new. Neither is it something extra you have to do just to be a member of the AAT or other professional bodies. It is any kind of learning as long as the subject and activity are relevant to your professional role and learning needs, and there are significant learning outcomes. It is something you will almost certainly already be doing as part of your everyday working life.

A CPD scheme will probably mean a certain amount of your learning will be in the form of 'structured' CPD. Structured CPD is learning where you get guidance from another knowledgeable person (e.g. a lecturer, trainer, speaker at a conference or seminar, experienced practitioner). It also means being able to participate by taking part in exercises, practice the skills being learnt, ask questions etc. Other activities that may qualify as structured learning include service as a member on a technical committee, writing technical articles, or presenting on a structured course (but not repeat presentations). In general, however, one single repetitive activity should not constitute the extent of a member's CPD activity.

Apart from participation in structured learning activities, there is a continuing need for members to keep abreast of a wide range of developments affecting their profession, clients and employers. This is achieved through unstructured CPD hours, such as regularly reading professional journals and the financial and business press. Other unstructured activities may include the use of video or audiotapes, computer based learning programmes, distance learning or alternative forms of learning where there is no interaction with other individuals and no assessment is provided.

Structured CPD	Unstructured CPD
· In house training · Other professional bodies · University courses · Conferences both local and international · Branch courses · National courses · Assessed distance learning · Outside providers · Other structured courses	· Reading professional/technical articles · Educational videos/tapes · Specific reading material that relates to practical work · Distance learning (with no assessment)

Although you have free choice of activities, it is recommended that you consider a reasonable spread of activities. For example, no one would expect all your CPD to be achieved just through research and reading.

Almost everyone's job is about much more than simply applying a particular set of technical knowledge and skills. Communicating with customers and colleagues, organising time and workload, delegating work to others and maintaining records are just some vital skills for all professionals. This is why the AAT does not dictate what subjects you should cover. They recognise that CPD covers a wide range of knowledge and skills.

The most common areas for AAT members are:
· accounting
· information technology
· supervision and management
· personal effectiveness.

Other increasingly covered subjects include customer service skills, learning languages, and health and safety/first aid. CPD can be on any subject you need to do your job properly or to develop your career in the future.

You can decide the relevant subjects for your CPD. But, as an AAT member you are responsible for making sure you are properly up to date and competent in all the key areas of your role.

1.4 Stakeholders involved in CPD

There are several parties with an interest or stake in CPD.
· Centrally there is yourself. CPD contributes to you keeping your skills, knowledge and experience up to date. Your CPD is without question something you should take personal responsibility for. You are the only one who can decide exactly what you need or want to learn, how you would prefer to learn about it, make sure you do learn it, and then put your learning to good use.
· Many employers see it as crucial to development. They use CPD as a means of giving power and focus to a range of human resource development (HRD) interventions. CPD helps with succession planning. For some organisations in

highly competitive sectors, CPD is a means of retaining staff. They go elsewhere if the organisation is not committed to their professional development.
- Universities and colleges also use CPD to help learners link their curriculum to the relevant and often pressing concerns of their current work or their future career.
- Academic institutions also develop CPD in response to the requirements of the professional bodies. These bodies advocate it as a way of supporting their members and as a means to underpin individual charter membership. The AAT can offer advice and guidance about your learning and provide many practical, free or low-cost CPD services and opportunities.

1.5 Why do CPD?

It is important that AAT members remain competent and develop new skills to remain effective in their jobs and careers. This will help maintain members' employability and their reputation with employers, clients and the public. It will also help maintain AAT's reputation for producing and supporting high calibre professionals.

Effective CPD can provide many benefits for individuals, employers, and society in general. Doing CPD will make sure you do not get left behind and that you stay effective. But more specifically, it also helps you to:
- maintain high professional standards for you and your team
- be more flexible and adapt to change/new opportunities
- adapt and move into new areas of practice
- develop the skills to set up or expand your own practice
- get into a better position for promotion
- help your existing organisation to become more successful
- give the best possible service (to colleagues and customers)
- get more enjoyment and personal satisfaction from your work
- help and support others more, e.g. colleagues, family and community.

You are also likely to find other indirect benefits such as:
- financial gain from promotion or setting up your own business
- reduced stress at work through being more effective/productive
- getting on better with people by improving management or inter-personal skills.

If you think about any other occupation, it is easy to see why lifelong learning is so important. Take your hairdresser for an example. Would you still use that person if you knew they did not keep up to date with the latest fashions, techniques and hair care products? Or what about your doctor – would you trust someone to take the best care of you if they still followed procedures and used treatments favoured when they qualified 20 years ago? No, neither would anyone else; and the same principle applies just as much to accountants.

1.6 Where and how to do CPD

The list of learning opportunities around us nowadays is almost endless. You can do CPD in many different ways, including:

- workshops, training courses, conferences
- AAT or other professional body branch/society meetings
- planned coaching from colleagues or specialists
- structured discussion groups
- studying for further qualifications
- on-line/CD-ROM courses
- planned reading/research using books, journals, press, Internet etc.
- using audio, video or IT resources
- special project work or job secondment
- hands-on development of skills (e.g. practising a new IT package or giving presentations)
- membership of local or professional groups
- special project or voluntary work.

2 Learning plan

2.1 Determining your development needs

It is important for members to determine what training and development is needed each year, to get maximum benefit from the professional development activities undertaken.

This is a four-step process:

1 **Appraisal – identify the skills and knowledge that you already have.**
This requires a critical analysis of work experience (skills practised and demonstrated) and previous education and study (knowledge).

2 **Planning – consider where you are heading in your career.**
Determine what your career goals and aspirations are, and consider the job roles within your industry or profession and the skills, knowledge and attributes they require. Perhaps discuss these with a mentor and learn more about the options available. If you haven't already, begin to set goals and identify career aspirations.

3 **Development – identify the 'gap' and plan how to achieve your objectives.**
By completing the previous steps you will have identified the areas in which you need further skill development or knowledge to achieve your career goal or aspiration. The 'gap' is your development or training need. You could plan how to address this gap by simply listing all your development and training needs down one side of a page and documenting all the options open to you on the other side. Consider also the support and resources you may need to address the gap and set actions to achieve your goals.

Research shows that the support of another individual, either a peer coach or mentor, or even support within a group is very advantageous.

- A colleague who you can ask for feedback on your performance and who can occasionally offer a different perspective on things can be very useful.
- Having access to someone with coaching skills and a commitment to working regularly with you can bring much energy and discipline to your development process.
- A mentor is someone who can act as a guide, advisor and counsellor at various stages in your career or perhaps during a particular period of your development, such as studying for a professional qualification. Your mentor may be a colleague or someone more senior in your organisation. Often people choose a mentor from outside their organisation, who can bring an objectivity and greater breadth to their professional development.

The achievement of development objectives requires involvement in a wide range of learning activities on a continuous basis. When arranging your CPD activities you will need to consider your preferred learning style.

4 Evaluation.
When reflecting on your activities you should consider whether or not you have experienced personal or business benefits from your efforts through the practical application of what you have learnt.

2.2 Step 1 – Appraisal

Where am I now? In order to identify future learning and development needs it is important to review your personal and professional experience to date. It is often said that there is no point in deciding where you are going until you have established where you are now. As with other areas in business, identifying what you have already achieved (in this case in terms of skills and knowledge) can provide a sound basis for planning for the future.

You can build a firm foundation for effective CPD by first taking stock of your achievements, experiences, skills and qualities. This is a simple activity, sometimes known as a SWOT analysis. SWOT stands for strengths, weaknesses, opportunities and threats.

Strengths – confirm what you can already do well. Identify your **strengths**, and your **positive assets**: physical, mental, behavioural and emotional. What are your core skills and what have you learnt so far? What do you do well? You may dress well, have a good memory, be good with the telephone, be honest, calm under pressure, a good listener and so on.

Capabilities may be categorised as:
- technical – involves working with tools and specific techniques
- human – the ability to work with people; it is co-operative effort; it is teamwork and the creation of an environment in which people feel secure and free to express their opinions
- conceptual skill – is the ability to see the 'big picture', to recognise significant elements in a situation and to understand the relationships among the elements.

· design skill – is the ability to solve problems in ways that will benefit the organisation.

The relative importance of these skills differs for the various positions in the organisational hierarchy, with technical skills being very important at the supervisory level, conceptual skills being crucial for top managers and human skills being important for all positions.

Weaknesses – identify obvious areas for improvement (either short-term or longer-term). Where are your skills/knowledge lacking? What would you like to improve – from your own point of view and from the point of view of other people?

Opportunities – identify the **opportunities** facing you. Think about what might help you develop further in some of these areas. What are the interesting new trends? Are there changes in markets and professional practice, emerging new specialisms, promotion opportunities or developments in technology?

Threats – acknowledge things that may make progress difficult, and where you might need special consideration or extra help. What **threats** and obstacles do you face? Is your professional role changing? Can you foresee competition from other businesses, legislative changes, and limited opportunities for progression or threat of redundancy?

Strengths	Weaknesses

· Current skills and knowledge
· List your advantages
  – Colleagues will identify these
· Outline what do you do well
  – Competence analysis will identify strengths and development needs
	· What could be improved?
	  – Assessment by supervisor will identify any weaknesses
	· What is done badly?
	· What should you avoid?

Opportunities	Threats

· What are the interesting trends?
  – Keep up-to-date with courses, colleagues and managers as well as publications
· Does your organisation have a high turnover of managerial staff?
  – Appraisals will outline the range of opportunities
	· What obstacles do you face?
	· Is changing technology threatening your position?
	· Is your job changing?

This tool is for an initial brainstorm to begin gathering some detail for your CPD action plan. It is unlikely to highlight everything you will need to focus on. But it will give you a good starting point. You could get even more out of it by asking a close colleague or friend to give you some thoughts on each of the areas.

A skills gap analysis is useful to rate your level of skill on a scale [e.g. scale 1-10; 1 as the lowest skill/knowledge level and 10 as the highest] for different subjects:

Accounting	Business and management
· Corporation tax	· Business start-up
· Personal tax	· Practice management
· VAT	· Employment law
· Inheritance tax	· Customer care
· Capital gains tax	· Leadership
· UK accounting standards	· Team building
· International accounting standards	· Motivation
· Financial reporting	· Coaching
· Charity accounting	· Delegation
· Payroll	· Managing performance
· Management accounting	· Developing others
· Business finance	· Managing meetings
· Auditing	· Objective setting
· Insolvency	· Business planning/strategy
· Financial services	
· Business and commercial law	
· Money laundering regulations	

Personal skills	Information technology
· Time/work management	· Using computers
· Assertiveness	· Computerised accounting systems
· Problem solving	· Spreadsheets
· Creative thinking	· Word processing
· Business writing	· Databases
· Presentations	· Presentations software
· Handling conflict	· E-mail
· Dealing with change	· Internet
· Networking	· Web publishing
· Improving own learning/performance	· E-commerce

2.3   Sample SWOT analysis

Strengths	Weaknesses
· significant experience in sales and purchase ledger functions	· lack of managementaccounts preparation experience (required to assist the management accountant with parts of this, but still quite limited knowledge)
· strong and up to date knowledge of VAT returns procedures	
· bank reconciliation	
· communicate well with colleagues	· contributing in meetings/get very nervous

Opportunities	Threats
· in-house assertiveness workshop · AAT Developing Professional Management Skills scheme 'getting the best out of your-self' module · join a general staff committee (e.g. social or health and safety) to develop experience and confidence of participating in meetings, and giving feedback back to my colleagues · structured on-the-job training plan for management accounts preparation · work with manager to produce Excel hints and tips pack for self and colleagues to use	· staff shortage due to long-term illness of colleague/have to spend lots of time training and supervising temps · heavy volume of work and competition between many different responsibilities · time for manager to help with the computerised accounting package and management accounts preparation · lack of confidence in putting myself forward/speaking up in meetings

There are a number of dimensions to this analysis for individuals.

· Do you have the skills necessary to do the job **today**? (You should have – but if not, training is essential.)

· Do you have the skills to do the job tomorrow? (This may be because of a change in the environment or an expansion of the department – if not, proactive training should be planned to ensure you are prepared.)

· Do you have the skills to do **tomorrow's job**? (Will you be promoted? If so, what new skills and knowledge will be needed? This is development and would be a pro-active approach to succession planning, or a personal strategy to increase the chances of promotion.)

· Do you have the skills for a **different job tomorrow**? (What will be the alternative employment options in the future and what skills and qualifications will be needed? This is the personal career development planning and investment for which many managers are today taking personal responsibility.)

This kind of SWOT analysis should enable you to determine areas of interest and ambitions, which can be used to shape plans for further development. Although there are clear benefits in planning CPD to develop knowledge and skills in new or weaker areas, you should not overlook the potential for further development in your stronger areas. Building on existing strengths is as relevant an aim for CPD as improving in areas of weakness.

It is also important to make a careful assessment of the external environment, including its opportunities and threats. For example, joining an expanding company usually provides more career opportunities than working for a mature company that is not expected to grow. E-learning might make it easier for some people to achieve their qualifications than attending classes at colleges, etc.

KAPLAN PUBLISHING

2.4 Step 2 – Planning

Where am I going? The first stage is to form an action plan before engaging in any development activities. The formation of this plan will assist in monitoring and reflecting upon the activity being undertaken. On completion of the activity, you can then review, reflect upon and evaluate your actions. This whole process should generate evidence that would be documented and fed back into the appraisal/assessment stage allowing for the cycle of activities to be continuously repeated.

Having established areas for action, the next step is to detail your priorities for development. Following the completion of the appraisal step, you should be able to identify gaps in your skills and knowledge where you can set specific development objectives. These objectives should contain an element of challenge so that they carry you on to new ground, but they must also be realistic.

At this stage it is useful to set targets in terms of required levels of competence.

> ☐ **DEFINITION** ☐☐☐
>
> A **competence** is an observable ability to complete a specific task successfully. Competencies are the critical skills, knowledge and attitude that a jobholder must have to perform effectively.

There are three different types of competence:
- behavioural competences include the ability to relate well to others
- occupational competences cover what people have to do to achieve the results in the job
- generic competences that apply to anyone, e.g. adaptability, initiative.

They are expressed in visible, behavioural terms and reflect the skills, knowledge and attitude (the main components of any job) which must be demonstrated to an agreed standard and must contribute to the overall aims of the organisation.

The term is open to various interpretations because there are a number of competence-based systems and concepts of competence. As a general definition, a competent individual can perform a work role in a wide range of settings over an extended period of time.

Some competence-based systems are achievement-led – they focus on assessment of competent performance – what people do at work and how well they do it. Others are development-led – they focus on the development of competence and are linked to training and development programmes to develop people to a level of performance expected at work.

For any competence based system the process is the same:

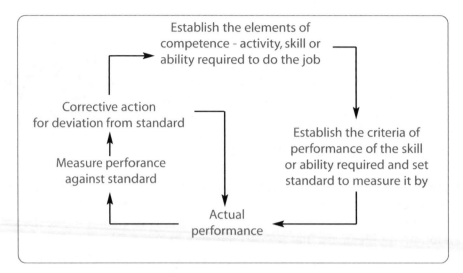

Decide what best describes your current level of competence and the level you now want to attain.

Unaware	· full training and development
Aware	· unaware of subject area and knowledge · possess little or no knowledge/skills · require full training and development
Capable	· possess adequate knowledge/skills · able to work with some autonomy · able to work effectively as part of team · require guidance/some further training
Skilled	· possess requisite knowledge/skills to perform effectively and efficiently · able to work with considerable autonomy · need occasional top-up training
Expert	· acknowledged by others as an authority · very substantial personal autonomy

When establishing your objectives, you should also work within practical constraints, which may influence methods of development. Factors you may wish to take into account include:

· What opportunities and support for learning are available?
· How much will it cost in terms of money, time, and conflict with other commitments?
· What added value will result – qualification, promotion, and new business?

Finally, objectives should be set within a realistic time frame. In some cases they will not be easily achievable within a 12-month cycle. However, it should be possible to determine some progress towards achieving an objective in this time period and to re-evaluate long-term objectives in the continuing cycle of development.

If this is the first time you have attempted to prepare such a plan, you may like to try a proven and easy to use method known by the acronym SMART. The letters will remind you of the five objective-setting rules as follows:

· **S**pecific – use as few words as possible
· **M**easurable – plan small steps with objectively discernable outcomes
· **A**chievable – stay within your physical and intellectual reach
· **R**ealistic – recognise the constraints of available time and resources
· **T**imed – set target dates for every step in your plan

▷ ACTIVITY 1   ▷ ▷ ▷ ▷

Effective personal development planning depends on setting appropriate objectives. What are effective objectives?

[Answer on p. 106]

2.5 Step 3 - Development

How will I get there? The achievement of development objectives requires involvement in a wide range of learning activities on a continuous basis. CPD may take the form of any appropriate learning activity and need not necessarily be biased towards course attendance. The decision as to what constitutes relevant learning and development must lie primarily with you as an individual.

Many people think CPD is just going on courses. While formal training can be a valuable part of professional development, there are countless other things that will help you keep up to date and further hone your knowledge and skills. Many of these other activities could be a lot more useful than the training courses you may have been relying on so much up to now.

Awareness of your preferred learning style, and other learning styles, will help you become a better all-round learner. With such awareness, you can tailor your CPD programme exactly to your own needs and preferences.

Peter Honey and Alan Mumford have identified four key learning styles. These are:

Activists – like to immerse themselves fully in new experiences, to take direct action, welcome new challenges, and try things out and actively participate. They are open-minded, enthusiastic, flexible and seek to centre activity around themselves.

Reflectors – like to stand back and observe, to think long and hard first, listen carefully, and learn from reading and re-reading. They are cautious, take a back seat and use information from past, present and immediate observations to maintain a big picture perspective.

Theorists – like to put things into the broader context, approach problems logically and objectively, and analyse in great detail. They are disciplined, aiming to fit things into rational order and keen on basic assumptions, principles, theories, models and systems thinking.

Pragmatists – like to see how ideas, theories and techniques work in practice, experiment, and go away to try out what they have learnt. They are impatient with endless discussion, act quickly and confidently on ideas, and get straight to the point.

Courses and seminars can be delivered in a variety of ways, including classroom style, multimedia presentations, and interactive group workshops. Not all delivery modes will match an individual's preferred learning style, and attending a course delivered in an inappropriate mode is a principal cause of frustration that course expectations were not met. Research shows that a large proportion of accountants prefer clear presentation of information, supported by underlying concepts and regulations. Also preferred is clear demonstration of technique and practice in real life applications.

The four major learning styles that are highlighted below may help to guide you in the choice of CPD activities.

1 Innovative – day-to-day learning
   · connect new information/skills with personal experience and real-life problems/situations
   · prefer co-operative methods of learning e.g. seminar groups, brainstorming, learning through project work, etc.
2 Analytic 'listening' learning
   · want to acquire knowledge to deepen understanding of concepts and processes
   · prefer to learn from what the 'experts' have to say e.g. lectures, conferences, further qualifications, etc.
3 Common sense – hands on learning
   · be interested in how things work and want to 'get in and try it'
   · prefer experiential methods of learning e.g. through hands-on tasks, on the job learning, etc.
4 Dynamic – teach yourself learning
   · rely on self-directed discovery and want to teach yourself
   · prefer independent study and training which involves simulations, role-play etc.

Many people will find that they have a mixed learning style, which involves two or more of the above. This situation provides a wide variety of possible methods for effective CPD.

Although the emphasis of CPD should be on planned activities, you should also be able to recognise and use unplanned opportunities that may arise. If you have been involved in any activity that did not feature in your development plans but from which you have learnt something, record it and consider whether it applies to any of your specified objectives or whether it may contribute to a new objective in the continuing development cycle.

KAPLAN PUBLISHING

When undertaking the activity, you need to maintain a progress file to record your achievements and review the actions you are taking. The record of achievement can be a vehicle for reviewing, making sense and perhaps for drawing implications for future practice and future learning.

▷ ACTIVITY 2   ▷ ▷ ▷ ▷

With reference to the four learning styles drawn up by Honey and Mumford, which of these styles do you think most closely resembles your own? What implications have this got for the way you learn?

[Answer on p. 106]

2.6 Step 4 – Reflection/evaluation

How will I know when I have got there? To gain the full benefit from any CPD activities undertaken, it is finally necessary to evaluate the outcomes and to establish whether you have achieved your objectives.

The evaluation stage deserves special attention as it produces a summary of the achievements that demonstrate how you have met your original objectives. For any areas of under achievement, you can consider whether or not the original target remains valid or if you simply require more time to achieve it. By reviewing the results of your CPD activity in this way you will continue the learning and development cycle into the next year.

Evidence of your achievement i.e. skills acquisition and improved competence, can be demonstrated in various ways as illustrated below.

Recognised qualifications:	· short course completion certificates · credits for accumulated qualification
Organisation:	· adoption of recommendations as policy · improved business performance · cost efficiency savings · safer working environment · achievement of quality standard
Self:	· measured against own criteria · discussion with manager/colleagues · favourable annual appraisal · recommendation for promotion · change in professional role/duties
Colleagues (peers/superiors):	· request to coach/advise colleagues · suggestion to join/lead project team

Public	· membership of other professional groups
	· solving problem for community group
	· publication of papers/research
	request for advice regarding policy/law
Client	· award of further work
	· award of commission in new area
	· recommendation to other organisation

Although we have described CPD in terms of steps, the reality is that it is a circular process.

Personal growth is both interactive and incremental. Consequently, all lifelong learning plans should be 'living' documents. They should relate to life in the real world, where people and conditions constantly change.

Once you have written your development plan you should revisit each part of the process from time to time. Just follow these simple guidelines:

· your plan when developments or circumstances so dictate
· together, these steps will ensure that you do not lose sight of your overall goals and that your development stays on track.

2.7 Keeping records

Planning, recording and reflecting are the real key to successful CPD so before starting you will need to decide the means of recording your plan and achievements that will suit you best. Remember, as important as record keeping is, it is only a means to an end. It is the process of planning, reviewing, learning and reflecting that matters, not the particular method or format you adopt. However, the very process of writing will help to distil experiences, recognise patterns and discern trends. It enables you to remember what has gone before and capture lessons for the future. It also becomes a valuable and objective measure of your professional competence and, as such, it can be useful when preparing for staff appraisals or tailoring your CV for a specific promotion or career move.

It is important to keep records in two key areas:
(i) A personal development plan – this looks ahead and sets out your objectives and the action and activities you plan to take to achieve them.
(ii) A record of achievements – this is a full record of the action and activities you have undertaken, together with their respective outcomes.

Your records demonstrate you have thoroughly reflected on your accomplishments to date, carefully assessed your present situation and coherently planned your future professional development.

Effective CPD is the production of a structured learning plan, which leads to increased and improved performance. The plan is a four stage cycle: appraisal, planning, development and reflection – that takes you through all the necessary steps to assess your current situation and identify your learning needs, set your learning objectives, find and participate in suitable activities and reflect on your progress.

▷ ACTIVITY 3   ▷ ▷ ▷ ▷

Professional development is a continuous process of reflection, planning and action. Briefly describe the stages of a CPD programme.

[Answer on p. 107]

3   Learning to improve your performance

3.1 Management of learning

Managing learning is about your ability to learn efficiently and be aware of your learning strategies, whether as an individual or as part of a group. You need to reflect on your own abilities and style as a learner, and how you can take responsibility for improving your own learning.

These skills represent possibilities – but please use any other ideas and descriptions that you have:
· use, evaluate and adapt a range of learning skills (analysis, synthesis, evaluation, argument, justification, problem-solving, etc)
· purposefully reflect on own learning and progress
· demonstrate awareness of learning processes
· use learning in new or different situations/contexts
· assist/support others in learning and learn from peers
· develop, evaluate and adapt learning strategies
· carry out agreed tasks
· work productively in a co-operative context
· learn through collaboration
· provide constructive feedback to colleagues
· assist/support others in learning
· interact effectively with supervisor/wider group
· develop business awareness
· evaluate own potential for employment.

3.2 Self-management

Self-management is about your personal organisational skills and being able to cope with the demands of managing your work, your studying, your college life, and beyond. It might also include addressing your personal values and commitments. You need to ask yourself, whether you:
· manage time effectively
· set realistic objectives, priorities and standards
· listen actively and with purpose
· show intellectual flexibility and creativity
· take responsibility for acting in a professional/ethical manner
· plan/work towards long-term aims and goals
· purposely reflect on own learning and progress
· take responsibility for own learning/personal growth
· demonstrate awareness of learning processes
· clarify personal values
· cope with physical demands/stress
· monitor, evaluate and adapt own performance.

3.3 Communication skills

Communication obviously underpins all aspects of life. At work it will often be oral but written and visual communication is equally important. How good are you at expressing ideas and opinions, at speaking or writing with confidence and clarity, at presenting yourself to a variety of audiences? You should be able to:

·   use appropriate language and form in a range of activities (reports, presentations, interviews, etc)
·   present information/ideas competently (oral, written, visual)
·   respond to different purposes/contexts/audiences
·   persuade rationally by means of appropriate information
·   defend/justify views or actions
·   take initiative and lead others
·   negotiate with individuals/the group
·   offer constructive criticism
·   listen actively and effectively
·   evaluate and adapt strategies for communication.

3.4 Team/group work/management of others

Do you fit well into a team? Are you a leader? Have you had a wide experience of working with different types of group, whether formal or informal? Have you been on a team development course? Do you work in study groups, or project groups, or manage meetings for a club or society? Consider your skills of co-operation, delegation or negotiation. How have you worked and learned with others? The following skills would indicate your group working abilities:

·   carry out agreed tasks
·   respect the views and values of others
·   work productively in a co-operative context
·   adapt to the needs of the group/team
·   defend/justify views or actions
·   take initiative and lead others
·   delegate and stand back
·   offer constructive criticism
·   take the role of chairperson
·   learn through collaboration
·   negotiate with individuals/the group
·   assist/support others in learning from peers
·   interact effectively with tutor/wider group
·   monitor, evaluate and assess processes of group/team work.

3.5 Problem solving

Do you like tackling and solving problems? How do you manage your job tasks? Can you identify the main features of a problem and develop strategies for its resolution? Are you able to monitor your performance and improve on strategies? Some subjects may traditionally be perceived as related to problem-solving (say, computing), but, for most of us, in any subject area, assignments such as reports or presentations present us with a variety of problems to be solved.

Problem solving skills means you need to be able to:
· identify key features of the problem/task
· conceptualise issues
· identify strategic options
· plan an implement a course of action
· organise sub-tasks
· set and maintain priorities
· think laterally about a problem
· apply theory to practical context
· apply knowledge/tools/methods to solution of problems
· manage physical resources (tools/equipment)
· show confidence in responding creatively to problems
· show awareness of issues of health and safety
· monitor, evaluate and adapt strategies and outcomes.

4 Test your knowledge ▷ ▷ ▷

1 What is CPD?

2 Briefly explain the difference between structured and unstructured CPD.

3 What is a SWOT analysis?

4 What do activists like to do?

5 People have different learning styles. What type of learning style is associated with wanting to acquire knowledge to deepen understanding of concepts and processes?

6 Why is it important to keep records of your CPD?

7 How would you evaluate your communication skills?

[Answers on p. 107]

5 Summary

CPD is the means by which members of professional associations maintain, improve and broaden their knowledge and skills and develop the personal qualities required in their professional lives. Your CPD should be driven by your need to improve or maintain competence in the areas needed to perform your role. Therefore, your CPD activities should relate to the knowledge and skills

3   You can build a firm foundation for effective CPD by first taking stock of your achievements, experiences, skills and qualities. This is a simple activity, sometimes known as a SWOT analysis. SWOT stands for strengths, weaknesses, opportunities and threats.

Strengths – confirm what you can already do well. Identify your **strengths**, and your **positive assets**: physical, mental, behavioural and emotional. What are your core skills and what have you learnt so far? What do you do well? You may dress well, have a good memory, be good with the telephone, be honest, calm under pressure, a good listener and so on.

Capabilities may be categorised as:
·   technical – involves working with tools and specific techniques
·   human – the ability to work with people; it is co-operative effort; it is teamwork and the creation of an environment in which people feel secureand free to express their opinions
·   conceptual skill – is the ability to see the 'big picture', to recognise significant elements in a situation and to understand the relationships among the elements.
·   design skill – is the ability to solve problems in ways that will benefit the organisation.

The relative importance of these skills differs for the various positions in the organisational hierarchy, with technical skills being very important at the supervisory level, conceptual skills being crucial for top managers and human skills being important for all positions.

Weaknesses – identify obvious areas for improvement (either short-term or longer-term). Where are your skills/knowledge lacking? What would you like to improve – from your own point of view and from the point of view of other people?

Opportunities – identify the **opportunities** facing you. Think about what might help you develop further in some of these areas. What are the interesting new trends? Are there changes in markets and professional practice, emerging new specialisms, promotion opportunities or developments in technology?

Threats – acknowledge things that may make progress difficult, and where you might need special consideration or extra help. What threats and obstacles do you face? Is your professional role changing? Can you foresee competition from other businesses, legislative changes, and limited opportunities for progression or threat of redundancy?

4   Activists – like to immerse themselves fully in new experiences, to take direct action, welcome new challenges, and try things out and actively participate. They are open minded, enthusiastic, flexible and seek to centre activity around themselves.

5   A person who preferred an analytic 'listening' type of learning would want to acquire knowledge to deepen understanding of concepts and processes and would prefer to learn from what the 'experts' have to say e.g. lectures, conferences, further qualifications etc.

6   Planning, recording and reflecting are the real key to successful CPD so before starting you will need to decide the means of recording your plan and achievements that will suit you best. Remember, as important as record keeping is, it is only a means to an end. It is the process of planning, reviewing, learning and reflecting that matters, not the particular method or format you adopt. However, the very process of writing will help to distil experiences, recognise patterns and discern trends. It enables you to remember what has gone before and capture lessons for the future. It also becomes a valuable and objective measure of your professional competence and, as such, it can be useful when preparing for staff appraisals or tailoring your CV for a specific promotion or career move.

7   You should be able to:
    ·   use appropriate language and form in a range of activities (reports, presentations, interviews, etc)
    ·   present information/ideas competently (oral, written, visual)
    ·   respond to different purposes/contexts/audiences
    ·   persuade rationally by means of appropriate information
    ·   defend/justify views or actions
    ·   take initiative and lead others
    ·   negotiate with individuals/the group
    ·   offer constructive criticism
    ·   listen actively and effectively
    ·   evaluate and adapt strategies for communication.

CULTURE AND ETHICS

INTRODUCTION

The second element of this unit is essentially concerned with your ability to demonstrate appropriate skills in ethical procedures as an employee. For example, you must be able to describe the culture of an organisation that would best support high ethical values. You should also be aware of the indicators of low ethical values within an organisation and what steps you can take to raise these ethical values – knowing your own limitations and the problems or issues this creates.

The contents of this chapter will help you to identify whether an organisation's culture is suitable for it and, if it is not, what aspects need to be changed.

The values of the people who lead and make up the organisation shape its culture, which determines the ethical behaviour of the organisation. Therefore, this chapter will give you an understanding of the nature and importance of organisational and professional ethics as well as recommending how ethical behaviour can be encouraged.

CONTENTS

1 Employer/employee situations
2 Culture
3 Sources of organisational ethical values
4 Resolving conflicting loyalties

PERFORMANCE CRITERIA

· Describe the type of culture within organisations that supports and promotes high ethical values and helps resolve any conflict of loyalties (32.2 A)
· Resolve conflicting loyalties where an employer may ask you to perform tasks which are illegal, unethical or against the rules or standards of the accounting profession (32.2 B)
· Follow appropriate procedures where you believe an employer has or will commit an act which you believe to be illegal or unethical (32.2 C)
· Respond appropriately to requests to work outside the confines of your own professional experience and expertise (32.2 D)

1 Employer/employee situations

1.1 Accounting technicians as employees

By the time accounting technicians qualify they will have learned to:
· prepare financial statements
· prepare financial reports and other management information
· compute tax liabilities for companies and for individuals
· set up and manage systems for budgets, stock control, cost accounting, cash reconciliation
· set up and manage credit control procedures
· use computers effectively in business environment.

There is a growing demand for accounting technicians in all areas, including accounting practice, commerce and industry, and the public sector. There are career opportunities in local or central government, educational institutions, the NHS, shops, hotels, charities and voluntary organisations.

Accounting Technicians are also active in the non-profit sector and growing numbers of large retailers, media, energy and manufacturing companies are now employing and training them. The opportunities have increased as the qualification's reputation has grown and now include areas such as internal audit, project accounting and financial and management accounting.

1.2 Contractual relationship

Under common law, the relationship of employer and employee generally exists when the person for whom services are performed has the right to control and direct the individual who performs the services, not only as to the result to be accomplished by the work, but also as to the details and means by which that result is accomplished. The right to discharge is also a factor indicating that the person possessing that right is an employer. Another factor characteristic of an employer, but not necessarily present in every case, is the supplying of tools and the providing of a place to work, to the individual who performs the services.

The relationship between employee and employer is a contractual one, based on agreement. Some may argue that by agreeing to take employment, it follows that the worker has undertaken to work to achieve shareholder profits, rather than pursue individual motivations.

In many cases, an employee's interests outside remuneration are widely acknowledged. For many employees a career path, development and growing responsibility are important. Whether a firm grants those things or not is, in itself, not an ethical issue, providing the firm's intentions are clear. For example, in a family firm, employees may simply have to accept that family members will hold senior positions, and there will never be developmental opportunities to advance beyond a certain point. As long as employees are aware of this, then it is a career judgement rather than an unethical issue.

KAPLAN PUBLISHING

Employees do not have a duty to remain with an employer until the employer no longer has a use for the worker. It is regarded as a legitimate right for employees to further their own interests by changing to another firm.

> ▷ **ACTIVITY 1** ▷ ▷ ▷ ▷
>
> A firm invests heavily in developing human resources in its research and development of a biotechnology drug. The key researchers are headhunted by a rival. What are the ethical issues involved?
>
> [Answer on p. 132]

1.3 The 'new' employer-employee contract

The fact that the business world is changing rapidly is a given. Nowhere in business have we seen greater change in the past few years than in the employer-employee area.

Some 'new' features include:
· skilled workers do not have to put up with abusive managers – they just leave
· the total employee package is becoming more crucial to obtaining and retaining the best employees
· skills, abilities and motivation count more than experience
· employers are demanding more accountability from employees
· employees are becoming the competitive advantage in the modern business world.
· the employee must bring value to the business every day. Trial and probation periods have gone from months to days.
· skills acquisition and continuous learning are essential for the employee to do the job. Job security and employability are now the employee's responsibility.
· work schedules are becoming more flexible

2 Culture

2.1 What is culture?

> ☐ **DEFINITION** ☐ ☐ ☐ ☐
>
> **Culture** is the general pattern of behaviour, shared beliefs and values that members have in common.

There is no shortage of definitions of organisational culture. It has been described, for example, as 'the dominant values espoused by an organisation' and 'the basic assumptions and beliefs that are shared by members of an organisation'. As it relates to organisations, culture is the general pattern of behaviour, shared beliefs and values that members have in common. Handy describes culture as the 'way things are done around here'.

Every organisation has a system of beliefs, values, norms of behaviour, symbols, myths and practices that are shared by members of the organisation. The key elements can be shown in a diagram:

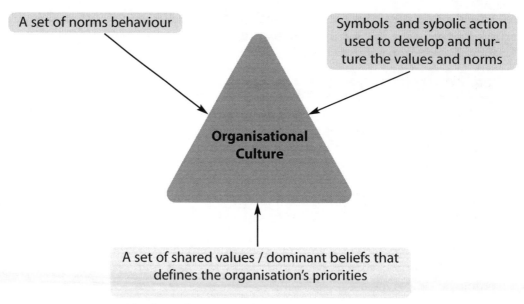

The key elements of organisational culture

Shared values or dominant beliefs – these underlie the culture by specifying what is important and need to be shared by everyone in the organisation so that they are reinforced and widely accepted. Examples of shared values include:

·   a belief in the importance of people as individuals
·   an operational focus such as guaranteeing delivery on time
·   a focus on output, e.g. zero defects.

Norms are an expected type of behaviour required within a given social group. They guide people's behaviour, suggesting what is or is not appropriate. The commitment to shared values must be strong enough to develop norms of behaviour or informal rules, which influence the decisions and actions throughout the organisation. For example, in a 'quality service' culture, fellow workers would informally police sloppy work affecting the product or service, without reliance on formal systems.

☐ **DEFINITION**   ☐☐☐☐

A **symbol** is something that stands for something else - whereas a sign is obvious and designed to be clear.

There are many examples of persistent, consistent and visible symbols and symbolic actions that make up an organisation's culture. These include:

·   the organisation's unique roots established by the personal style and experience of the founder and the original mission, e.g. the concept of entertainment developed by Walt Disney.
·   the organisation's logos and slogans
·   the activities of an executive can send a strong signal throughout the organisation, e.g. regularly visiting the factory floor to establish problem areas and speak to employees
·   rituals such as recruitment techniques, eating lunches and giving impromptu awards help to define a culture.

·   organisational structure can be an attention-focussing process. For example, replacing tables that seat four with ones that seat six in the canteen increases the chances of employees from different departments meeting and interacting with each other.

2.2 Cultural values

Management and leadership guru Stephen Covey suggests that values identify our highest priorities. Values drive our actions, they are what we esteem, what we give worth to. They are the 'unwritten rules' of how people interact including as shoulds and should nots, musts and must nots, rights and wrongs, and things that are important and unimportant. Values are unwritten in that we all have them and they are reflected in what we actually do. An organisation is no different, and should have values that define the character and drive the decisions of the organisation. Writing them down is a good thing only to the degree to which these are communicated and supported by the company hierarchy.

Cultural values may include the following:

Openness – proactive communications, straightforward messages, direct and timely feedback, early expectation setting, sharing the good and the bad and 'no surprises' are all part of a commitment to openness. Organisations should create a culture of open and honest communications where everyone should feel comfortable to speak his or her mind.

Trust – can be defined as 'the assurance that one can count on the good will of another to act in one's best interest'. To build trust and credibility we must do what we say and say what we do. The five elements of trust are benevolence, integrity, openness, reliability and competence.

Trust techniques include:
·   sharing thoughts, feelings and rationale
·   making commitments you can keep
·   admitting mistakes
·   requesting and accepting feedback
·   testing assumptions.

Trust traps include:
·   making assumptions
·   breaking promises
·   covering yourself
·   spreading rumours
·   by-passing people.

Integrity – no matter what type of business it is, integrity must be the primary core value, providing the foundation for all other values. Without integrity other values will lack credibility. Organisations must do what they say they will do and be trustworthy and honest in all their dealings. Honesty and integrity are bedrocks of a value system that is applied not only to how the organisation relates to people, but also to how they keep their business records. Integrity is key to empowerment. We empower people we trust.

Empowerment – is made possible by ensuring that business processes are in place, communication channels are clear and unblocked and relevant measurement and control systems are transparent and adhered to. Empowerment is delegation not abdication of responsibility. Instead, empowerment is sharing responsibility to achieve goals, the means to achieve the goals, accountability for the goals and the means employed, and the authority (power) to accomplish the task within the given set of means. The empowered must act resolutely, stand up for what they believe in, tell the truth and be willing to challenge the status quo. Those who empower must be good listeners, open-minded, empathetic. Fundamental empowerment principles include:

· 'letting go' of things others can do
· developing a sense of enthusiasm, pride, and community
· ensuring appropriate recognition and reward
· encouraging initiative, ideas and risk taking
· ensuring that people have goals and know how they are doing
· coaching to ensure success
· reinforcing good work and good attempts
· sharing information, knowledge and skills
· valuing, trusting and respecting each individual
· providing support without taking over
· practising what you preach.

Accountability – refers to the ability to call public officials, private employers or service providers to account, requiring that they be answerable for their policies, actions and use of funds. It also means holding employees accountable for their behaviour as well as their outcomes, rewarding them for correct behaviour and applying consequences to those not meeting behaviour expectations.

Respect – means being absolutely committed to creating a work environment in which all individuals are treated with respect and dignity. Each of us has the right to work in a professional atmosphere that promotes equal employment opportunities and prohibits discriminatory practices, including harassment. Respect demands that:

· individual actions support the creation and maintenance of a respectful workplace
· everyone understands their obligations for ethical behaviour and seeks help and guidance if they are unsure in any given situation
· when anyone observes any potential wrongdoing, they will take appropriate action and ensure that the situation is addressed, and
· any employee reporting wrongdoing will be protected from retaliation.

It also means respecting diversity, inclusion, civility and individual uniqueness and recognising the strength these factors bring to the workplace and learning environment.

2.3 The organisational iceberg

One way to recognise why people behave as they do, is to view an organisation as an iceberg, having overt, formal aspects on the tip of the iceberg and covert, behavioural aspects hidden underneath.

· The formal aspects (the visible bits) include aspects such as organisational design, financial resources, customers, technology, formal goals, rules and regulations.
· The covert, behavioural aspects (the hidden bits) include attitudes, personalities, conflict, informal team processes and political behaviour.

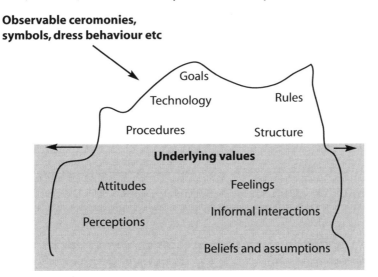

There is a distinction between observable and underlying symbols. By looking at the observable ones you can get an idea of an organisation's corporate culture.

The pervasive nature of culture, in terms of 'how things are done around here' and common values, beliefs and attitudes, will have a significant effect on organisational processes such as decision-making, design of structure, group behaviour, work organisation, motivation and job satisfaction, and management control.

2.4 The growth and maintenance of organisational culture

Organisation culture develops with the influence, style and goals of the creators of the organisation. The founders begin with an original idea, unconstrained by previous ways of doing things and therefore able to impose their vision of how and why things should be done. They play a major role in establishing customs and traditions.

We can distinguish three main sources of the maintenance of culture:
· **Top management** – because of their power and influence, top managers have a considerable influence in either sustaining or modifying organisational culture. Other employees will observe their behaviour and they will establish norms of behaviour that will filter throughout the organisation.
· **Selection** – the selection/rejection decision can be taken on the basis that a potential recruit will or will not help in maintaining the existing culture.
· **Socialisation** – organisational socialisation is the process of indoctrination into the culture of the organisation. Frequently this is done by some form of induction training but in many organisations there are also informal practices which serve a similar function. Typically the new employee is told 'how things are done around here' both in the training situation and as words of advice from superiors and colleagues.

2.5 Types of culture

Handy, in his book Understanding Organisations, elaborates on Harrison's four basic classifications of the types of culture one might expect to find in an organisation – the power culture, the role culture, the task culture and the person culture, characterised by the concentration of power and hierarchy, the relationship of the individual to the organisation and the centrality of tasks of the individual.

The power culture – features strong central leadership, which is competitive and challenging, and where money and status are important. There are few procedures and rules of a formal kind. Such cultures are typical of small entrepreneurial firms and of stockbroking, investment banking, and similar rather risky enterprises.

The role culture – when we think of an 'organisation' it is usually this culture that we envisage. It is a culture that bases its approach around the definition of the role or the job to be done, not around personalities. It is a bureaucratic organisation, where the structure determines the authority and responsibility of individuals and there is a strong emphasis on hierarchy and status. Procedures and rules are important. Examples include the civil service, banks and large supermarkets.

The task culture is best seen in teams established to achieve specific tasks, e.g. project teams. Influence is based on expertise, not status. People describe their positions in terms of the results they are achieving. Nothing is allowed to get in the way of task accomplishment. If individuals do not have the skills or technical knowledge to perform a task they are retrained or replaced. These cultures are suited to organisations that are concerned with problem solving and short-term one-off exercises – often found in rapidly changing organisations, where groups are established on a short-term basis to deal with a particular change. Examples include the entertainment industry and computer software design and market research organisations.

The person culture is characterised by the fact that it exists to satisfy the requirements of the particular individual(s) involved in the organisation. Although not a common culture for an entire organisation to be based, it is however found in small areas of large companies. The culture is that of educated and articulate individuals – specialists who have come together because of common interest – solicitors, academic researchers, consultants etc. They may use some common office services but generally operate independently. In some instances, a key individual heads a support team of different skills. An example is barrister in chambers.

▷ **ACTIVITY 2**   ▷ ▷ ▷ ▷

Name the following types of orientation:
(a) where the organisation is dominated by a single powerful figure
(b) where the organisation serves the person
(c) where there is a strong emphasis on close role definition and the features of bureaucracy are largely present
(d) where the focus is on task and goal accomplishment.

[Answer on p.132]

3   Sources of organisational ethical values

3.1 The role and importance of culture

First and foremost, a culture defines identity. It is the set of values, beliefs and understandings and ways of thinking that are shared by members of an organisation and is taught to new members as the correct way to operate (values and norms). A culture's strength is the degree of agreement among employees about the importance of specific values. The fact that it is shared by members gives a feeling of belonging and being part of an organisation. It creates boundaries as to 'this is the way we do things here, not everywhere else'. People in an organisation with a defined culture live and breathe this culture whether they are at work, at home, or at play.

Culture reinforces organisational design and structure by internal integration or external adaptation. For example, Ben & Jerry's was founded by two hippies that created funny names for the ice cream flavours. All the employees supported the alternative life-style. However, the organisation was taken over by Unilever and, despite the fact that it tried to preserve its alternative culture, it changed, which resulted in people deserting the organisation.

The external adaptation of culture determines:
·   how the organisation meets its goals
·   how it deals with outsiders
·   how it responds to customers' needs
·   how it deals with competitors
·   how it helps in encouraging employee commitment to core purpose of organisation, specific goals, accomplishing goals.

The culture of an organisation has the potential to enhance organisational performance, individual satisfaction, and a variety of expectations, attitudes, and behaviour in organisations. Culture seems to determine things like loyalty and commitment, how hard people work and how far they are prepared to take risks.

The effects of organisational culture on employee behaviour and performance include:
·   it allows employees to understand the firm's history and current methods of operation
·   it fosters commitment to corporate philosophy and values
·   it serves as a control mechanism for employee behaviour
·   a culture emphasising ethical norms provides support for ethical behaviour
·   top managers play a key role in fostering ethical behaviour by exhibiting correct behaviour
·   the presence or absence of ethical behaviour in managerial actions both influences and reflects the culture
·   it can imprint a set of unwritten rules in minds of employees eg, in Japanese firms there is an emphasis on team collaboration, open communication, security and equality.

3.2 Ethics and social responsibility

> **□ DEFINITION**
>
> **Ethics** is the set of standards and code of conduct that define what is right, wrong, and just in human actions.

Managers' decisions and actions affect the health, safety, morale, and behaviour of all members of the organisation. Unfortunately, ethical issues often do not fall neatly into categories of right and wrong. Attempts to do what is ethical can be complex, revealing that there are varying degrees of rightness and wrongness.

Suppose, for example, that two students each missed passing their ethics exam by only five marks. The first student wants the teacher to adjust the grade in exchange for sexual favours and the second student wants the grade adjusted because his/her spouse had just died and she/he had passed all the other exams except the one taken on the same day as the funeral. Most people would agree that the teacher who agrees to adjust the first student's grade is acting unethically. The second student's case is not so clear-cut.

Of course, behaving ethically involves more than just performing individual acts of helping others and behaving honestly. Ethics arise in all issues associated with human relationships. For managers, ethical issues surface in numerous interactions with an organisation's external and internal stakeholders.

> **□ DEFINITION**
>
> **Social responsibility** is an organisation's obligation to engage in activities that protect and contribute to the welfare of society.

Although there are several specific definitions and interpretations of social responsibility, an organisation's social responsibilities are always shaped by its culture and the historical period in which the organisation operates.

The appropriate nature of an organisation's social responsibility is a matter of intense debate. At one extreme are those who strongly believe that organisations are in business solely to produce goods and services that societies want – be they atomic weapons, legal advice, or life-saving drugs – and that they are entitled to make a profit in return. For these people, social responsibility is simply not an issue. At the other extreme are those who believe that organisations should be allowed to do business only if they help solve social problems, do no harm, and put some of the profits they earn back to work for society. This disagreement is not one that lends itself to quick and easy resolution.

> **▷ ACTIVITY 3**
>
> Do ethical considerations differ from those of social responsibility?
>
> [Answer on p. 132]

3.3 Forces that shape ethical and socially responsible behaviour

While individuals come to an organisation with a set of values developed over time, the most influential factor affecting their ethical behaviour after they arrive is the way they are led. Leadership is what determines the organisational climate or culture, and it has a major impact on the way all the organisation's members do their work.

One of the most important tasks of any leader is to create an environment where ethical behaviour and decision making is standard operating procedure. This can be achieved through alignment of the personal ethical values of the individual employees with those of the organisation. The leader can develop this organisational climate by:

· clarifying the organisation's core ethical values so all employees know what is expected of them
· making values alignment a key part of the hiring decision for new employees
· developing policies so employees know how to deal with foreseeable ethical issues
· providing training and support systems to help employees build a more ethical organisation.

Taking those steps will increase the degree of ethical alignment or congruence in the organisation. Organisations with high ethical congruence 'walk their talk', meaning their day-to-day behaviour matches their stated values.

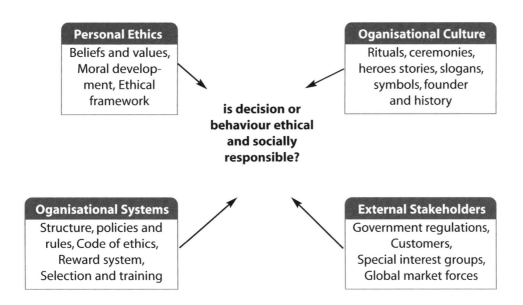

> ACTIVITY 4   ▷ ▷ ▷ ▷

A visitor to a factory notices that a machine operator is using the machine without the safety guard in place. What are the social obligations?

[Answer on p. 132]

3.4 Attitudes to corporate ethics

The diagram below shows how US academics Eric Reidenbach and Donald Robin have established a sort of moral pyramid to demonstrate the range of corporate attitudes to corporate ethics.

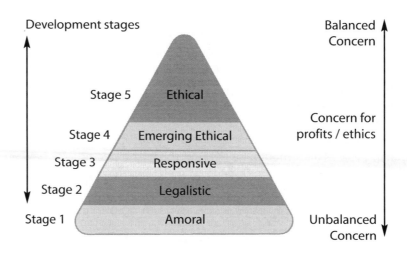

This model proposes a two dimensional form that considers the developmental stages that a company may grow through, tempered against a concern for profits and ethical standards.

Stage 1 Amoral

At the base are the amoral or ethically challenged companies. Amoral organisations are around strictly for the short term. They are prepared to condone any actions that contribute to the organisation's aims and pursue winning at any cost. Obedience is valued and rewarded and there is little concern for employees other than their value as an economic unit of production. The ethical climate of a stage one organisation can be summed up by phases like:

· They'll never know
· Everybody does it
· We won't get caught.

At the heart of this organisation is the philosophical conviction that business is not subject to the same rules as individuals and that there is no set of values other than greed.

Stage 2 Legalistic

Legalistic organisations obey the law, though ethical concerns are judged on the basis of adherence to the letter if not the spirit of it, if that conflicts with economic performance. Economic performance dominates evaluations and rewards. A legalistic company's code of ethics – if it exists – would be dominated by 'don't do anything to harm the organisation' statements.

Some legalistic companies have no ethics code, and do not accept the necessity. Often they see little purpose in expressing explicit ethical standards, and indeed some feel any such statements could lead to difficulties and complication.

Stage 3 Responsive

Responsive organisations are those that take a view – perhaps cynically – that there is something to be gained from ethical behaviour. They are interested in being responsible corporate citizens, mainly because it is expedient and have codes of conduct that begin to look more like codes of ethics. Managers understand the value of not acting solely on legal basis, even though they believe they could win.

Although a reactive mentality may remain, it is coupled with a growing sense of balance between profits and ethics. Management begins to test and learn from more responsive actions. A responsive company's ethics code would reflect a concern for other stakeholders, but additional ethics support vehicles, such as hotlines, are less likely to be found.

Most stage three companies would leave ethical concerns aside until they become a problem only then would they consider remedial action.

Stage 4 Emerging ethical

Emerging ethical (or ethically engaged) organisations take an active (rather than a reactive) interest in ethical issues. They recognise the existence of a social contract between business and society, and seek to instil that attitude throughout the corporation. Managers have an active concern for ethical outcomes and want to do the right thing. Values are shared across the organisation. Ethical perception has focus but may still lack organisation and long term planning.

Ethical values in such companies are part of the culture. Codes of ethics are action documents, and contain statements reflecting core values.

These organisations accept that their code of ethics is a starting point – any code not monitored and enforced rapidly becomes a dead letter. One leading UK bank has put in place a range of instruments for enlisting staff commitment to its code, including ethics hotlines and regular assessment of code effectiveness.

Stage 5 Ethical organisations

Ethical organisations have a 'total ethical profile' with carefully selected core values (and an approach to hiring, training, firing and rewarding) that reflect it. They have a philosophy that informs everything that the company does and a commitment on the part of everyone to their core values. They balance profits and ethics throughout their culture.

Although the concept of social responsibility may change from time to time, the pyramid model gives us a framework for understanding the evolving nature of the firm's economic, legal, ethical and philanthropic performance.

3.5 The Carroll model of social responsibility

Carroll's 4-level model encompasses the economic, legal, ethical and discretionary (philanthropic) expectations that society has of organisations at a given point in time. It has a number of similarities to that of the Reidenbach and Robin model. Carroll's pyramid of social responsibility model is outlined below.

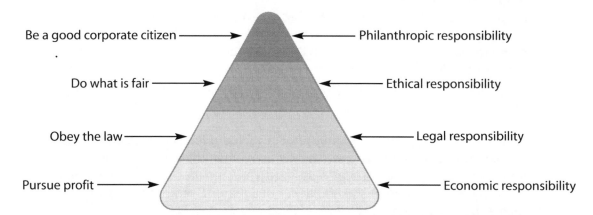

Economic responsibility – is fundamental to the firm, as the overriding need is to be profitable and to protect the longevity and success of the firm. However this does not preclude the firm from behaving in an ethical manner.

Legal responsibility – the need is for the firm to be a law-abiding entity. The law, Carroll argues, offers society a codification of a set of standards to which firms and individuals are bound. The firm should respect both the letter and the spirit of the law.

Ethical responsibility – the onus on the firm is to behave and act in an ethical manner and to avoid harm in its actions.

Philanthropic responsibility – the firm should behave as a good corporate citizen and make a contribution to the community in which it operates.

Carroll's pyramid is a sort of Maslow's hierarchy of needs for the business corporation in that the pursuit of higher level needs can only be met once the fundamental needs at the bottom of the pyramid have been satisfied. Based on this logic it would not seem possible to think about tackling ethical issues until economic needs have been satisfied. This line of thought misses however one key point. The ability to deliver profit is ultimately dependent on the market. All businesses are predicated on satisfying the evolving needs of society, which give rise to the entrepreneurial inventions on which all businesses depend. As the demands of society are increasingly for products and services that satisfy their moral and ethical values the economic responsibilities of businesses are becoming increasingly tied to their performance as corporate citizens.

Carroll also discusses three different manager typologies within the pyramid model – Immoral, Amoral and Moral. Briefly these manager types are described and characterised as follows:

Immoral Managers – are managers whose decisions, actions and behaviour suggest an active opposition to what is deemed to be right and ethical. These managers care only about their or their organisation's profitability or success. Legal issues are there to be circumvented and loopholes in the law actively sought. Strategy is to exploit opportunities for personal or organisational gain at any cost.

Amoral Managers – are neither immoral nor moral but are not sensitive to the fact that their everyday business decisions may have a deleterious effect on others. These managers may lack an ethical perspective in their organisational lives. Typically their orientation is to the 'letter of the law' as their ethical guide. Amoral managers may not consider a role for ethics in business.

The Moral Manager – in moral management, ethical norms that adhere to a high standard of right behaviour are employed. Moral managers not only conform to accepted and high levels of professional conduct, they also lead on issues of ethical behaviour.

The law is seen as giving a minimal guide to ethical behaviour. The 'spirit of the law' is more important than the 'letter of the law'. The objective is to operate well above what the law mandates the firm to do. Moral managers want to be profitable and ethical. Moral managers will use ethical principles to base their judgements upon – justice, rights, the Golden Rule etc. When ethical dilemmas arise, moral managers and moral companies will tend to assume leadership in their companies and industries.

▷ ACTIVITY 5

A pharmaceutical chemist knows that early trials on a drug have shown that, at best, the drug requires much more development and at worst, the drug is ineffective. However, publicity used by the company to raise capital sums still proclaims that it is a wonder drug and close to launch. Is this an ethical issue?

[Answer on p. 132]

---

4 Resolving conflicting loyalties

4.1 Duties

Accountants owe a duty of loyalty to their employer as well as to their profession and from time to time members encounter situations that give rise to conflicts of interest. Such conflicts may arise in a wide variety of ways, ranging from the relatively trivial dilemma to the extreme case of fraud or similar illegal activities. It is not possible to attempt to itemise a comprehensive checklist of potential cases where conflicts of interest might occur, although we will outline a few special areas in the next section. Members should be constantly conscious of and be alert to factors that give rise to conflicts of interest. However, there can be particular factors that occur when the responsibilities of a member may conflict with internal or external demands of one type or another. For example:

· There may be the danger of pressure from an overbearing supervisor, manager, director or partner, or when there are family or personal relationships that can give rise to the possibility of pressures being exerted upon them. Indeed, relationships or interests that could adversely influence, impair or threaten a member's integrity should be discouraged.

- A member should not mislead his or her employer as to the degree of expertise or experience he or she possesses, and where appropriate expert advice and assistance should be sought.
- A member may be asked to act contrary to technical and/or professional standards.
- A question of divided loyalty as between the member's superior and the required professional standards of conduct could occur.
- Conflict could arise when misleading information is published which maybe to the advantage of the employer or client and which may or may not benefit the member as a result of such publication.

4.2 Types of unethical and/or illegal business actions

Under normal circumstances, an accountant cannot legitimately be required to:
- break the law
- breach the rules and standards of their profession;
- lie to or mislead (including by keeping silent) those acting as auditors to the employer, or
- put their name to or otherwise be associated with a statement which materially misrepresents the facts.

The range of tasks that are illegal, unethical or against the rules or standards of the accounting profession includes the following:
- **Fraud and other illegal activities** – fraud is a term that is often used to describe such acts as deception, bribery, forgery, extortion, corruption, theft, conspiracy, embezzlement, misappropriation, false representation, concealment of material facts and collusion. Fraud comprises both the use of deception to obtain an unjust or illegal financial advantage and intentional misrepresentations affecting the financial statements by one or more individuals among management, employees, or third parties. It can range from minor employee theft and unproductive behaviour to misappropriation of assets and fraudulent financial reporting. Examples of fraud are:
  – falsification or alteration of accounting records or other documents
  – misappropriation of assets or theft
  – suppression or omission of the effects of transactions from records or documents;
  – recording of transactions without substance
  – intentional misapplication of accounting policies, or
  – wilful misrepresentations of transactions or of the entity's state of affairs.

Material financial statement fraud can have a significant adverse effect on an organisation's market value, reputation, and ability to achieve its strategic objectives. A number of highly publicised cases have heightened the awareness of the effects of fraudulent financial reporting and have led many organisations to be more proactive in taking steps to prevent or deter its occurrence. Misappropriation of assets, though often not material to the financial statements, can nonetheless result in substantial losses to an organisation if a dishonest employee has the incentive and opportunity to commit fraud.

Consider the following dilemma:
A safety inspector has found several safety violations in the manufacturing plant where you work. Correcting these violations will cost £30,000. The inspector has offered to ignore the violations in return for a secret payment of £5,000, which your boss has asked you to organise. The workers will never be told about the safety violations and the inspector will file a report stating that the plant passes all the safety regulations. What would you do?

- **Supply of information or statements**, which are misleading, false, or deceptive – means that someone has been misled or deceived if the information they received about goods or a service gave them a false impression or they have had a false representation made to them when the information they received about goods (or services) is not true.

Consider the following scenario:
To avoid an end of year loss, you have been asked by your boss to revise many accounting estimates to lower expenses and increase net income. These include re-evaluating the allowance for bad debts to look at the possibility of lowering the allowance, examining the depreciation life estimates to see how they relate to industry norms. If some depreciation life estimates are on the low end of the range of industry norms, you have been asked to consider increasing those estimates. You have also been asked to look at the estimates for warranty expenses, environmental cleanup expenses, and so forth. In short, many estimated expenses might be lowered a little on closer scrutiny.

Would you falsify some data if your boss asked you to? Would you go along with the boss, although you know it is both illegal and misleading to falsify the data, because it would seem to help the organisation? Or would you refuse, although this may adversely affect your promotion prospects? Here is a case of a clash between the organisation (in the shape of the boss) and the individual. Of course, as with much in ethics it is not clear-cut. If the 'adjustment' that the boss wants is a complete and very misleading falsehood, then the individual may, and indeed should not, do as requested. But what if it is an omission that is called for or a massaging of the data or being economical with the truth or engaging in creative accounting? Then there is a real dilemma – one between the organisation and the individual (and another between the business and external stakeholders).

- **Client influence** – means disclosing at the earliest opportunity any special relationships, circumstances or business interests which might influence or impair, or could be seen by the client or others to influence or impair, your judgment or objectivity on a particular assignment.
- **Employer influence** – examples of malpractices that are subject to the employer's influence include health hazards, security risks, unethical conduct, deceiving the authorities, government officials or the public, or deliberately concealing, destroying or manipulating information.
- **Actions of delegated staff** – members who are formally delegated responsibility for the custody of financial resources should be competent to carry out such responsibilities and are held accountable for their proper execution.

4.3 Detecting fraud

The starting point for most fraud detection is to ask yourself how someone could go about making money by defrauding your employer. Someone who knows a lot of detail about the way the business works will probably be able to think of several ways in which a suspected fraud could have been committed. For each possible method of fraud a series of questions should then be asked.

- Who might be involved in this fraud?
- Why would this person risk his job, reputation and future livelihood by committing the fraud?
- How would the person attempt to cover up the fraud?
- Where would the loss appear in the company's accounts?
- Would the fraudster need accomplices either inside or outside the company to carry out the fraud?
- What would be the tell tale signs to look for?
- Who is the best person in the company to look for suspicious signs of fraud?
- Is the company's policy to prevent future frauds or punish existing frauds?

By answering the above questions for each method of perpetrating the suspected fraud, the company will be well on the way to evolving a fraud detection plan with clear objectives.

Fraud is found to be more frequent in organisations with some or all of the following characteristics:
- High staff turnover rates in key controlling functions. Long-service staff in stores/purchasing departments.
- Chronic understaffing in key control areas.
- Frequent changes of legal advisers, auditors or professional advisers.
- Remuneration based very significantly on financial performance.
- Inadequate segregation of duties e.g. where an individual orders goods, approves the invoices and then authorises the payments.
- Low staff morale/lack of career progression/weak management.
- Excessive hours worked by key staff with insufficient delegation of duties.
- Lack of effective procedures in HR, credit control, inventory control, purchasing or accounts departments. Consistent failure to correct major weaknesses in internal control.
- Frequent transactions with related parties/no checking that suppliers are appropriate.
- Overly secret dealings with certain clients or suppliers.
- Mismatch between profitability and cash flow.
- Excessive pressure to meet budgets, targets or forecast earnings.
- Personnel not required to take their holiday entitlement.
- When an employee is on holiday leave the work is left until the employee returns.
- Inadequate responses to queries from management, suppliers, auditors or bankers.
- An employee's habits change or his/her lifestyle is more affluent than would be expected from his/her employment.
- Lack of common-sense controls such as changing passwords frequently, requiring two signatures on cheques or restricting access to sensitive areas.

· Effective fraud detection requires management to be sufficiently knowledge-able about the mechanics of the business and constantly aware of the need to be vigilant against fraud.

4.4 Procedures for resolving conflicting loyalties

When faced with identified and significant ethical issues in an employed situation members should, in the first instance, look to the grievance or other established policies of the organisation and follow these wherever possible. If following these policies does not resolve the problem or the member is unable to use such procedures he or she has three choices when confronted with unethical behaviour – voice, loyalty or exit.

Voice – means expressing disquiet with and opposition to the observed unethical or illegal behaviour. But where do you voice your objections? The obvious choice is your supervisor or manager. But what if he or she condones the unethical behaviour, or worse, is its source? You may be jeopardising your position, and maybe your membership in the organisation. A second choice is to go to senior management. This also has potential risk. They may be excusing or even directing the unethical behaviour. This action may bring your loyalty into question. If so, your objections may be covered up or ignored, and you may end up being forced out of the organisation.

On the other hand, it may be that the senior leadership is unaware of the unethical behaviour and you may have initiated an organisational response eliminating the unethical behaviour and restoring ethical standards. A third option is to go public, to engage in 'whistleblowing.' This is also risky, because it can lead to reprisals with negative consequences. The level of risk depends on the commitment of the organisation to high ethical standards and on its willingness to encourage whistleblowing in its own best interests. Many organisations have shown commitment to ferreting out unethical individuals and maintaining high ethical standards by establishing procedures for anonymous reporting of ethical breaches and safeguards to protect whistleblowers. Recently, the law in the UK has been changed so that whistleblowers will be eligible for unlimited compensation. The guidelines shown below provide an approach to whistleblowing.

· Make sure that you are fully aware of the facts and that ideally you have some evidence to support them. There is nothing worse than going to all the trouble only to be told later that there was a reasonable explanation for something you were concerned about. Keep accurate records of meetings and discussions. Seek out other people who could corroborate your story.

· Make a rough estimate of the harm that could be done if the issue were ignored.

· Reflect on your own motives for whistleblowing, ensuring that they are not dominated by self-interest e.g. out of spite for someone.

· Do you have internal procedures within the organisation that you have to follow if you want to report any concerns?

Exit is the most direct response. If you cannot resolve any material issue involving a conflict and you cannot live with behaviour that does not meet your own ethical standards you may, after exhausting all other relevant possibilities, have no other recourse but to leave.

However, exit is not only a direct response, it is a final one, so the personal and organisational consequences must be considered. The most important personal consequences are the costs. Where do you go from there? What other options are available? How marketable are you? Can you afford the financial loss?

There are specific organisational consequences as well. Will the ethics of the organisation's leaders change? Will they do business with someone else who does not have the high standards you do? In leaving, one gives up the ability to influence the organisation directly. When considering exit, one must ask, 'Could I have had more of an impact by remaining in the organisation and trying to change it from within?'

Before resigning it is strongly recommended that members should obtain appropriate legal advice. The recently-approved Public Interest Disclosure Act, 1998 gives protection, including protection from dismissal, to employees in the UK who disclose otherwise confidential information internally or to a prescribed regulator in good faith.

Exit and voice may be combined. An individual resigns in protest and goes public with his or her reasons for leaving. This leaves the individual vulnerable to the label of an employee who quit before being fired, but it also can lead to increased credibility as someone acting on conviction in spite of personal cost.

However, exit combined with voice is most effective if taken by someone at the upper levels of the organisation. An organisation can more easily ignore the 'exit and voice' of a lower level employee than it can the resignation of a strategic leader, especially if it is followed immediately by a press conference.

Loyalty. The final response to unethical behaviour in an organisation is loyalty. This is the alternative to exit. Instead of leaving, the individual remains and tries to change the organisation from within. Loyalty thus discourages or delays exit.

Loyalty also may discourage public voice, since being loyal to the organisation means trying to solve problems from within without causing public embarrassment or damage. Loyalty can also encourage unethical behaviour, particularly in organisations that promote loyalty above all. These organisations discourage exit and voice, and basically want their members to 'go along' with organisational practices.

KAPLAN PUBLISHING

5 Test your knowledge ▷ ▷ ▷

1 How does Handy define culture?

2 Describe the cultural values of integrity and accountability.

3 Describe the role culture.

4 List some of the effects of organisational culture on employee behaviour and performance

5 What are the characteristics of amoral or ethically challenged companies?

6 Which organisational systems shape ethical and socially responsible behaviour?

7 Give four differences between moral and immoral management.

8 When faced with identified and significant ethical issues in an employed situation what should members do initially?

[Answers on p.133]

6 Summary

As this chapter deals with employer/employee situations, we began by determining what is meant by this relationship. An organisation operates in a social and ethical environment which offers constraints over what to can do. However, the areas in which responsibilities must be exercised are not clear. Organisational culture refers to the shared understandings and meanings that members have concerning an organisation.

Handy outlined the four basic classifications of the types of culture one might expect to find in an organisation as power, role, task and people cultures.

Ethical behaviour depends on the personal ethics or values of its members, which shape its culture. A person's own values have a considerable influence on their ethical standards; these are often reinforced and supported by the actions of superiors and peers.

Professionals are also considerably influenced by the ethical standards maintained within the various institutions of which they are members. Organisations have to ensure they obey the law but they also face ethical concerns because their reputations depend on a good image and because employees need guidance in cases of uncertainty.

When faced with identified and significant ethical issues in an employed situation there are certain procedures for members to follow for resolving conflicting loyalties.

Answers to chapter activities & 'test your knowledge' questions

△ ACTIVITY 1   △ △ △ △

In spite of the investment in human capital, the employees cannot be obliged to remain in their company. In some cases, the cost of the development can be recovered, but the intellectual capital can only be protected by legal means. The expertise walks with the employees. This is not an ethical issue, but a business risk, common in many sectors.

△ ACTIVITY 2   △ △ △ △

(a)   Power orientation
(b)   People orientation
(c)   Role orientation
(d)   Task orientation

△ ACTIVITY 3   △ △ △ △

The two are similar in that both revolve around concerns for the well being of others; however, ethical considerations differ from those of social responsibility in certain ways. Ethical judgments are based on personal values that have been learned over a number of years. They usually are involved in situations that do not influence society as a whole. Frequently, in fact, ethical judgments affect only one person, the people in a manager's organisation, or an organisation's stakeholders, rather than society as a whole. Ethics usually involve one person's judgment and behaviour; social responsibility usually involves those of entire organisations. In short, ethics are primarily a personal issue; social responsibility is more an organisational issue.

△ ACTIVITY 4   △ △ △ △

There is no legal reason why the visitor should involve himself or herself. However, doing nothing would violate all three principles of social responsibility. In the first place, it is reasonable to suppose that the visitor would prefer to be told of an unsafe action were the position reversed. Bringing it to the operator's attention will not inconvenience or harm the visitor in any way. By acting politely, there is no reason why the affair should lead to embarrassment or loss of dignity.

Note that with a social obligation, there is not an obvious penalty if no action is taken. However, society would be much the worse if everyone did so.

△ ACTIVITY 5   △ △ △ △

It is an ethical issue. Although the research chemist does not have a duty to shareholders and potential investors, the firm is behaving unethically by knowingly misinforming people about something of importance.

The dilemma for the chemist is whether to do anything. He might start by wondering if the poor performance of the drug is widely known within the firm. If it is, and the publicity is deliberately misleading or fraudulent, he is in a difficult position.

Test your knowledge

1   Handy describes culture as the 'way things are done around here'.

2   Cultural values identify our highest priorities and no matter what type of business it is, integrity must be the primary core value, providing the foundation for all other values. Without integrity other values will lack credibility. Organisations must do what they say they will do and be trustworthy and honest in all their dealings. Honesty and integrity are bedrocks of a value system that is applied not only to how the organisation relates to people, but also to how they keep their business records. The cultural value of accountability refers to the ability to call public officials, private employers or service providers to account, requiring that they be answerable for their policies, actions and use of funds. It also means holding employees accountable for their behaviour as well as their outcomes, rewarding them for correct behaviour and applying consequences to those not meeting behaviour expectations.

3   The role culture bases its approach around the definition of the role or the job to be done, not around personalities. It is a bureaucratic organisation, where the structure determines the authority and responsibility of individuals and there is a strong emphasis on hierarchy and status. Procedures and rules are important.

4   Some of the effects of organisational culture on employee behaviour and performance include:
· it allows employees to understand the firm's history and current methods of operation
· it fosters commitment to corporate philosophy and values
· it serves as a control mechanism for employee behaviour
· a culture emphasising ethical norms provides support for ethical behaviour
· top managers play a key role in fostering ethical behaviour by exhibiting correct behaviour
· the presence or absence of ethical behaviour in managerial actions both influences and reflects the culture
· it can imprint a set of unwritten rules in minds of employees eg, in Japanese firms there is an emphasis on team collaboration, open communiciation, security and equality.

5   The characteristics of the amoral or ethically challenged company are:
· They are prepared to condone any actions that contribute to the organisation's aims and pursue winning at any cost.
· Obedience is valued and rewarded and there is little concern for employees other than their value as an economic unit of production.
· At the heart of this organisation is the philosophical conviction that business is not subject to the same rules as individuals and that there is no set of values other than greed.

6   The organisational systems that shape ethical and socially responsible behaviour are:
· structure

- policies and rules
- code of ethics
- reward system
- selection and training.

7 **Immoral Managers** – are managers whose decisions, actions and behaviour suggest an active opposition to what is deemed to be right and ethical. These managers care only about their or their organisation's profitability or success. Legal issues are there to be circumvented and loopholes in the law actively sought. Strategy is to exploit opportunities for personal or organisational gain at any cost.

The Moral Manager – in moral management, ethical norms that adhere to a high standard of right behaviour are employed. Moral managers not only conform to accepted and high levels of professional conduct, they also lead on issues of ethical behaviour.

The law is seen as giving a minimal guide to ethical behaviour. The 'spirit of the law' is more important than the 'letter of the law'. The objective is to operate well above what the law mandates the firm to do. Moral managers want to be profitable and ethical. Moral managers will use ethical principles to base their judgements upon – justice, rights, the Golden Rule, etc.

8 When faced with identified and significant ethical issues in an employed situation in the first instance, members should look to the grievance or other established policies of the organisation and follow these wherever possible. If following these policies does not resolve the problem or the member is unable to use such procedures he or she has three choices when confronted with unethical behaviour – voice, loyalty or exit.

KAPLAN PUBLISHING

ETHICS IN PUBLIC PRACTICE

INTRODUCTION

Accounting technicians work in a variety of organisations, large and small. Those with more experience can become self-employed, providing a range of accountancy services to different business. These tend to be in a specialist area of accounting and may include advising on budgets and taxation issues, calculating end of year accounts and consultancy.

In this chapter we look at the guidelines applicable to self-employed members covering the initial engagement through to earning a fair reward for the services rendered.

In all professional work there are two main risks: the risk of an error being made; and the risk of that error being overlooked. We aim to highlight the likely risks within each area, and provide organised work methods, which will keep those risks to a minimum level.

This chapter also recognises that the practice is a commercial enterprise, and that the standardisation of systems will improve efficiency. Wherever appropriate, relevant regulations and ethical guidance have also been taken into account.

CONTENTS

PERFORMANCE CRITERIA

· Prepare appropriate letters of engagement and develop and implement a fair fees policy for your professional services. Recognise and explain why certain types of information should be regarded as confidential (32.3 A)

· Identify and explain how specific situations can undermine professional independence (32.3 B)

· Prepare a policy to be followed for handling client's monies. (32.3 C)

· Maintain independence and objectivity and impartiality in a range of circumstances (32.3 D)

· Make recommendations for a policy statement in relation to a client wishing to change accountant (32.3 E)

· Identify scope of professional liability (32.3 F)

· Prepare clear guidelines that should be followed to advertise your accounting services in a professional and ethical manner (32.3 G)

· Give advice to clients on retention of books, working papers and other documents (32.3 H)

1   Public practice

1.1 Services provided in practice

Not all firms engage in general practice. Increasingly, there is a tendency for sole practitioners and even partnerships to specialise in particular areas of work or to particular types of organisation. Services provided by specialists include:

- taxation - corporate, personal, VAT
- financial planning
- business finance
- training services
- computerised systems.

Before starting to practise, accountants have to decide which areas of work they have the skill and experience to perform and what work they will refer to others. Practitioners with specialist skills, e.g. expertise in VAT, may be able to charge higher hourly rates than they could for more general work.

No practitioner can offer a complete range of services to clients in great depth, because they would not have the knowledge and experience to do so and certainly could not keep up to date in all subjects. It can be extremely dangerous to perform services for clients in which the practitioner's mistakes can lead to financial loss for the client. For example, taxation is an area in which legislation is constantly changing and a failure to monitor changes effectively may lead to the practitioner giving advice that is wrong.

1.2 Benefits

As a member in practice, there are a number of benefits including free promotion by the AAT through the Directory of Members in Practice. However, all members in practice are strictly governed by the AAT and must conform to rigorous professional and ethical standards.

All full and fellow members who wish to offer accountancy, taxation or related consultancy services to individuals and organisations must be a member of the AAT scheme. This demonstrates to the public that they are committed to high standards of ethics and professionalism and it enables the AAT to promote their services, giving them the additional credit of the AAT's good name.

Joining the scheme for members in practice adds a great deal of credibility to your services, showing potential clients that you are competent and highly trained, and that you have the AAT seal of approval. And as a member you benefit from:

- recognition by external organisations, such as mortgage lenders
- access to free business support and technical helplines
- ethical advice
- twice-yearly newsletter full of useful articles, information and technical updates

- competitive rates on professional indemnity insurance (PII)
- specially organised CPD events
- inclusion in the Directory of Members in Practice – searchable by members of the public looking for individuals to do their accounts, also useful for networking purposes
- a dedicated support team within the AAT

In addition to all these benefits, licensed members in practice also benefit from:
- a licence certificate for display purposes
- the entitlement to market their services using the AAT name, logo and approved wording on business stationery.

2 Fees and commissions

2.1 Charging methods

The ways of charging clients are numerous. There are hourly rates, by the job fixed rates, contingency, percentage or performance arrangements, flat fee plus expenses, daily fee plus expenses, and many other methods of charging for your consulting services. Which one is best?

Many practitioners charge by the hour or day. Members determine their fees primarily on the basis of the time expended multiplied by the standard billing/charging rate of the professional involved. Occasionally, members will apply a premium rate where there is weekend or holiday work or other extraordinary circumstances. To establish an hourly or daily rate, practitioners try to calculate the number of chargeable hours in a year. Many hours will be spent marketing and in administrative and other functions, so this time is not chargeable to the client. Also, holiday time, holidays, sick days, and so on, cannot be directly charged to the client. Your hourly or daily rate may be limited by what your competition charges, especially if you have not positioned yourself as different from them.

A contingency or percentage fee is an arrangement where no fee will be charged unless a specified finding or result is obtained eg, savings have been achieved or a percentage of a debt recovered, or when the fee is otherwise dependent on the findings or results of such services. Lawyers can enter risk-sharing arrangements with their clients on a contingency fee agreement – this allows a lawyer to charge you a percentage of what is recovered. No fee will be payable if there is no recovery. Financial reporting does not generally lend itself to this type of charging. However, in bankruptcies, liquidations, receiverships, administrations, voluntary arrangements and similar work the remuneration may, by statute or tradition, be based on a percentage of realisations or a percentage of distributions. Consequently, it may not be possible to negotiate a fee in advance.

Some accountants charge by the job or a flat rate. For example, a tax consultant might charge £250 to prepare a tax return for you, including an unaudited income statement for your business from information supplied by you. If the consultant takes only one hour to do this, he or she grosses £250 per hour. If, though, the tax consultant miscalculates the time required, it could take 20 hours to complete the job and he or she would make only £12.50 per hour.

2.2 Determining what to charge

No matter how you charge clients, you first need to calculate how much to charge per hour – even if you charge a fixed fee for the whole project. You cannot determine how much your fixed fee should be unless you know roughly how many hours the job will take and what you need to earn per hour to make it worth your while.

Where a time charge is levied, adequate time records must be maintained in order to calculate accurate and realistic fees, recognising circumstances where a high incidence of research time is encountered, where little prior notice is given or where, in providing special services such as winding up an investment portfolio, staff with particular skills are required.

If you are experienced in your field, you probably already know what to charge because you are familiar with market conditions. However, if you are just starting out, you may have no idea what you can or should charge and you may have to calculate what your rate should be based on your expenses and investigate the marketplace to see if you should adjust your rate up or down.

Setting a fee or a price for your services involves several steps:
· establishing your daily or hourly labour rate – the value of your time and the time of others involved in the project
· determining your overhead – the expense of being in business
· setting your profit – the value you place on the risk you take by being in business.

To the new practitioner it may seem that the fees charged by established firms are high but large firms have high overheads.

Calculate your hourly rate
There is a standard formula for determining an hourly rate: Add together your labour and overhead costs; add the profit you want to earn, then divide the total by your hours worked. This is the minimum you must charge to pay your expenses, pay yourself a salary, and earn a profit. Depending on market conditions, you may be able to charge more for your services – or you might have to adjust your rate downwards.

To determine how much your labour is worth, decide on a figure for your annual salary. This can be what you earned for doing similar work when you were an employee, what other employees earn for similar work, or how much you would like to earn (as long as your goal is reasonable).

Compute your annual overhead
Overheads include the expenses that you have regardless of how much work

you do. These expenses are fixed at pretty much one level whether you are working on one project or several. Of course, if your business expands greatly, the overhead will increase accordingly. Overheads usually include the rent and utilities for the office, clerical assistants' salaries, heating and lighting, telephone charges, business insurance, professional association memberships, stationery and supplies and legal and accounting fees, and advertising and marketing costs – for example, the cost of a yellow pages advert or brochure marketing expenses.

Overhead also includes the cost of your fringe benefits, such as medical insurance, disability insurance, and retirement benefits, as well as your income taxes and self-employment taxes.

If you are just starting out, you will have to estimate these expenses or ask other practitioners in the same field what they pay in overhead, then use that amount in your calculations.

You are also entitled to earn a profit over and above your salary and overhead expenses. Your salary does not count as profit; it is one of the costs of doing business. Profit is the reward you get for taking the risks of being in business for yourself. It also provides money to expand and develop your business. Profit is usually expressed as a percentage of total costs. There is no standard profit percentage, but a 10% to 20% profit is common.

Finally, you need to determine how many hours you will work and get paid for during the year. Assume you will work a 40-hour week for purposes of this calculation, although you may end up working more than this. If you want to take a two-week holiday each year, you will have a maximum of 2,000 chargeable hours per year (50 weeks x 40 hours). If you want to take more holidays, you will have fewer hours to charge for.

However, you will probably spend at least 25% to 35% of your time on tasks that you cannot charge to clients, such as bookkeeping and invoicing, drumming up business, and upgrading your skills. This means you will probably have only 1,300 to 1,500 hours for which you can get paid each year, assuming a two-week holiday.

Investigate the marketplace

As well as calculating how much you would like to earn per hour, you also need to determine whether this figure is realistic. This means finding out what other practitioners are charging for similar services – and what your potential clients are willing to pay. You can gather this information by:

·   contacting a professional organisation, which may be able to give you good information on what other practitioners are charging in your area
·   asking other practitioners what they charge. You can communicate pricing concerns over the Internet
·   talking to potential clients and customers – for example, attend trade shows and business conventions.

KAPLAN PUBLISHING

You may discover that your ideal hourly rate is higher than what other practitioners are charging in your area. However, if you are highly skilled and performing work of unusually high quality, you can ask for more than other practitioners with lesser skills charge. One approach is to start out charging a fee that is at the lower end of the spectrum for practitioners performing similar services, then gradually increase it until you start meeting price resistance. Over time, you should be able to find a payment method and fee structure that enable you to get enough work while adequately compensating you for your services.

▷ **ACTIVITY 1**

Sam, a self-employed accounting technician, earned £25,000 per year as an employee and feels that he should receive at least the same annual salary as an independent consultant. He estimates that his annual overhead will be about £10,000 per year. He wants to earn a 10% profit and estimates that he'll work about 1,500 chargeable hours each year. Determine Sam's hourly rate.

[Answer on p. 169]

2.3 Develop a fair fees policy

Fees should reflect the value of the professional services performed for the client, taking into account:
· the skill and knowledge required
· the level of training and experience required to perform the services
· the time required by each person engaged in performing the services, and
· the degree of responsibility that it entails.

Determining your fee structure is probably one of the most important steps in building and maintaining a consulting practice. You will be selling your services to other people in business and, if you want to be seen as responsible, reliable and in demand, you have to know and communicate the real value of your services. It is not improper for a member to charge a client a lower fee than has previously been charged for similar services, provided the quality of the work does not suffer. However, members in public practice who obtain work at fees significantly lower than those charged by an existing accountant, or quoted by others, must be aware that there is a risk of a perception that the quality of work could be impaired.

By explaining the basis of your charges, you let a prospective client know how valuable your consultation is. A low fee may get you some business initially but it will cost you in the long run because it forces you to work at a rate of compensation that cannot support your practice. It also sets you up for future business at the same low unrealistic rates.

The time to set fees is at the very outset of your business. Your fee is based on your skills, the need for your talents and the assumption that you will give your clients state of the art services. Then you should regularly review and adjust your fees based on market realities and your increasing knowledge and skill.

An outline fees policy might include the following sections and explanations:

Hourly fees	Most of the legal services we provide are billed on an hourly basis. For more information on our rates, please contact our offices to request a copy of our current Fee Brochure
Fixed fees	We may agree to set a fixed fee in advance when a client asks us to perform a narrow task or a carefully defined service.
Contingency fees	As a rule, we will not agree to a contingent fee in matters involving the recovery of money. To compensate for the risk of little or no recovery, we must require payment of a relatively high percentage of any amount you receive. We believe contingent fees are rarely in our clients' best interests, and we generally discourage their use.
Expenses	As a client, you are responsible for paying all costs and out-of-pocket expenses connected to your accountancy matters, in addition to the firm's professional fees. Such expenses include, but are not limited to telephone calls, postage, copying and messenger services. We will not incur unusual or major costs without your advance approval.

2.4 Commissions

Accountants often give advice to a client. If acted upon, this will result in commission being earned by the practice or anyone in it. Under these circumstances special care should be taken that the advice is in fact in the best interests of the client. The client must be informed, in writing, both of the fact that commission will be received and, as soon as practicable, of the amount and terms of such commission.

2.5 Invoicing clients

There is much advice given on the subject of invoicing. Much of it is common sense, for example:
· do not allow work in progress to accumulate without charging
· try to get the work done promptly and the client invoiced as soon as possible
· if accountancy work is being provided on a regular basis, weekly bills should be rendered.

If you render bills regularly, the client will know what the services are costing him/her and will not raise complaints about your charges in the same way as he/she may do if faced with a large bill once a year.

Regular billing helps your cash flow and reduces the need for working capital.

If clients do not pay bills, do not provide further services. When you withdraw services it is essential to inform the client that you are not continuing with work until your invoices are paid as agreed in your letter of engagement. The client should be told that he/she is responsible for meeting deadlines for filing accounts and meeting the HM Revenue and Custom's deadlines for filing tax returns and paying tax and VAT on time.

Many clients are now agreeable to paying fees on a monthly basis by direct debit or credit transfer.

Your letter of engagement should set out your terms of trade and should state that:
· invoices should be paid within 30 days of submission
· you reserve the right to charge interest at, say, 4% over bank base rate on unpaid amounts.

3   Letters of engagement

3.1 Duty of care to the client

A letter of engagement should identify the work to be done, the responsibilities of the client and the practitioner in relation to the work; and the basis upon which fees will be charged.

A clear and concise letter of engagement is part of the practitioner's duty of care to the client. The letter should identify:
· the work and scope of the work to be done
· the respective responsibilities of the client and the practitioner in relation to the work; and the basis upon which fees will be charged.

A letter of engagement also aids the clients' understanding of their responsibilities, the work, and the practitioner's role working on the client's behalf and can provide some protection to the practitioner against incurring liability for negligence.

3.2 Discussion with the client

A letter of engagement documents expectations of both practitioner and client. It can be a means through which both feel comfortable in their business relationship. In this way, a prompt response following your first meeting with a potential client can seal the deal and provide you with a safety net as you move forward in your business.

Before the letter is drawn up there should be a discussion about the service(s) the client wants the practitioner to provide (and vice versa). During the process there will be a mutual understanding reached and this is what the letter of engagement will then record.

It is the responsibility of the practitioner to be clear about the matters agreed with the client, and to record these in the letter of engagement. To achieve this, the practitioner must have a thorough understanding of the client's requirements and have clarified any doubtful points. This means listening carefully to the client, asking the client's opinion where appropriate and recognising that a letter of engagement will often encompass matters raised by, and important to, the client as well as to themselves. The client must be aware of any work that must be done, or any information they must provide, so that the practitioner can act on their behalf. Under no circumstances must practitioners promise what they are incapable of delivering!

3.3 Prepare appropriate letters of engagement

A short letter will often be sufficient if it properly reflects the understanding reached between the practitioner and the client. A longer more formal proposal may sometimes be necessary, either because this is what the client wishes or because the practitioner recognises that this is necessary in order to set out the matters mutually agreed. The following features are recommended for inclusion:

· **The nature of the assignment,** the **scope of the work** to be undertaken and, if appropriate the **format and nature of any report** which has to be produced. Start the letter by stating – 'enclosed is a list of my services as per our conversation today. If there is anything that I have missed or neglected to include, please contact me immediately as these are the services I am currently prepared to provide.' This avoids any misunderstanding as to what you agreed to do. Your client cannot come back months later and say, 'I thought you were also going to…' This letter provides your client with the opportunity to ask for additional services upfront if necessary, and it protects you from doing work you had not originally planned on.

· **Timing** – the date the work is expected to start, (and whether these dates are dependent on information to be gathered by the client or others), the duration of the work and the dates on which reports are to be delivered. In managing your clients you will need flexibility in order to accomplish all the tasks associated with your business. For example, if you are collecting information from your client weekly, do not give an exact day or time. If you have specified a pick-up time and are late by even a day you are in breach of the contract. Simply state that you will collect the information weekly; perhaps you could say the 'end of the week' or the 'beginning of the following week'.

· In your letter you must **formalise the necessary reporting mechanisms** you plan to use with your client. Provide a time when you will have the month-end prepared and ready to deliver; based on the client's needs – this can be monthly or perhaps quarterly. Again, do not be specific as to the times you will meet, as this could change. For example, you may want to state that you will meet with them by the 15th of each month with the previous month's data. This allows for you to schedule a new appointment each month with leeway as to when the actual meeting time is.

· **Duration of assignment** – monthly or annual and whether the engagement will continue unless specifically terminated by the client.

· **Client's responsibilities** – as to the production of information such as records and books, their format and timing. The client should also be advised that, for example, in relation to tax compliance work a member will only be acting as an agent for the client and that the client is responsible for the tax returns, etc. submitted.

· The **basis, frequency and rate of charge for services** rendered together with the treatment of expenses incurred in connection with the assignment. The incidence of any taxes should also be specified. State the fee charged for your services and the accepted method of payment. You also need to state when the payment is due. If you require payment 'at the time of delivery,' you expect to be paid before you handover the reports in your monthly meeting with the client.

· **Detection of irregularities** – the responsibility for the detection of irregularities and fraud rests with the client's management and this would normally be outside the scope of the engagement. Nevertheless it should be made clear, under the terms of the engagement letter that, the client is obliged to provide full information to the member.

· **Ownership and lien** – the ownership of books and records created in the engagement and whether the member will exercise a lien over such items if fees remain unpaid or are disputed. A lien is a legal claim or charge against property for satisfaction of a debt. A lien allows the creditors a means of preventing the property from getting sold or obligated without their consent until their lien has been satisfied. The member's policy on retention, destruction and return of records should, if appropriate, be specified.

· **Unpaid fees** – the practitioner's actions on a fee remaining unpaid after presentation of the invoice should be dealt with – including the charging of interest and at what rate, the cessation of work and, as above, the exercise of a lien over the client's books and records.

· **Third parties** – the usage of the member's work by the client for third parties should be specified and suitable disclaimers employed.

· A letter of engagement might also usefully cover other mutually agreed matters as appropriate:
    – the practitioner's method of approach
    – the benefit(s) to be gained
    – the resources required, including involvement by any staff employed by the practitioner, and/or
    – staff employed by the client
    – the practitioner's qualifications to do the job
    – disclaimers (e.g. responsibility for a particular result)
    – confidentiality
    – copyright, patents, royalties. Firms also need to be vigilant regarding the requirements of the Data Protection Act 1998, especially where they operate a payroll service for clients.

Send the letter to the potential client by recorded delivery. This signifies to your client the letter's importance and provides you with notification that it has been received. Once you have a receipt, you can rest assured that your client has access to the document and will notify you if any changes are necessary.

A letter of engagement records how matters stand at the commencement of the relationship between the practitioner and the client – what will be done, by whom, by when and for what fee.

At any point after the practitioner starts work for the client the letter of engagement may become obsolete – perhaps because the client requires some additional work to be undertaken that is not reflected in the letter of engagement or the practitioner may recognise that the agreed deadline for the completion of the work cannot be met for reasons that the client needs to know and understand.

When this happens, the practitioner should ensure that the letter is updated as appropriate and agreed by the client.

▷ ACTIVITY 2   ▷ ▷ ▷ ▷

You have been having discussions with a client who is blind. Outline the rule-based approach and the principle based approach to the letter of engagement (see Chapter 1 for revision on rule-based and principle-based approaches).

[Answer on p. 169]

▷ ACTIVITY 3   ▷ ▷ ▷ ▷

Why must the practitioner send his or her client a letter of engagement?

[Answer on p. 169]

4   Obtaining professional work

4.1 Publicity

Self-employed practitioners can seek publicity in the following ways:

- They may be listed in trade and professional directories provided it does not bring the AAT into disrepute or bring discredit to the member, his/her firm or the accountancy profession.
- They may inform interested parties through any medium that a partnership or salaried employment is being sought and may write to or make a direct approach to another when seeking employment or professional business.
- They may pay their employees a bonus or another accountant/third party a fee for the introduction to a new client.
- They may approach clients and non-clients by direct mail provided that communications sent this way are addressed to named individuals.
- They may use telephone communications or personal visits but no call should be made at an unsocial hour. Callers should give their names and that of the practice at the outset and should immediately and courteously terminate the call if the person called indicates that they do not wish the discussion to continue, and they shall not attempt to make any further call on that person without being invited so to do.
- Members may seek a personal introduction to an appropriate executive or prospective client through the medium of a person known to both parties but must not make any unethical payment.
- Members may also publicise their name, qualifications and other relevant information in connection with books, articles, interviews, technical releases, etc.

Promotional material may contain any factual statement, the truth of which a member is able to justify, but should not make disparaging references to, or disparaging comparisons with, the services of others.

4.2 Advertising

Advertisements must comply with the local law and in the UK should conform as appropriate with the requirements of the British Code of Advertising Practice, and the ITC and Radio Authority Code of Advertising Standards and Practice, in particular as to legality, decency, clarity, honesty and truthfulness.

These considerations are of equal application to other promotional material, and to letterheads, invoices and similar practice documents.

If reference is made in promotional material to fees or the basis on which fees are calculated, the greatest care should be taken to ensure that such reference does not mislead as to:

· the precise services to be covered, and
· the basis of current and future fees.

Where members seek to make comparisons in their promotional material between their practices or services (including fees) and those of others, great care will be required. In particular, members should ensure that such comparisons;

· are objective and not misleading
· relate to the same services
· are factual and verifiable, and
· do not discredit or denigrate the practice or services of others.

Particular care is needed in relation to claims of size or quality. For example, it is impossible to know whether a claim to be 'the largest firm' in an area is a reference to the number of partners or staff, the number of offices or the amount of fee income. A claim to be 'the best firm' is subjective and incapable of substantiation, and should be avoided.

The advertisement itself should not, either in content or presentation, seek to promote services in such a way, or to such an extent, as to amount to harassment of a potential client. This is likely to deter the potential client and in the event of a complaint of harassment the burden of demonstrating that approaches of a repetitive and direct nature did not amount to harassment is likely to rest with the member.

4.3 Names and letterheads of practices

The name of a practice, which may feature on advertisements, letterheads, business cards and publications directed to clients or potential clients, must be consistent with the requirements of professional standing and with the dignity of the profession in the sense that it should not project an image inconsistent with that of a professional practice bound to high ethical and technical standards. It must comply with partnership and company law as appropriate, and, in the UK, with the Business Names Act 1985. The name must be one that is not likely to:

· be misleading as to the nature or structure of the firm or the status of any person named in such letterhead or publicity. It should not, for instance, give an impression to the public that the firm is multi-partnered and broadly based when in fact it might be a very small firm. A practice with a limited number of offices should not describe itself as 'international' merely on the grounds that one of them is overseas. Similarly it would be misleading for a sole practitioner to add the suffix 'and Associates' to the name of his practice unless formal arrangements were agreed with two or more consultants or firms. It would be misleading if there were a real risk that the practice name could be confused with the name of another practice, even if the member (s) of the practice could lay justifiable claim to the name. The name should not identify any service provided by the practice as being of a specialised nature, unless a member can clearly demonstrate expertise in that particular area.

· bring the profession into disrepute; or

· be unfair to other practitioners or the public.

It should be clear from the letterhead of a practice whether any person named on it, other than persons named only in the name of the member firm, is a partner of the practice, a sole practitioner or a director.

5 Professional appointments

5.1 Accepting new assignments

An accountant or firm of accountants in public practice should only undertake work that they can expect to complete with professional competence. It is essential therefore for the profession in general and in the interests of their clients that accountants be encouraged to obtain advice when appropriate from those who are competent to provide it.

However, an existing accountant without a particular skill may be reluctant to refer a client to another accountant who may possess that skill, because of the fear of losing existing work to the other accountant. As a result, clients may be deprived of the benefit of advice that they are entitled to receive.

The wishes of the client should be paramount in the choice of professional advisers, whether or not special skills are involved and an accountant should not attempt to restrict in any way the client's freedom of choice in obtaining special advice, and when appropriate should encourage a client to do so.

When a member is asked to provide accounting services or advice, he or she should enquire whether the prospective client has an existing accountant. There are three possible answers:

· The client has no existing accountant.

· There is an existing accountant who will continue to provide professional services.

· The client wants to change accountant.

5.2 New client packages

There are a number of procedures that a firm needs to go through when taking on a new client with no existing accountant. It is common for firms to put together a 'new client pack' of forms and information likely to be needed at the initial interview. Typically this might include:
· new client set-up form
· money laundering checklist
· engagement letter
· assessment authority to the HM Revenue and Customs
· joint notification form and CA5601 direct debit payment form
· Class 2 NIC small earnings exception request
· VAT registration form
· letters of authority to supply information – addressed to the bank, etc. and signed by the client.

5.3 Specific assignments with existing accountants

In cases where there is an existing accountant who will continue to provide professional services, the newly approached (receiving) accountant should limit the services provided to whatever specific assignment has been requested. This will probably be an assignment of a type that is clearly distinct from that being carried out by the existing accountant and should be regarded as a separate request to provide services or advice.

The receiving accountant also has the duty to take reasonable steps to support the existing accountant's current relationship with the client and should not express any criticism of his or her professional services without obtaining all the relevant information.

Before accepting any appointments of this nature, the newly appointed accountant should advise the client of the professional obligation to communicate with the existing accountant and should do so immediately in writing, advising of the approach made by the client and the general nature of the request. Where appropriate the existing accountant should maintain contact with the newly appointed accountants and co-operate with them in all reasonable requests for assistance.

Communication is meant to ensure that all relevant facts are known to the member who, having considered them, is then entitled to accept the nomination if he or she so wishes. However, care must be taken when communicating all relevant facts to a member in situations where the existing accountant knows or suspects that their client is involved in money laundering or a terrorist activity. Under the Money Laundering Regulations 2003 and the Terrorism Act 2000, it is a criminal offence to 'tip off' a money launderer or terrorist. In the Republic of Ireland, the offence of 'prejudicing an investigation' under the anti-money laundering provisions of the Criminal Justice Act, 1994 (as amended) is established by section 58 of that Act. It is an offence for a person, knowing or suspecting that a report has been made under the money laundering reporting obligations of that Act, to make any disclosure likely to prejudice an investigation. Disclosure of money laundering or terrorist suspicion reporting to your potential successor should be avoided because this information may be discussed with your client or former client.

5.4 Replacing/changing accountants

Clients have the right to choose their professional advisers, and to change to others if they wish. There are many reasons why clients would wish to change accountants – it could be that:

· they are unhappy with the service
· they can get a better/cheaper service elsewhere
· their current supplier is closing their business
· the company has grown and the current accountant cannot cater for their expanded needs. Since it is impracticable for any one professional accountant in public practice to acquire special expertise or experience in all fields of accountancy some professional accountants in public practice have decided that it is neither appropriate nor desirable to develop within their firms the complete range of special skills that may be required.

While it is essential that the legitimate interests of the client be protected, it is also important that an accountant who is asked to replace another accountant has the opportunity to check if there are any professional reasons why the appointment should not be accepted. This cannot effectively be done without direct communication with the existing accountant. In addition, this helps to preserve the good relationships that should exist between all accountants.

Before accepting an appointment involving recurring professional work previously carried out by another accountant in public practice, the new accountant should check if the prospective client has advised the existing accountant of the proposed change and has given permission, preferably in writing, to discuss the client's affairs fully and freely with the proposed accountant.

Then the new accountant will, as a matter of professional ethics and routine, write to the previous accountant to request professional clearance and all relevant information and documents which will be required to fully take over the case.

The existing accountant, on receipt of the communication should reply, preferably in writing, advising whether there are any professional reasons why the proposed accountant should not accept the appointment, and, if there are any such reasons or other matters which should be disclosed, ensure that the client has given permission to give details of this information to the proposed accountant.

The fact that there may be fees owing to the existing accountant is not a professional reason why another accountant should not accept the appointment. The existing accountant should promptly transfer to the new accountant all books and papers of the client which are or may be held after the change in appointment has been effected and should advise the client accordingly, unless the accountant has a legal right to withhold them.

KAPLAN PUBLISHING

After these procedural steps have been taken, the proposed successor should consider whether to accept the appointment or to decline it. in the light of the information received from the existing adviser or from any other source, including any conclusions reached following discussion with the client.

An example of a typical letter, which would be sent from the new accountant to the existing accountant, is shown below.

Dear Sir or Madam

COMPANY NAME

We have been approached by the above to act as accountant, and we are therefore writing to confirm whether or not there are any professional reasons why we should not accept the appointment.

Assuming there are none, we would appreciate providing us with the following information/documents:

- Letter of resignation.
- Latest set of accounts prepared and submitted to HM Revenue and Customs.
- Trial balance as at the last balance sheet date.
- Bank reconciliation statement as at the last balance sheet date.
- Breakdown of company fixed assets.
- Detailed breakdown of debtors and creditors as at the last balance sheet date.
- Reconciliation of Corporation Tax creditor.
- Last copies of Corporation Tax computation and CT600 prepared and agreed by HM Revenue and Customs and any agreed and amended assessments.
- Corporation Tax District and reference number if CT600 not yet submitted.
- Outstanding Correspondence with HM Revenue and Customs
- Photocopy of the last Annual Return.
- Statutory books and records including copies of forms 88(2), 288 and 287, Memorandum and Articles of Association and Certificate of Incorporation.
- Photocopies of the last tax return and supporting documentation submitted on behalf of the directors.
- Latest income tax assessments and any outstanding appeals or correspondence.
- PAYE Inspector and reference.
- Copies of the last P35 and P11D.
- Copies of VAT returns.
- Any other relevant information that may be helpful to us in taking over this case.

If you are holding any records belonging to the company, for example VAT returns/summaries and payroll documents, we would appreciate your ensuring that they are sent either directly to the company or to ourselves, in order that they may be available in the event of a future HM Revenue and Customs enquiry.

We hope to receive an early response and thank you in anticipation of your assistance.

Yours faithfully

5.5 Defamation

Under UK law an existing adviser who communicates to a potential successor matters damaging to the client or to any individuals concerned with the client's business will have a strong measure of protection were any action for defamation to be brought against him or her, in that the communication is likely to be protected by what is called 'qualified privilege'. This means that the existing appointee should not be liable to pay damages for defamatory statements even if they should turn out to be untrue, provided that they are made without what the law regards as 'malice'. There is little likelihood of an adviser being held to have acted 'maliciously' provided that:

· he or she states only what he or she sincerely believes to be true, and
· he or she avoids making reckless allegations against a client or connected individuals which he or she could have no reason for believing to be true.

Examples of statements that have been determined by the courts to be defamatory are those that involve; allegations of embezzlement, lying, irresponsibility, lack of integrity, dishonesty, laziness, incompetence, not being eligible for rehire, insubordination, being a traitor to the company, or having committed a criminal act.

6 Independence, objectivity and impartiality

6.1 Guidelines

Independence is defined as being 'a quality which enables a member or associate in public practice to apply unbiased judgement and objective considerations to establish facts in arriving at an opinion or decision'. To be recognised as independent, the member or associate in public practice must be free from any obligation to, or interest in the client, its management or its owners. Members or associates in public practice, when undertaking a reporting assignment, should be independent in fact and appearance.

When undertaking a financial reporting assignment, a self-employed member should be independent both in fact and appearance

To safeguard their independence, before deciding whether to accept a new appointment or continue with an existing appointment, members contemplating any such assignment should consider:

· the expectations of those directly affected by the work;
· the environment in which the work is to be conducted, including the environment within the member's practice and the profession;
· the threats to objectivity which may actually arise or may appear to arise because of any expectations and the environment, and
· the safeguards which can be put in place to offset the risks and threats.

The guidelines on objectivity emphasise the need for the member to maintain objectivity at all times. This is particularly so in financial reporting, and similar roles. In general, members should be able to reach a proper and responsible decision whether or not to accept or continue an engagement based on a realistic assessment and weighing of the threats to objectivity which arise and of the generally accepted safeguards that may be employed to negate those threats to objectivity or to reduce them to acceptable proportions.

6.2 Specific situations and professional independence

Performance in this element relates to the following situations:

Simultaneous engagement in other related business

A practitioner should not take part in any other related business, occupation or activity at the same time if:

· it harms or might damage integrity, objectivity, independence, or the good reputation of the profession

· it would be incompatible with the provision of professional services.

The rendering of two or more types of professional services concurrently will not by itself impair integrity, objectivity or independence. It is only where it has the effect of not allowing the member in practice to conduct a professional practice properly in accordance with the fundamental ethical principles of the accountancy profession that it should be regarded as inconsistent with the practice of accountancy.

It is economic in terms of skill and effort for members in practice to be able to offer other financial and management consultancy services to their clients since they already have a close familiarity with the clients' businesses. Many companies, particularly smaller ones, would be adversely affected if they were denied the right to obtain other services from their accountants or auditors.

The preparation of accounting records is a service that is frequently requested of a member in practice, particularly by smaller clients, whose businesses are not sufficiently large to employ an adequate internal accounting staff. It is unlikely that larger clients will need this service other than in exceptional circumstances. In all cases in which independence is required and in which a member in public practice is concerned in the preparation of accounting records for a client, the following requirements should be observed:

· The practitioner should not have any relationship or combination of relationships with the client or any conflict of interest that would impair integrity or independence.

· The client should accept responsibility for the statements.

· The practitioner should not assume the role of employee or of management conducting the operations of an enterprise.

· Staff assigned to the preparation of accounting records ideally should not participate in the examination of such records. The fact that the practitioner has processed or maintained certain records does not eliminate the need to make sufficient audit tests.

Ownership or interest in client's companies

Financial involvement with a client will affect independence and may lead a reasonable observer to conclude that it has been impaired. Such involvement can arise in a number of ways such as:

· **by direct financial interest in a client** – a direct financial interest includes an interest held by the spouse or dependent child of the member in public practice and in some countries may be extended to include other close relatives. Shares in a client may be involuntarily acquired as when a member in public practice inherits such shares or marries a shareholder, or in a take-over situation. In these cases the shares should be disposed of at the earliest practicable date or the member should decline any further reporting assignment on that company

· **by indirect financial interest in a client** e.g. by being a trustee of any trust or executor or administrator of any estate if such trust or estate has a financial interest in a client company;

· **by a loan to or from the client** or any officer, director or principal shareholder of a client company – neither a member in practice nor his spouse or dependent child should make a loan to a client or guarantee a client's borrowings or accept a loan from a client or have borrowings guaranteed by a client

· **by holding a financial interest in a joint venture with a client** or employee(s) of a client.

Personal and family relationships

Personal and family relationships can affect independence. There is a particular need to ensure that an independent approach to any assignment is not endangered as a consequence of any personal or family relationship.

Agency commission, fees, goods and services

Commission – a member who receives a commission or other reward in return for the introduction of a client should be aware that where it is made in the course of a 'fiduciary relationship' with the client, the member would be accountable for the commission or reward to the client. A 'fiduciary relationship' between a member and client will arise where the accountant acts as the client's agent or where the accountant gives professional advice to the client so as to give rise to a relationship, which the law would regard as one of 'trust and confidence'.

That means that the member will be bound to inform the client of the nature and amount of the commission or reward and pass it over, unless the client agrees that the member can keep it.

Fees – when the receipt of recurring fees from a client or group of connected clients, represents a large proportion of the total gross fees of a member in practice or of the practice as a whole, the dependence on that client or group of clients should inevitably come under scrutiny and could raise doubts as to independence.

Goods and services – acceptance of goods and services may be a threat to independence. Acceptance of undue hospitality poses a similar threat. Goods and services should not be accepted by members in practice, their spouses or dependent children except on business terms no more favourable than those generally available to others. Hospitality and gifts on a scale that is not in keeping with the normal courtesies of social life should not be accepted.

6.3 Potential threats to objectivity/independence

As we noted in the first chapter, the potential threats to objectivity and hence independence can be categorised in various ways.

Self-interest – when practitioners could benefit from a financial interest in, or other self-interest conflict with, a client. Examples include:
· Dependence by the practice as a whole or by an individual partner on total fees from this client.
· Serious concern about the possibility of losing the engagement.
· Significant amount of unpaid fees from prior engagements.

Self-review – when practitioners audit or review their own work. Examples include:
· The practice performed services for this client that directly affect the subject matter of the engagement.
· The practice prepared any original data or records that are the subject matter of the engagement.

Advocacy – when practitioners promote a client's position or opinion. Examples include:
· The practice dealt in or promoted shares or other securities of this client.
· The practice acted as an advocate on behalf of an assurance client in litigation or in resolving disputes with third parties.

Familiarity – when practitioners becomes too sympathetic to a client's interests. Examples include:
· A former partner of the firm is a director, officer or employee of the client in a position to exert direct and significant influence over the subject matter of this engagement.
· There is a long association of a senior person on the engagement team with the client.

Intimidation – when practitioners are deterred from acting objectively, by actual or perceived threats from a client. Examples include:
· Client threatened to replace the practice due to a disagreement with the application of an accounting principle.
· Client applied pressure to inappropriately reduce the extent of work performed in order to reduce or limit fees.
· There is actual or threatened litigation between the practice and this client.

6.4 Safeguards and procedures

Where threats to a member's independence exist, members should always consider the use of safeguards and procedures that may negate or reduce them. In certain countries, the law or professional rules provide for safeguards or requirements. In those cases, the member has to comply with the existing rules. Failure to comply with these rules leads to professional disciplinary proceedings. Safeguards and procedures might include:
· educational and experience requirements for entry into the profession

· continuing professional development requirements
· policies and procedures intended to promote quality control of reporting engagements and external or internal review of a firm's quality control system
· arrangements to ensure that staff are adequately aware and empowered to communicate any issue of independence and objectivity that concerns them
· where available, the involvement of an additional principal who did not take part in the conduct of the reporting assignment
· where possible:
  – the involvement of an additional principal who did not take part in the conduct of the reporting assignment
  – consulting a third party such as a committee of independent directors, or a professional regulatory body
  – arrangements to reduce the risk of conflict by compartmentalising responsibilities and knowledge in specific cases
  – rotation of senior personnel
· publicly visible steps, possibly including a public announcement, to explain how the risk of conflict is recognised and mitigated in a specific situation
· refusal to perform the assignment where no other appropriate course can decrease the perceived problem.

All members in practice are strongly recommended to arrange adequate professional indemnity insurance, unless their work is entirely covered by insurance arranged by a third party.

6.5 A principles-based approach to safeguard independence

When independence is required for a particular engagement, a principles-based approach would mean the member or firm completing the following four steps:

1 **Identify threats to independence** – which we identified above.

2 **Evaluate the significance of any threat** and for each threat identified determine if there are safeguards that can be applied to eliminate the threat or reduce it to an acceptable level. Possible safeguards include:
  · professional, legislative, or regulatory safeguards
  · safeguards within the entity
  · safeguards within the firm.

3 **Determine if there are prohibitions that preclude performing the engagement.** Prohibitions describe circumstances and activities that members and firms must avoid when performing an engagement because there are no adequate safeguards that will, in the view of a reasonable observer, eliminate a threat or reduce it to an acceptable level. A checklist of general prohibitions can be designed (see below) to assist sole practitioners and small firms in their review engagements and should be completed prior to accepting a new engagement and on an annual basis for each existing review engagement.

KAPLAN PUBLISHING

Description of general prohibition

Direct financial interest or material indirect financial interest in client by firm, member or student.

Loan or guarantee from or to the client where the client is not a bank or similar institution.

Close business relationship with client or its management.

Immediate family members of member or student serving as directors, officers, or employees of client.

Recent service of member or student with client as an officer or director or employee during the period covered by the engagement.

Serving as officer, director or company secretary for client.

Performing management activities or making any management decisions (such as authorising transactions) for the client.

Preparation or changes to journal entries or other accounting records without client management approval.

Provision of legal services to the client that is material to the financial statements during the period covered by the engagement.

Provision of corporate finance or similar services to the client during the period covered by the engagement.

Fee for this engagement significantly lower than that charged by the prior accountants.

Acceptance of significant gifts or hospitality by member or student from the client

If you answered yes to any of the above, you have identified a problem with your independence that cannot be managed. You will need to review the related guidelines in depth and very carefully consider and document all the circumstances. If the circumstances cannot be resolved, it is likely that you may not provide these services to the client and must decline or discontinue the engagement.

4 For each threat that is identified as not clearly insignificant, document:
- a description of the nature of the engagement
- the threat
- a description of the safeguard applied to eliminate the threat or reduce it to an acceptable level and
- an explanation of how the safeguard eliminates the threat or reduces it to an acceptable level.

6.6 Agency

The acceptance by a member of any agency may present a threat to professional independence. Before accepting an agency, from a building society or other body, members should be satisfied that their professional independence would not be compromised. Acceptance of an appointment as an agent should comply with all statutory and regulatory requirements and members should satisfy themselves that their acceptance is not made inappropriate by the manner in which the service they are to provide may be publicised or brought to the attention of the public. They should take all reasonable steps to assure themselves that the undertaking they may represent is properly conducted and financially sound.

Particular problems occur with building society agencies because of the expansion of their range of services beyond deposit and similar business to the inclusion of insurance and unit trust investments. Members in the UK should note that involvement in such business requires authorisation under the **Financial Services Act 1986**. A member who is not authorised under the Act may, however, act as a 'bare introducer', ie. refer an enquirer to, for example a list of providers of financial services, provided that the member gives no recommendation of any kind.

Although a member's operation of a building society agency restricted to simple forms of deposit taking would not require authorisation under the Act, the mere presence of agency signs and literature, together with the public perception of the increasing range of building society products and services, could produce a real danger that the member might be perceived to be running an investment business. Should an unauthorised UK member actually engage in investment business as defined by the Financial Services Act, that member could be committing a criminal offence.

For these reasons, in normal circumstances it will be inappropriate for members, unless authorised, to enter into or continue any form of agency or other arrangement with a building society

6.7 Handling client's monies

> ☐ **DEFINITION**   ☐☐☐☐
>
> **Clients' monies** can be defined as any monies received by a professional accountant in public practice to be held or paid out on the instruction of the person from whom or on whose behalf they are received.

The definition of clients' money is extremely wide. It is any monies – including documents of title to money e.g. bills of exchange, promissory notes and documents of title which can be converted into money e.g. bearer bonds – received by a professional accountant in public practice to be held or paid out on the instruction of the person from whom or on whose behalf they are received. It includes all money over which you have exclusive control yet which does not belong to you or your practice. Examples include rents, fees received from a client for payment to another agency, money due to be paid to other contractors and monies held by members appointed as Receiver under the Law of Property Act 1925.

In some countries the law does not permit a professional accountant in practice to hold clients' monies and in other countries there are legal duties imposed on professional accountants who do hold such monies. Members operating in the UK cannot hold investment business clients' monies as defined in the UK Financial Services Act 1986 unless they are regulated under authorisation schemes in accordance with that Act. Members should not hold clients' monies if there is reason to believe that they were obtained from, or are to be used for, illegal activities.

Policy for handling monies belonging to others:
A member in public practice entrusted with monies belonging to others should:
· keep it separately from personal or firm monies
· use it only for the purpose for which they are intended, and
· at all times, be ready to account for it to any persons entitled to such accounting.

A member in practice should maintain one or more bank accounts for clients' monies. Such bank accounts may include a general client account into which the monies of a number of clients may be paid. A client account can be defined as any bank account that is used solely for the banking of clients' monies. Clients' monies received by a member in public practice should be deposited without delay to the credit of a client account, or – if in the form of documents of title to money and documents of title which can be converted into money – be safeguarded against unauthorised use.

Monies may only be drawn from the client account on the instructions of the client.

Fees due from a client may be drawn from client's monies provided the client has been notified of the amount of such fees and has agreed to such withdrawal. Payments from a client account shall not exceed the balance standing to the credit of the client.

When it seems likely that the client's monies will remain on client account for a significant period of time, the member in practice should, with the concurrence of the client, place such monies in an interest bearing account within a reasonable time. All interest earned on clients' monies should be credited to the client account.

Members in public practice should keep such books of account as will enable them, at any time, to establish clearly their dealings with clients' monies in general and the monies of each individual client in particular. A statement of account should be provided to the client at least once a year.

7 Legal considerations

7.1 Retention of books, working papers and other documents

> ☐ **DEFINITION** ☐☐☐☐
>
> A **'document retention policy'** is a set of guidelines that a company follows to determine how long it should keep certain records, including e-mail and Web pages.

The policy is important for many reasons, including legal requirements that apply to some documents.

It is difficult to specify how long individual files should be retained. It may be advisable to retain all files for a minimum of six years from when the subject matter was wholly completed. At the end of the six-year period, you should review the files again according to the nature of the particular transactions, and the likelihood of any claims arising.

Every business needs to have a good record retention policy. Failure to retain documents for the use of HM Revenue and Customs can result in fines of up to £3,000. Other records which have no statutory retention period may be essential in later years for historical or research purposes.

Either way, you must ensure that you manage your business documents effectively, and, above all, that you keep the right ones.

Which records should be kept?

The documents that should be kept will vary from business to business, according to size, status and in some cases, personal preference. Some items should be kept permanently, such as deeds and title papers, accounting ledgers, incorporation documents and, all of the company's statutory records. Others can be discarded after allocated periods of time. The following is not an exhaustive list, but a rundown of common records that will be relevant to the majority of businesses.

Tax records – all business records must be kept for eight years from the last date by which the relevant tax return was to be filed. So, for example, a completed tax return for the year to 5 April 2000 will be returned to HM Revenue and Customs by 31 January 2001 and the relevant documents should be kept until 31 January 2009. But remember, this is only the minimum statutory requirement. You may wish to keep records for longer periods. Records include:

· daily takings, including paid invoices, credit card receipts and cheques
· expenses, including purchase of capital items (such as machinery), general overheads (such as heating), materials and stock
· banking and cash transactions, including withdrawals, payments in, bank statements, cheques issued and cheque book stubs
· amounts paid into the business, such as loans and grants from personal sources.

You may also wish to retain personal financial papers for a similar time.

The Value Added Tax Act 1994, states that records and papers relevant to VAT liability have to be kept for six years after the current date, although in certain limited circumstances agreement can be made with HM Revenue and Customs to retain documents for a shorter period.

Records used to compile annual accounts normally need to be retained for five years. Annual accounts that have been audited should be kept permanently.

Wages and personnel records - documents related to wages, such as P45, must be retained for six years. Records of income tax, pay details and payroll, as well as national insurance contributions and annual earnings summaries should also be kept for this period.

A confidential personnel file for every employee should be maintained. This will include such items as personal details, application forms and offer letters, national insurance number, payment details and holiday/sickness information. For legal and reference purposes, this file should be kept for seven years after the end of the person's employment. You might also include medical records, accident reports, expense accounts and overtime details.

Limitation period

The law requires that persons with a legitimate cause should make their claim within a reasonable time. The essential purpose of a limitation period is to place a time limit on the period within which a party can commence legal proceedings, or in some circumstances, to require notice of a claim to be given to the other party to potential legal proceedings. If a limitation period has expired for a particular claim, the claim will be 'statute-barred'

Limitation periods are imposed by statute, primarily the Limitation Act 1980. There are different limitation periods for different types of cause of action. For example, for breach of an ordinary contract, the limitation period is six years from the date of the breach but 12 years if the contract was created by deed. For deliberately caused personal injury, the limitation period is six years from the date of the injury. For negligently caused personal injury, the limitation period is three years from the date the plaintiff discovered or ought to have discovered the injury but the court can extend time if it is just and equitable to do so.

For negligently caused property damage or economic loss, the limitation period is 3 years from the date the plaintiff discovered or ought to have discovered the damage.

For libel, the limitation period is one year from the date of the publication but the courts can extend time if it is just and equitable to do so.

Before deciding to destroy a file it is essential to consider who owns which documents. No documents should be destroyed without the prior consent of the owner. You may always invite clients to take possession of their own papers, balancing the potential saving of space and expense against a possible loss of goodwill.

Original documents, such as deeds, guarantees or certificates, which are not your own property, should not be destroyed without the express written permission of the owner. Where the work has been completed and the bill paid, other documents, including your file, may be stored, for example, on a CD ROM, computer system or microfilm and then destroyed after a reasonable time. In cases of doubt the owner's written permission should always be sought. If it is not possible to obtain such permission you will have to form a view and evaluate the risk.

> **▷ ACTIVITY 4** ▷ ▷ ▷ ▷
>
> Why should members retain books, working papers and other documents for the period of limitation i.e. no less than six years?
>
> [Answer on p. 170]

Members who are in doubt about the time limits applicable to the retention of books, working papers or other documents should consult their legal advisers

7.2 Ownership of books and records

Members should be aware that the terms books and records are not confined merely to documents stored on paper, but extend to any information that can be understood by the senses or is capable of being made intelligible by the use of equipment. The term therefore covers information that is stored on microfilm or electronically, for example on hard or floppy disks, including messages sent by electronic mail.

To determine whether documents and records belong to the member or the client it may be necessary to consider:
·   The capacity in which the member acts in relation to his client – as a general rule, under UK and other common-law based systems, where the member is acting as a principal (and not as an agent) in relation to the client, only documents brought into being by the member on the specific instructions of the client belong to the client. Documents prepared, acquired or brought into being by the member, solely for the member's own purpose as a principal, belong to the member. For example, if the work is to prepare accounting

records for the client, the records belong to the client. If the work is to prepare for the client financial statements from the client's records, the financial statements belong to the client, while the member's draft and office copy of those financial statements belong to the member. If, however, the client has specifically asked for drafts to be prepared for him, they will belong to the client as the drafts are the 'product' that is required by the client. Similar considerations apply in connection with the preparation of other documents such as reports, memoranda and notes.

If the work is of a tax compliance nature, (the preparation and submission of accounts, returns and computations or VAT returns to the Revenue and Customs and the agreement of the client's tax liabilities) the accounts, schedules and computations belong to the client but if the work to be done is to give tax advice, the member is acting as principal and drafts, internal memoranda and similar documents in connection with that work belong to the member. However, letters or documents giving the advice belong to the client.

- **The contract between the member and his client usually as evidenced in an engagement letter** – any specific agreement reached between the member and his client relating to the ownership of documents produced by the member will override the principles referred to above. Although such an agreement does not have to be in writing in order to affect the rights of ownership of documents created by the member, in the interests of certainty, any express agreement with the client should be documented in writing.

- **The purpose for which the documents and records exist or are brought into being** – letters received by a member from a client belong to the member. A member's copy of any letter written to a client also belongs to the member. Ownership of copies of communications between a member and third parties depends on the relationship between a member and the client. Where the member is an agent, the copies belong to this client. An example is tax correspondence on behalf of the client. Similarly, where a member seeks specialist advice (as opposed to information) from a third party such as a solicitor, he or she will normally be doing so on the client's behalf and the resulting communications will normally belong to the client. On the other hand, where the member is acting as principal, it is probable that the courts would hold that copies belong to the member. During the course of an engagement, a member is likely to create file notes that may document telephone conversations, internal discussions or the results of procedures. The ownership of such documents depends on the relationship between the member and the client. Where the member acts as an agent, [and if the time spent creating the documents is reflected in the fees charged to the client] the document is likely to belong to the client. On the other hand, where the member is acting as principal, it is likely that such documents would belong to the member.

7.3 Rights of access

Members are reminded that, regardless of whether particular documents are owned by a member or the client, confidentiality is an implied term of every client engagement. In consequence, voluntary access to information or documents should be given only after obtaining the client's consent, or where the member's duty of confidentiality to the client is overridden by the powers of third parties

to require access to documents, or where the member feels obliged to volunteer information. Members should also be alert to the overriding nature of statutory and other provisions when considering confidentiality.

If a client requests access to documents that belong to him or her then, subject to any considerations of lien, access should normally be given. A member's response to a request by a client for access to papers generated on a client engagement but owned by a member is more difficult to determine: a member's willingness to assist the client will depend on the circumstances in which and the reason for which access is being sought. In the litigious climate now facing the profession, members should be alert to the possibility that giving access may increase the potential risks of litigation against the member, even where no obvious likelihood exists. On the other hand, there are circumstances where allowing access can result in the client being better informed, thereby reducing such potential risks.

7.4 Lien

A lien is a form of security. It is a right of a creditor to retain possession of goods belonging to a debtor until the debt has been cleared. For example, an accountant is engaged to prepare and balance a general ledger and prepare a draft income tax return. If the accountant performs these services and the client refuses to pay, the accountant may be entitled to exercise a lien over the documents until such time as payment is made.

Liens come in two types – general and particular. A general lien gives the creditor the right to hold on to any of the debtor's goods. A particular lien relates only to the goods involved. This means that, under UK law, when a member has carried out work on the documents of a client and the bill presented for the work has not been paid, the member will have a particular lien over those documents and will be able to retain possession of the documents until his or her fees have been paid.

However, a right of particular lien will exist only where all of the following circumstances apply:
· the documents retained must be the property of the client who owes the money and not of a third party, no matter how closely connected with the client
· the documents must have come into the possession of the member by proper means
· work must have been done by the member upon the documents and a fee note rendered and
· the fees for which the lien is exercised must be outstanding in respect of such work and not in respect of other unrelated work.

The exercise of a lien in fee disputes is perfectly legal, but members should remember that its nuisance value is likely to promote ill-will not only between the parties, but also towards the profession as a whole. Members should, however, take legal advice before seeking to exercise a lien in any but the most straightforward of cases. Similarly a client disputing the right of lien of a member should be advised to take legal advice. Where the member's right is well founded the advice the client receives may change his or her attitude both to the lien and the bill.

7.5 Scope of professional liability

The risks inherent in an accountancy practice vary with the type of work undertaken. Some of this work may expose the member to the risk of a claim for damages due to his or her alleged negligence in the performance of it. Negligence in this case means some act or omission that occurs because the member concerned or an employee or associate of the member has failed to exercise the degree of reasonable care and skill that is reasonably expected of him or her in the circumstances of that case resulting in financial loss to a person to whom a duty of care is owed

There is a contractual relationship between a member and client even if the contract is not in writing, or is evidenced in writing but has not been signed. Regardless of the other terms in the contract, there is an implied term that the member will perform the tasks in terms of the contract with reasonable care and skill. The care and skill required will be judged primarily on the nature of the work undertaken. Where a member undertakes work of an unusually specialised nature, or work of a kind whose negligent performance is particularly liable to cause substantial loss, he or she will usually be taken to have assumed a duty to exercise a higher degree of care and skill reasonably to be expected of any accountant undertaking such demanding work, especially if the member has held out as being experienced in the kind of work in question. Opinions expressed or advice given will generally not give rise to liability merely because in the light of later events they prove to have been wrong, even if they amounted to an error in judgement, provided they were arrived at using the care and skill that was reasonable for an accountant undertaking such work.

A member may and usually will be liable to his client for negligence not only in contract but also from other causes e.g. criminal acts, breaches of trust or breaches of contract, other than the negligent performance of its terms, and certain heads of liability arising by statute independently of contract. He or she will also be liable for negligence to a third party to whom a duty of care was owed and who has suffered a loss as a result of the member's negligence.

It is not possible either in law or in fact to guard against every circumstance in which a member may risk incurring liability for professional negligence. When entering into contracts with clients, where there appears to be any doubt about the extent of the member's liability, the member is recommended to seek legal advice. However, as discussed below, there are a number of steps that members can take to assist them in managing their liability.

- **Identifying the terms of the engagement**

  Before carrying out any work for a client a member should ensure that the exact duties to be performed and in particular any significant matters to be excluded have been agreed with the client in writing by a letter of engagement or otherwise, including the actual services to be performed, the sources and nature of any information to be provided and to whom any report should be addressed and supplied. These terms should be accepted by the client by signing and returning a copy of the engagement letter, so as to minimise the risk of disputes regarding the duties assumed. If the client subsequently asks a member to carry out any additional duties, or in any other way varies the terms of the engagement, the changes should also be defined and agreed by the member and the client, once again preferably in writing.

- **Defining the specific tasks to be undertaken**

  Besides reporting in terms of the Companies Act (1973) and other statutes, members are called upon to give opinions and advice in connection with many matters, and undertake a great variety of assignments. A member should make clear in the letter of engagement the extent of the responsibilities he or she agrees to undertake, making particular reference to any information supplied by the client and relied on as a basis for the work, for which the client or others are responsible, setting out in detail the specific tasks to be undertaken and, where appropriate, excluding those tasks that are not to be undertaken. Where the circumstances appear to warrant it because of the complexity of an assignment or otherwise a member should either seek specialist advice or suggest that the client should do so.

Members should guard against the situation where they undertake to perform particular tasks, then during the course of the work find that it is impossible or unnecessary to perform all the tasks originally envisaged but do not agree with the client the change in the scope of the work. Where members undertake to perform tasks that they do not then perform, they are in breach of contract and to be safe from legal action, should obtain a variation of the contract (preferably in writing) to cover the change in scope before submitting their reports. In any event, they should make clear in their reports precisely which tasks have and have not been undertaken. Members should also ensure that the description of the work done in any invoice sent to clients is consistent with the terms of the engagement letter, any subsequent variation, and the report.

- **Defining the responsibilities to be undertaken by the client**

  A member should make it clear in the engagement letter where responsibilities are to be undertaken by the client e.g. a report or statement prepared by a member for issue by the client in circumstances where the client could reasonably be expected to check it for completeness or accuracy before any use is made of it involving third parties. Financial statements prepared for the purpose of being submitted to the Receiver of Revenue for the assessment of taxation will frequently, although not invariably, fall within this category.

Ensuring that the client is aware of his responsibilities should help to protect the member from any subsequent dispute with the client. In such cases, the effective cause of any loss suffered by a third party may be reliance on a document that is the responsibility of the person in whose name it was issued, and who ought to have checked the document, and not that of the member. Therefore, where the member considers that some matter needs to be checked by the client, this should be made clear.

· **Specifying any limitations on the work to be undertaken**
   It may be appropriate to alert the client to limitations or restrictions on the scope of the member's work in response to risks unique to a particular engagement. The most common example is where the client requires an immediate answer to a complicated problem. In giving informal advice or advice which must necessarily be based on incomplete information, a member should make it clear that such advice is subject to limitations and that consideration in depth may lead to a revision of the opinion or advice given.

The member should also state that the client is responsible for the accuracy and completeness of the information supplied. In all cases, the client should be warned about the risk of acting on the advice tendered before further investigation has been carried out.

When publishing documents generally a member may find it advantageous to include in the document a clause disclaiming liability. Such a clause cannot however be relied on in all circumstances. For example, a court might hold that such a disclaimer represented an unreasonable exclusion of liability.

When submitting unaudited accounts or financial statements to the client a member should ensure that any special purpose for which the documents have been prepared is recorded on their face, and in appropriate cases should introduce a clause recording that the document is confidential and has been prepared solely for the private use of the client.

When giving a reference to a third party with regard to future transactions (eg. payment of rent) a member should state that it is given without financial responsibility on the part of the member.

7.6 Professional Indemnity Insurance

The attention of all self-employed members is drawn to the need to maintain an adequate level of Professional Indemnity Insurance cover in accordance with the scheme for self-employed members.

The simplest definition of liability insurance is 'insurance which protects a person or entity from claims initiated by another party'.

The purpose of professional liability insurance is to protect those seen as professionals or 'experts' in a given field, who may not be protected by general liability due to their expertise. When you are seen as a professional, you are held to a higher standard and are therefore often considered to hold greater liability towards your clients. Consequently, you need more coverage than general liability insurance offers.

8 Test your knowledge ▷ ▷ ▷

1 Why might a practitioner charge a premium rate for some services?
2 What are overheads? What expenses are likely to be included?
3 When might an accountant charge a fixed fee in advance?
4 Give some examples of how a practitioner could use the letterhead to mislead.
5 Distinguish between an existing and a receiving accountant.
6 Explain the term 'qualified privilege'.
7 Describe a 'fiduciary relationship' between an accounting practitioner and a client.
8 Outline some of the threats to independence.

[Answers on p. 170]

9 Summary

We began this chapter on the **ethical guidance** applicable to self-employed members in the UK by identifying the types of work undertaken by practitioners and the benefits associated with being a member in practice.

The factors leading a member to self-employment are varied. Independent practice may offer flexibility, autonomy, and the opportunity to focus on work that the member finds satisfying. Whatever the appeal, it brings with it responsibilities for defining practice and setting policies that otherwise would be the responsibility of an employer. There are numerous issues that are crucial for self-employed members to consider and it is wise to do so before embarking on independent practice.

We noted that a helpful starting point is to identify the basis for all charges, giving a reasonable estimate of projected fees and expenses, pointing out any uncertainties involved, so that clients may make informed decisions with regard to using the member's services. As a matter of good practice, members should ensure that a letter of engagement is agreed for each client. This provides written confirmation of the work to be undertaken and the extent of the member's responsibility.

When obtaining professional work a member may promote and advertise the practice subject to guidance. The restrictions we outlined relate principally to the maintenance of professionalism. The Code of Ethics sets out forms of unacceptable promotion, eg use of coercion, material not in good taste, creating false or unjustified expectations, unfavourable comparisons with other members, etc.

Members have the right to choose for whom they act and the appropriate procedure for any practitioner who is invited to act in succession to another, whether the changeover is at the insistence of the client or of the existing accountant, is to explain to the prospective client the professional duty to communicate with the existing accountant; regarding his or her involvement with the client and request disclosure of any issue or circumstance which might be relevant to the successor's decision to accept or decline the appointment.

KAPLAN PUBLISHING

An accountant or firm of accountants in public practice should only undertake work that they can expect to complete with professional competence whilst maintaining independence and objectivity and impartiality in a range of circumstances. We identified specific situations that could undermine professional independence and looked at the potential threats to objectivity. For each of the threats there are procedures and safeguards to negate or reduce them.

Finally we discussed some legal considerations – identifying the rules concerning the ownership of books, working papers and other documents and the general position regarding their retention.

Professional liability insurance provides protection to accountants against exposure to claims that a member may incur because of an act or default, which results in financial loss to a person to whom a duty of care is owed.

Answers to chapter activities & 'test your knowledge' questions

△ ACTIVITY 1 △△△△

Sam determines his hourly rate as follows:
He adds his salary and overhead together: £25,000 + £10,000 = £35,000.

He then multiplies this total by his 10% profit margin and adds this amount to his salary and overhead: 10% of £35,000 = £3,500; £35,000 + £3,500 = £38,500

Finally, he divides the total by his annual chargeable hours to arrive at his hourly rate: £38,500 ÷ 1,500 = £25.67.

Sam rounds his hourly rate up to £26. However, depending on market conditions, Sam might be able to charge more – or have to accept less.

△ ACTIVITY 2 △△△△

From a rule-based approach, you would need to send them a written letter of engagement. However, the purpose of a letter of engagement is to make each party aware of their rights and responsibilities (this is the principle). Although blind people cannot read a written letter of engagement, they could still be made aware of their rights and responsibilities if it is in Braille. Therefore, you would send them the letter in Braille.

△ ACTIVITY 3 △△△△

On accepting an appointment, the practitioner must send the client a letter of engagement. This forms the basis of a contractual relationship between the practitioner and the client.

A properly worded letter of engagement establishes the framework in which the client relationships are managed. It should set out the work that is to be performed and the basis on which fees will be levied. It is rarely worthwhile suing a client for non-payment of fees if you do not have a letter of engagement in place.

△ ACTIVITY 4   △△△△

Members should retain books, working papers and other documents for the period of limitation, i.e. no less than six years because a disaffected client or other person could issue a writ against the firm before the end of the expiry of the six-year period, and delay serving it for up to a year. Seven years might, in fact, be the most prudent retention period.

Test your knowledge △ △ △

1   Occasionally, members will apply a premium rate where there is weekend or holiday work or other extraordinary circumstances. Many firms are engaging in international activities with their clients – most commonly, by providing tax services. Maintaining the expertise for these clients can be difficult and time-consuming and members may charge premium fees for these services.

2   Overheads include the expenses that you have regardless of how much work you do. These expenses are fixed at pretty much one level whether you are working on one project or several. Of course, if your business expands greatly, the overhead will increase accordingly. Overheads usually include the rent and utilities for the office, clerical assistants' salaries, heating and lighting, telephone charges, business insurance, professional association memberships, stationery and supplies and legal and accounting fees, and advertising and marketing costs – for example, the cost of a yellow pages advert or brochure marketing expenses. It will also include the cost of your fringe benefits, such as medical insurance, disability insurance, and retirement benefits, as well as your income taxes and self-employment taxes.

3   An accountant may charge a fixed fee in advance when a client asks him or her to perform a narrow task or a carefully defined service.

4   A letterhead can be misleading as to the nature or structure of the firm or the status of any person named in such letterhead or publicity. For example, it could give an impression to the public that the firm is multi-partnered and broadly based when in fact it might be a very small firm. A practice with a limited number of offices could describe itself as 'international' merely on the grounds that one of the offices is overseas. Similarly it could be misleading if a sole practitioner added the suffix 'and Associates' to the name of the practice without the formal arrangements being agreed with two or more consultants or firms. It could be misleading if there were a real risk that the practice name could be confused with the name of another practice, even if the member (s) of the practice could lay justifiable claim to the name. The name should not identify any service provided by the practice as being of a specialised nature, unless a member can clearly demonstrate expertise in that particular area.

5   An existing accountant is an accountant in public practice currently holding an appointment or carrying out accounting, taxation, and consulting or similar work for a client. A receiving accountant or newly appointed accountant is a professional accountant in public practice to whom the existing accountant or client of the existing accountant has referred audit, accounting, taxation, consulting or similar appointments, or who is consulted in order to meet the needs of the client.

6 The defence of 'qualified privilege' applies when you have an interest or a legal, social or moral duty to communicate something to a person and that person has a corresponding interest or duty to receive the information. An existing accountant who communicates to a prospective accountant matters damaging to the client or to any individuals concerned with the client's business will have a strong measure of protection were any action for defamation to be brought against him in that the communication will be protected by qualified privilege. This means that he should not be liable to pay damages for defamatory statements even if they turn out to be untrue, provided that they are made without malice. There is little likelihood of an existing accountant being held to have acted maliciously provided that he states only what he sincerely believes to be true; and he does not make reckless imputations against a client or connected individuals which he can have no reason for believing to be true.

7 Members have duties to their clients that arise from the nature of the relationships with the clients. Members have a professional duty to act with integrity and due care and a contractual duty to provide services as defined by the terms of the engagement. In certain cases, the relationship between a member and a client could also be one that the courts describe as a fiduciary relationship that gives rise to fiduciary duties. The concepts of fiduciary relationship and fiduciary duty are derived from the law of trusts. The obligations of a fiduciary can be onerous and the implications of being in breach of a fiduciary duty can be significant. In determining whether a fiduciary relationship does exist, a court will look at all of the factors but, in a professional engagement situation, will particularly focus on the purpose and nature of the service being provided; the extent of the reliance which the client places on the member; any lack of sophistication of the client; the vulnerability of the client to the influence of the member; and, the discretionary authority, if any, granted by the client to the member. The court will also consider the extent of the disclosure to the client of the member's interest in the matter and whether the member has put himself or herself in a position of conflict or has an opportunity to receive a benefit unknown to the client.

8 Threats to independence include:
- *Self-interest* – when practitioners could benefit from a financial interest in a client
- *Self-review* – when practitioners audit their own work
- *Advocacy* – when practitioners promote a client's position or opinion
- *Familiarity* – when practitioners becomes too sympathetic to a client's interests
- *Intimidation* – when practitioners are deterred from acting objectively, by actual or perceived threats from a client.

KEY TECHNIQUES
QUESTIONS

Chapter 1
Ethics – Principles and procedures

▷ ACTIVITY 1

You work for a medium-sized company that has just appointed a new manager who is of the opinion that simply stating a code of conduct (or ethics) is not enough. He believes the organisation should appoint an ethics committee, consisting of internal and external directors, to institutionalise ethical behaviour. What do you think the duties of the committee will involve?

▷ ACTIVITY 2

Can you explain the difference between compliance-based codes of ethics and integrity-based codes of ethics?

▷ ACTIVITY 3

You have been asked by your supervisor to prepare six slides to use in a presentation on professional ethics for the forthcoming employee induction meeting. They will outline the main points of the fundamental principles set out in the Code of Ethics for professional accountants.

▷ ACTIVITY 4

Professional and technical competence can be divided into two phases: attainment and maintenance. Describe what each phase means to you as an accounting technician.

▷ ACTIVITY 5

What is the difference between a 'gift' and a 'bribe?'

What is a 'kickback?'

▷ ACTIVITY 6

From time to time, you may receive or give gifts that are meant to show friendship, appreciation or thanks from or to people who do business with your company. You know you should never accept or offer gifts or entertainment when doing so may improperly influence or appear to influence your or the recipient's business decisions. If you are involved in any stage of a decision to do business with another company or person, you also know that you must refrain from accepting or giving any gift or entertainment that may influence or appear to influence the decision to do business.

Jot down some 'quick tips' that colleagues would find helpful in deciding whether to accept or reject a gift.

Chapter 2
Ethical conflict

▷ ACTIVITY 1

Is the following statement true or false?
'Knowing the Code of Business Conduct (Ethical guidelines) will cause you to recognise all ethical dilemmas and resolve them.

▷ ACTIVITY 2

There are four characteristics of an ethical dilemma and all four must be present to satisfy the definition that an ethical dilemma exists. What are they?

▷ ACTIVITY 3

Is the following statement true or false?

'The Code of Business Conduct is an essential guide in helping recognise and resolve ethical dilemmas.'

▷ ACTIVITY 4

What should an employee do after receiving confidential information that could affect the stock price of his or her employer?
A Talk to one's manager and get some advice. Anyone with material insider information about a public company is prohibited from trading its stock.
B Wait until after the quarterly earnings are released and then sell the shares.
C Go ahead and sell. Rumours like this come up all the time and if you are not an officer or director of the company there are no restrictions on trading.

▷ ACTIVITY 5

Is the following statement true or false? 'You may legally buy or sell company shares as long as you are not aware of any material non-public information concerning the company.'

▷ ACTIVITY 6

Is the following statement true or false? 'A ten-day period beginning three days after the release of quarterly earnings is a good time for employees of a publicly traded company to buy or sell shares.'

Chapter 3
Communications and interpersonal skills

▷ **ACTIVITY 1**

Draw an outline organisation chart of your department. Show its sections and the job titles and names (if you know them) of individuals that you deal with regularly – peers, superiors and subordinates.

▷ **ACTIVITY 2**

You are arguing with a colleague at work over who gets the desk by the window because you both want it.

Discuss the possible outcomes using the following chart.

	You get what you want	You do not get what you want
Your colleague gets what he/she wants	WIN-WIN	WIN-LOSE
Your colleague does not get what he/she wants	LOSE-WIN	LOSE-LOSE

▷ **ACTIVITY 3**

You work in the accounts department of a manufacturing company and you have a number of work-related matters that you need to discuss.
· A temporary domestic problem makes it difficult for you to arrive at work at the usual starting time.
· You have recently been given the task of preparing a report analysing the manufacturing cost of some of your company's products. You have little experience of product costing and are a little unsure of how to proceed.
· You have recently missed a deadline because information you requested from a subordinate was not given to you in time.

Who would be the appropriate person or persons to discuss each of these matters with?

Chapter 4
Continuing professional development

▷ **ACTIVITY 1**

Explain how Continuing Professional Development (CPD) brings benefits to the individual and to the organisation.

▷ **ACTIVITY 2**

Identify Honey and Mumford's four learning styles. How can these preferred learning styles be accommodated when designing training programmes?

▷ ACTIVITY 3

Effective personal development planning depends on setting appropriate objectives. How would you identify effective objectives?

▷ ACTIVITY 4

What are the stages in the CPD development cycle? Why is it a cycle?

▷ ACTIVITY 5

'Real world, problem-solving' has been described in the following manner:

Take the mess that confronts you, organise it into a problem, figure out what to do, and implement your decisions-modifying them as you go. To organise the messes into problems and develop solutions, you must ignore the irrelevant, eliminate the false, recognise the incomplete, and find the missing pieces. Only then can you devise logical, justifiable solutions.

A simple, five-step system that we can easily apply and use everyday is:
1.   Describe the problem situation.
2.   Define the problem.
3.   Choose a solution.
4.   Apply a solution.
5.   Evaluate the result.

Use this problem-solving technique for the following problem situation:

'My employer just finished explaining how to operate a machine. I understand most of the details, but I am confused about one of the procedures.'

Chapter 5
Culture and ethics

▷ ACTIVITY 1

A production technique is illegal in Europe, but not in parts of the third world, because of the health risks it poses to workers. Is it ethical for a global company use the technique?

▷ ACTIVITY 2

A manufacturer buys large volumes of a component through a distributor. A pressure group finds out that children in an Asian factory make these parts. Upon investigation, this turns out to be the case. What are the company's ethical responsibilities?

▷ ACTIVITY 3

What is the difference between loyalty and whistle blowing and how are they related?

▷ ACTIVITY 4

In an industry that is noted for dubious behaviour, most of the companies subscribe to an industry code of practice and have ethical guidelines displayed in all company premises. A young manager realises that he cannot meet his performance targets without breaking these guidelines, and seeks help from an older manager. In a formal meeting, he is told that his performance will be judged by the ability to meet his targets within the guidelines, but informally he is told that the performance indicators are more important providing he is not caught. Can the young manager behave ethically?

Chapter 6
Ethics in public practice

▷ ACTIVITY 1

A letter of engagement is shown below:

> JACK BLOGGS & Co
> Certified Bookkeepers
> Partners: Jack Bloggs and Jill Bloggs
> 21, Upton Hill, Trumpton
>
> 1st April 2006
>
> Mr Colin Client
> 32, The Fairway
> Halifat
>
> Dear Colin,
>
> Thank-you for instructing us as your bookkeepers. We look forward to working with you. As we agreed, we will write up your sales ledgers every month for you.
>
> We are happy to agree a special flat rate for these services for you at a rate of £200 per month, plus VAT.
> If you decide you want us to do other work for you, we are, of course, happy to do this at our usual hourly rate of £15 per hour, plus VAT.
>
> We will, of course, send you an invoice of any fees you have run up each month so that you can keep a tight rein over what you are spending.
>
> We work on the following item:
>
> · All sums must be paid within 28 days of the date of invoice

· We can both end this agreement by either of us given the other 30 days written notice of our intention to end the agreement
· If the invoice is not paid within 28 days, we charge compond interest on the unpaid bill at a rate of 2% per calendar month until is paid in full.
· We reserve the right to stop work if you fail to make any payment when and as it falls due.

Yours sincerly,
Jack
For Jack Bloggs & Co.

I agree to the terms and conditions set out in this letter of engagement

Signed

Colin Client   Date:

List the important information the letter evidences.

▷ ACTIVITY 2

An old school friend of yours is thinking of starting up on his own and has shown you his advert (see opposite) that he is going to have printed off and distributed locally.

Can you point out where he might have gone wrong?

ROYAL INTERNATIONAL BOOKKEEPERS – THE BIGGEST AND BEST IN TOWN

FED UP WITH THE HEADACHE OF ACCOUNTING?
VAT man causing you problems?
Let us handle **everything** for you...

· 'creative' accounting · VAT returns · annual accounts · cash flow	· reducing your tax bill · monthly figures · bank reconciliation · using your system or starting from scratch

Good rates – friendly service – fully qualified – holder of LOADS of Certificates – fully insured – any size of business – special rates for start-up businesses – discounts for introductions to friends – cheapest fees around

Derek Debit
123 Somewhere Lane
Anywhere
London
Telephone: 07822865867

▷ ACTIVITY 3   ▷ ▷ ▷ ▷

Although you are not an auditor, you have recently been attending a training seminar where the following scenarios were presented for discussion:

On 20 May 2004, the audit engagement partner of Porter and Co visited the offices of Clubbers Limited to plan the final audit procedures for the year ending 31 July 2004. A week later, each of the five partners of Porter and Co received an unsolicited letter from the Managing Director of Clubbers Limited offering one year's free membership at one of its golf and country clubs with effect from 1 August 2004. Individual annual membership normally costs £3,000 and the offer was not made to anyone else.

The wife of one of the audit managers at Bosworth and Company – a large audit firm and auditors of Thomson Limited – has recently been appointed as the Financial Director of Thomson Limited. Immediately prior to her appointment she had been employed by one of Thomson's competitors. Each of the directors of Thomson Limited is entitled to an annual bonus based on the reported profit of the company.

Olivers, a long established firm, audit the financial statements of two private limited companies owned by Thomas Ash, an entrepreneur with a very dominant personality. The annual total fee income of Olivers is £830,000 and the combined audit fees attributable to the two companies is £72,000. Thomas Ash has recently approached Olivers with a view to appointing them as auditors to a third limited company under his control. The projected annual fee attributable to the third company is £80,000.

Comment on any concerns you may have regarding the threat to auditor independence and objectivity.

Recommend the appropriate action to be taken by the audit firm to safeguard against any threat identified.

KAPLAN PUBLISHING

PRACTICE SIMULATION 1
QUESTIONS

The situation

You are an accounting technician employed by a firm of chartered accountants based in a small town. You have responsibility for several clients, reporting to a partner who oversees your work, but you are the main contact for the clients.

TASK 1

You have been asked to present a training session on professional ethics to some new trainees at your firm.
(a) Use your answer booklet to give a brief explanation of what is meant by each of the following.
·   Confidentiality
·   Integrity
·   Independence and objectivity
·   Professional and technical competence
·   Professional behaviour
·   Due care
(b) Read the 'client background information' given and the 'personal matters' given, and set out in your answer booklet how you can use these situations to demonstrate ethical issues that arise in everyday practice.

You should allow 40 minutes to complete this task.

TASK 2

During your presentation one of the trainees makes the following comment.

"One of the reasons I wanted to get into accountancy was because I've heard you can get some really good deals from clients – I have a friend who even got a holiday because the client was so pleased with what he did for them"
Use your answer booklet to set out your response to this remark.

You should allow 10 minutes to complete this task.

TASK 3

Another trainee who is present at your presentation starts to tell everyone about the company where he previously worked. He explains how they used to pay people beneath the minimum wage, and how he had to pay people for a certain number of hours so that they would be entitled to state benefit, and made the rest up in cash. He also started to talk about the fact that the company didn't comply with regulations regarding the use of the machinery in the work place.

Use your answer booklet to set out how you could use what he is saying to illustrate some ethical issues.

You should allow 10 minutes to complete this task.

TASK 4

At the end of your training session it has been decided that you should include a session on claiming expenses and completing time sheets.

Use your answer booklet to set out why is it appropriate to include this in an ethics training session.

Your should allow 10 minutes to complete this task.

TASK 5

Having completed your training session you return to you desk to find a fax from a lending institution asking for financial information about one of your clients. The fax asks for an immediate response to enable the finance to be arranged as soon as possible, this is the first you have heard of this.

Use your answer booklet to set out the ethical issues which arise in this situation.

You should allow 10 minutes to complete this task.

TASK 6

Your art gallery client has asked for some very specific advice on VAT issues. You know a bit about this, but have not dealt with it for three years and are not totally confident that you will give the right information. The client does not want to pay for this extra advice as they feel it should be part of the whole service.

Use your answer booklet to set out how you should deal with this situation and the issues that it raises.

You should allow 15 minutes to complete this task.

TASK 7

In the evening you go to your local pub for a drink and, by chance, meet a client of the firm. He asks you several questions about inheritance tax and capital gains tax and then mentions that he has just come into quite a large sum of money and asks you to give him some advice on what would be the best thing to do with it.

Use your answer booklet to set out how you would respond to these questions, highlighting the ethical issues that come out of this.

You should allow 10 minutes to complete this task.

TASK 8

(a) You are conducting a meeting with a potential client. Use your answer booklet to set out how you respond to the following questions:
· How much will you charge?
· How do I get the information from my previous accountant?
· A friend of mine said his accountant would not release any information once he changed accountants, are they allowed to do that?
· I would like you to hold some money on my behalf for reasons that I would rather not discuss. Can you do this for me?
· The sign of a good accountant is the amount of tax they save you, how much tax do you think you will be able to save me?

(b) Later in the day you receive a phone call from the potential client saying that he would like to change to your firm but he asks you not to write to his previous accountants. He says he will get all the information you require.

Use your answer booklet to set out what you should do in this situation.

You should allow 35 minutes to complete this task.

TASK 9

You receive a phone call from an existing client asking you to prepare a funding proposal to assist in raising finance for their business. He says this is very urgent and would like you to start work on it straight away, but he asks that your fee be dependent on the success or otherwise in raising finance.

The client has specifically stated that it is only the proposal which he requires from you and will not need any further help with the raising of the money.

Set out in your answer booklet the matters that need to be agreed before you commence work including whether his suggestion regarding the fee is acceptable.

You should allow 10 minutes to complete this task.

TASK 10

Your firm has decided to launch a new marketing campaign with the aim of increasing the number of clients and the fee income. The partners have asked for suggestions from all employees for ways of gaining new clients.

Some of the suggestions are set out below:
· point out how much lower our fees are than the other local firms
· point out that we give a better service than the other local firms
· offer a 25% discount for the first year to all new clients
· offer a commission to all staff for any clients introduced to the firm
· when new employees join the firm from another practice, give them an extra incentive to bring clients from their old firm with them

· offer a free initial consultation for every potential client
· offer commission to existing clients for any new clients they introduce.

Use the table in your answer booklet to comment on the appropriateness of these suggestions in relation to professional ethics.

You should allow 30 minutes to complete this task.

Client background information

Boat builders

This client is a limited company owned by a father and son. The company owns a property of relatively high value which was purchased three years ago and has since significantly increased in value. The property is now on the market as the company is struggling financially and needs to sell it quickly.

The son, who has the boat building expertise, wishes to leave to do other things. The father and son have fallen out over the exit route for the son and you are trying to mediate.

Over the years you have acted for them you have formed a good relationship with the son, but have always found the father difficult to talk to, and he shows little interest in or understanding of the financial aspects of the business. The son is planning to go into partnership in a new venture outside the area but he has said he would very much like you to continue to act for him. His ability to buy into the new venture depends a great deal on the settlement from the existing family business.

In passing you have heard the son say that he does not invoice for all jobs and puts the money straight into his personal account.

You have also been told that there is one employee who is not on the payroll and is paid in cash. He is particularly skilful and would be difficult to replace, and he will not work unless he is paid in this way.

Care home

This is a care home for old people run by a married couple who happen to live in the same road as you do.

The maintenance of the road you live in is the joint responsibility of the residents. The road has recently been maintained, and you are all supposed to be sharing the cost, however, the owner of the care home arranged for the work to be done and you know that he had similar work carried out at the care home at the same time. You have asked him for a copy of the invoice for your own records, and although you have paid him, he keeps finding reasons not to show you the invoice. You therefore are beginning to suspect that the total cost will be put through as a business expense.

From looking at the books of the boat builders (above) you know that the husband has recently had a boat built. This is common knowledge, but his wife has told you that he has spent Ł1,000 on this, whereas you know from the boat builders records that the boat cost Ł3,000.

This week you are preparing quarterly management accounts for the care home and you notice a 'boat builder' invoice in amongst repairs and maintenance which has been described as 'welding work', it is for Ł3,000.

The care home has a residential flat above it which the clients let out. When preparing their tax return, they say they have not let it out for the whole year, but there is something in the way he says it which makes you think this may not be true.

Property developer

You have a meeting arranged with a local property developer. He wants to discuss plans for future investments and he has asked you to bring along ideas for potential properties. He is always interested in getting a good deal and tends to let people hang on until they are desperate to sell.

He lets one of his properties out to another client of yours who runs an art gallery (details below). The developer has told you that he plans to sell very soon.

Art gallery

Your clients have been talking about their long term plans for their gallery and how their present location is ideally suited to their plans. They are thinking about investing a large amount of money in changing the premises to the way they need it for their business and are currently spending a lot of time on planning this at the expense of their existing business.

A personal friend of yours exhibits at the gallery and is paid a commission for any sales made. From the work you have done on the accounts it appears that the gallery have been taking prints of your friend's pictures and selling them without her knowledge.

Personal matters

Your brother-in-law

Your brother-in-law has recently been offered a job with one of your larger clients. He and your sister are very excited and see it as a major career move; the additional money he will be earning will enable them to start a family and buy a larger house.

You were aware that your client was looking to recruit, but the level of pay that your brother in law has been told is far higher than the figure you had been given by your client.

The last set of accounts you prepared for the company were qualified on a going concern basis and you know the company has serious financial difficulties.

Your house

You are having an extension built by a local builder who is not a client. This is completely outside your professional work. He offers to do the build for cash so that you don't have to pay VAT.

Coverage of performance criteria

The following performance criteria are covered in this simulation. An indication of which performance criteria are covered by the individual tasks is given in the task assessment criteria.

Element	PC Coverage
32.1A	Identify and apply the fundamental principles of honesty and integrity.
B	Highlight situations within professional work that require objectivity and fairness, and where judgements and actions could compromise personal or organisational integrity and reputation.
C	Recognise the principles of effective Continuing Professional Development (CPD) to maintain professional and technical competence (to include sources of advice and information outside formal learning).
D	Recognise and explain why certain types of information should be regarded as confidential.
E	Identify circumstances when it would be appropriate to disclose confidential information.
F	Identify the key issues which ensure professional services are performed within the scope of professional ethics guidance.
G	Make critical decisions to identify appropriate ethical behaviour when interacting with others in a variety of circumstances.
H	Refer and seek advice from relevant sources for issues beyond own professional competence.
I	Describe the types of contractual obligations you would have in providing services to clients to include due care and carrying out assignments within a reasonable timescale.
J	Discuss agree and resolve any ethical conflict.

32.2 A	Describe the types of culture within organisations which supports and promotes high ethical values and helps resolve any conflict of loyalties.
B	Resolve any conflicting loyalties where an employer may ask you to perform tasks which are illegal, unethical or against the rules or standards of the accounting profession.
C	Follow appropriate procedures where you believe an employer has or will commit an act which you believe to be illegal or unethical.
D	Respond appropriately to requests to work outside the confines of your own professional experience and expertise.
32.3 A	Prepare appropriate letters of engagement and develop and implement a fair fees policy for your professional services.
B	Identify and explain how specific situations can undermine professional independence.
C	Prepare a policy to be followed for handling clients monies.
D	Maintain independence and objectivity and impartiality in a range of circumstances.
E	Make recommendations for a policy statement in relation to a client wishing to change accountant.
F	Identify scope of professional liability.
G	Prepare clear guidelines which should be followed to advertise your accounting services in a professional and ethical manner.
H	Give advice to clients on retention of books, working papers and other documents.

PRACTICE SIMULATION 1
ANSWER BOOKLET

TASK 1
(a)

	Explanation
Confidentiality	
Honesty and integrity	
Independence and objectivity	
Professional and technical competence	
Professional behaviour	
Due care	

(b)

Boat builders

Care home

Property developer

Art gallery

Your brother in law

Your house

TASK 2

TASK 3

TASK 4

TASK 5

TASK 6

TASK 7

TASK 8

(a)

Client's question / comment	Your response
How much will you charge?	
How do I get the information from my previous accountant?	
A friend of mine said his accountant would not release any information once he had changed accountants.	
I would like you to hold some money on my behalf for reasons that I would rather not discuss. Can you do this for me?	
The sign of a good accountant is how much tax they save you, how much tax do you think you will be able to save me?	

(b)

TASK 9

TASK 10

Suggestion	Your response
Point out how much lower our fees are than other local firms	
Point out that we give a better service than other local firms	
Offer a 25% discount for the first year to all new clients	
Offer a commission to all staff for any clients introduced to the firm	
When new employees join the firm from another practice, give them an extra incentive to bring clients from their old firm with them	

KAPLAN PUBLISHING

Offer a free initial consultation for every potential client	
Offer a commission to existing clients for any new clients they introduce to the firm	

PRACTICE SIMULATION 2
QUESTIONS

The situation

You are an accounting technician employed in the accounts department of Cutting Edge – a medium sized manufacturing company. You work very closely with the sales team and report to the accounts supervisor.

TASK 1

You have applied for promotion to a supervisory position within the same company and are preparing for the interview for the post. Another colleague has mentioned that the manager interviewing you is very fond of asking questions on members' responsibilities regarding ethical principles.

Write brief revision notes for the interview on the following:

Ethical principles	I have a responsibility to:
Professional and technical competence	
Confidentiality	
Integrity	
Objectivity	

You should allow 20 minutes to complete this task

TASK 2

You share a house with two other girls and, while you are getting on with your notes, one of your room mates comes in and she wants to talk to you about work. She has recently been promoted in the accounts office of the company she works for and it seems that over a discussion on the sales forecast that she will be preparing a senior sales person had told her confidentially that the company was way under target sales for the next quarter. You ask your room mate if she is worried about losing her job but she assures you that hadn't occurred to her but what she was concerned about was whether she should sell her shares in the company and advise her family to sell theirs before the price dropped. She didn't want to do anything illegal so was asking for your advice.

What ethical situations are described and what would you advise her to do?

You should allow 15 minutes to complete this task

TASK 3

At your interview the manager asks you if you have ever experienced unethical behaviour at work. You tell her about a placement with a small company you did when you were a student and about how you were enjoying it very much until you become aware that your employer was 'fixing the books' by incorrectly recording expenses and revenue to his benefit for taxation purposes. When you asked about the practice, he just laughed and said that the government would never miss it and they make it so hard for small businesses to survive that he had to do what it took to stay viable. He also mentioned that a lot of other companies do it too and that, in order to continue to be able to hire students such as you, these were a few of the things he had to do. Finally, he suggested that this business was part of a small community and that your observations and opinions might best be kept to yourself.

The manager asks you about the issues and how you would deal with the situation if it were happening at Cutting Edge:
Is it any of your business?
What should you do?
Who should you speak with about your situation?
What will be the likely impact on your employment?

You should allow 20 minutes to complete this task

TASK 4

The following topics are also raised during your interview:
(a) The manager mentions that in today's competitive business climate the offering or receipt of promotional materials or gifts is not unusual and questions whether you can distinguish between a gift and a bribe.
    Explain the difference between a gift and a bribe and why offering or accepting gifts or benefits from customers, suppliers and others may present a conflict of interest.
(b) Because Cutting Edge has customers in many foreign countries there is a need to prevent involvement in transactions possibly related to money laundering.

Give some examples of what could be a sign of suspicious behaviour relating to money laundering in the case of new clients as well as regular and established clients

You should allow 30 minutes to complete this task

TASK 5

A fellow employee is being harassed at work and is afraid to say or do anything about it. If you 'blow the whistle' the company may retaliate against you. You could even lose your job.
(a) When is disclosure justifiable?

(b) What must the company include in its policy on harassment to support the workforce?

You should allow 15 minutes to complete this task

TASK 6

(a) Knowing you are an accountant, a customer (who is also a good friend) has asked you to perform a business valuation for insurance purpose. He is prepared to pay you for the time you spend doing it. You have never formally performed a business valuation before and have no expertise in this area. Would you provide this service?

(b) Realising that this is an area that you could include in your continuing development programme, draw up a plan to show how you would incorporate it into your development cycle.

(c) Why is reflection a necessary part of your development plan? Explain the benefits of completing a reflective account.

You should allow 35 minutes to complete this task

TASK 7

As part of your job you oversee a number of customer accounts and you like to check that everything is going well. You notice that a new customer has just returned 5,000 units – a quarter of his order – and you are curious why. You have a chat with the salesperson that took the order and it transpires that the customer only wanted 15,000 units and was authorised to spend up to £15 on each unit. For that size of order, the price would have been £16 per unit. Customers need to order 20,000 units to get them at the lower price of £15 so the salesperson had suggested to the customer that he ordered 20,000 units to obtain a discount and bring the price down to £15 each and return the 5,000 he didn't need. The way the return policy works meant he could give back the 5,000 units during the first two weeks of the contract and the price would remain the same. He would get 15,000 units at £15 each. The salesperson's commission is based on the sales total after the two-week period so no one was being misled.

Can the requirement to compete and deal ethically be breached by this kind of arrangement – one that actually benefits the customer?

You should allow 10 minutes to complete this task

TASK 8

You and two others in your department have just had a message regarding your computers. They are all three marked as surplus and are going to be destroyed. You are going to get new ones even though the three of you, compared with the other eight in the department, have the most up-to-date units already and they all contain sensitive information. You are really concerned because you know the company has a shareholder court case pending and destroying information might be seen as an effort to cover-up and you share your concern with your supervisor – whose attitude is that the equipment belongs to the company and not to you. She told you she didn't have time to go into the details and asked you to just follow the instructions. What issues are causing you concern and what elements should an organisation's document creation and retention policies specify?

You should allow 10 minutes to complete this task

TASK 9

A friend of yours is in public practice and, knowing you are looking to improve your position at Cutting Edge and have still not heard anything about the new job since your interview, asks you to join him. He is more qualified than you and has had to turn away potential clients because he feels that his fees would be too high for the type of services they require.
If you were in public practice there are several areas that you would be lacking in experience. These include:
(a) Letters of engagement;
(b) Methods of charging for your consulting services;
(c) Obtaining professional work; and
(d) Handling client's monies

Outline the main points to be aware of for each of the above.

You should allow 25 minutes to complete this task

PRACTICE SIMULATION 2
ANSWER BOOKLET

TASK 1

Ethical principles	I have a responsibility to:
Competence	
Confidentiality	
Integrity	
Objectivity	

TASK 2

TASK 3

Is it any of your business?

What should you do?

Who should you speak with about your situation?

What will be the likely impact on your employment?

TASK 4

(a)

(b)

TASK 5

(a)

(b)

TASK 6

(a)

(b)

(c)

TASK 7

TASK 8

TASK 9

(a) Letters of engagement

(b) Methods of charging for your consulting services

(c) **Obtaining professional work**

(d) **Handling client's monies**

KEY TECHNIQUES
ANSWERS

Chapter 1
Ethics – Principles and procedures

△ ACTIVITY 1 △△△△

The duties of the committee must be to:
·   hold regular meetings to discuss ethical issues
·   deal with 'grey' areas
·   communicate the code to all members of the organisation
·   check for possible violations of the code
·   enforce the code
·   reward compliance and punish violations
·   review and update the code.

△ ACTIVITY 2 △△△△

A compliance-based approach is designed to ensure that the organisation complies with the relevant law. Compliance means doing what one must do, because it ought to be done. Codes usually only address employee conduct, and are designed primarily to protect a company from prosecution or litigation. They emphasise following rules or written procedures and seeking guidance if a specific rule cannot be found. Any violations are prevented, detected and punished.

An integrity-based approach enables legal and responsible conduct. Codes emphasise knowing the basic values or principles which are intended to drive decisions and actions within a group. The activities assimilate values into company systems, provide guidance and consultation, identify and resolve problems and oversee compliance. The approach emphasises managerial responsibility for ethical behaviour, as well as a concern for the law. Integrity means wanting what ought to be done.

△ ACTIVITY 3 △△△△

Presentation on professional ethics

Slide 1 – Integrity

Members should be straightforward and honest in performing professional work

Do not subvert the organisation's legitimate objectives

Communicate unfavourable as well as favourable info.

Avoid activities that could affect your ability to perform duties

INTEGRITY

Avoid conflicts of interest and advise others of potential conflicts

Refuse gifts or favours that might influence behaviour

Recognise and communicate personal and professional limitations

Refrain from activities that could discredit the profession

KAPLAN PUBLISHING

Slide 2 – Objectivity

Members should be fair and should not allow prejudice or bias or the influence of others to override objectivity

Slide 3 – Professional and technical competence

Members should refrain from undertaking or continuing any assignments which they are not competent to carry out unless advice and assistance is obtained to ensure that the assignment is carried out satisfactorily.

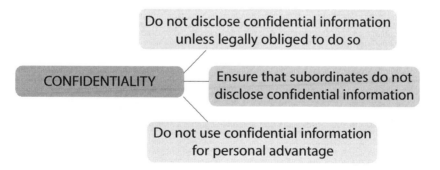

Slide 4 – Confidentiality

Members should respect the confidentiality of information acquired during the course of performing professional work and should not use or disclose any such information without proper and specific authority or unless there is a legal or professional right or duty to disclose.

Slide 5 – Professional behaviour

Members should act in a manner consistent with the good reputation of the profession and refrain from any conduct, which might bring discredit to the profession.

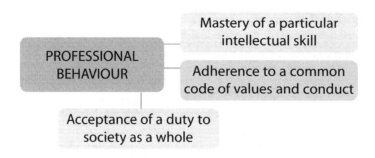

Slide 6 – Due care

A member, having accepted an assignment, has an obligation to carry it out with due care and reasonable despatch having regard to the nature and scope of the assignment.

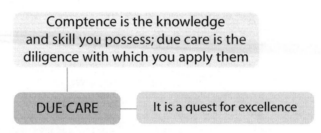

△ ACTIVITY 4 △ △ △ △

Professional competence may be divided into two separate phases:
Attainment of professional competence – this requires specific education, training, assessment or examination in professionally relevant subjects and, whether prescribed or not, a period of relevant work experience in finance or accountancy.

Maintenance of professional competence – this requires a continuing awareness and application of developments in the accountancy profession including relevant national and international pronouncements on accounting, auditing and other relevant regulations and statutory requirements. To achieve this, a programme of a minimum of thirty hours continuing professional development (CPD) is recommended each year.

Members should adopt review procedures that will ensure the quality of their professional work is consistent with national and international pronouncements that are issued from time to time.

△ ACTIVITY 5 △ △ △ △

A 'gift' is made with 'no strings attached' in the interest of, for example, building a business relationship or expressing thanks.

A 'bribe' occurs if you accept or give something of value to someone in return for something else, such as the award of business or the exercise of the other's discretion or influence.

A 'kickback' is something of value provided for the purpose of improperly obtaining or rewarding favourable treatment in connection with the award of a contract.

KAPLAN PUBLISHING

△ ACTIVITY 6   △ △ △ △

Here are some helpful tips when considering whether to accept a gift:
- Cash gifts are never appropriate.
- Do not accept a gift if it could cause you to feel an obligation.
- Do not accept a gift from a vendor if it may give the vendor, other suppliers or sub-contractors the impression that they have to provide similar gifts or favours in order to obtain company business
- Do not justify accepting a gift by arguing, 'Everybody else does it,' 'I deserve a break today,' or 'No one will ever find out.'

Chapter 2
Ethical conflict

△ ACTIVITY 1   △ △ △ △

The answer is false. No single communication can list all the ethical dilemmas that will be encountered or how to resolve them. Knowledge of the laws, our policies and the Code is important in recognising and resolving ethical dilemmas, but practicing these lessons and building them into everyday behaviour is the way they have meaning. This helps create a culture of integrity and 'doing the right thing'. When this occurs we are able to spot and resolve less common ethical dilemmas even if they are not specifically listed in the Code.

△ ACTIVITY 2   △ △ △ △

There are four characteristics of an ethical dilemma. All four must be present to satisfy the definition that an ethical dilemma exists:
1. There must be at least two courses of action from which a choice must be made as to the action to be taken.
2. There must be significant consequences for taking either course of action.
3. Each of the courses of action can be supported by one or more ethical principles.
4. The ethical principles supporting the unchosen course of action will be compromised.

△ ACTIVITY 3   △ △ △ △

The answer is true. The Code of Business Conduct deters wrongdoing, promotes honest and ethical conduct and compliance with laws, rules and regulations. Knowing the code helps you identify ethically challenging situations and make the right decisions. It also encourages and governs prompt internal reporting of potential violations and ensures accountability for everyone it covers. The Code of Business Conduct is one of the most important communications you will ever receive regarding workplace conduct.

△ ACTIVITY 4   △ △ △ △

The employee is right to be concerned about the situation. Even though he or she is not a director, officer or even in management, insider trading laws and employer policies apply to all employees. It is not clear whether the information received would be classed as material information that would disqualify a person from buying or selling shares in the company. The best advice would be to consult the manager.

△ ACTIVITY 5 △△△△

The answer is true. Generally this statement is correct. However, some employees may be required to comply with company policies for pre-clearance of transactions. Insider trading is a very serious charge that can lead to civil and criminal prosecution. If you have any doubt check with your manager or legal department.

△ ACTIVITY 6 △△△△

The answer is true. The 'window period' is generally a good time for trades, but it is not a 'safe harbour'. There is always a risk of liability for insider trading if you are in possession of material non-public information about the company.

Chapter 3
Communications and interpersonal skills

△ ACTIVITY 1 △△△△

We obviously cannot draw an organisation chart of your organisation but the one shown below is a general overview of one.

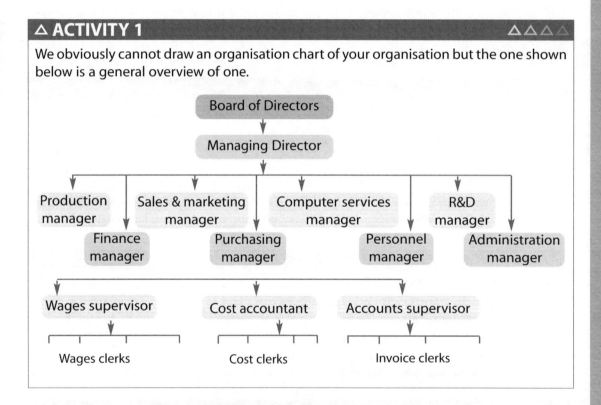

△ ACTIVITY 2 △△△△

· Win-lose or lose-win – one of you gets the window seat and other does not. The result could be a broken relationship within the team.
· Lose-lose means that neither of you get it. Someone else from the team may have taken advantage of you arguing and benefited. This will be another cause for a breakdown in the working relationship.
· A compromise would be to get the window seat on alternative days or weeks. This would result in half satisfied needs.

· Win-win would be to discuss what each of you want from the seat. You may want the view; your colleague may want better light. This offers options to explore e.g., what other ways are there for improving the lighting conditions; can your desk be moved so that you have a better view. This result shows a positive intention to respect both parties wishes equally, with benefits for team communication and creative problem-solving.

△ ACTIVITY 3 △△△△

Your domestic problem should be explained to your line manager.

There are several possibilities here. You could discuss it with more experienced colleagues; or you could find out who used to prepare the report before it was assigned to yourself; or you could ask your line manager for a suitable briefing or training.

You will certainly need to discuss this with the subordinate concerned. You may also need to refer the matter to a higher authority – your own line manager perhaps, or the personnel department – if this kind of shortcoming is persistent.

Chapter 4
Continuing professional development

△ ACTIVITY 1 △△△△

Continuing Professional Development brings benefits to the individual:
· It has a positive impact on job satisfaction and motivation.
· It increases skill levels and flexibility.
· It can confer professional recognition and enhance career prospects.
· It empowers individuals to take responsibility for their own development.
· It can increase self awareness, self confidence and respect from colleagues.

And to the employing organisation:
· It can save money as investment in development becomes more focussed and cost effective.
· It can improve retention. Employees who are given development opportunities are more likely to stay with the organisation.
· Organisations benefit from up to date skills and knowledge.
· It can make recruitment easier. Employers who offer development opportunities gain good reputations.

△ ACTIVITY2 △△△△

There are different ways of learning and people learn more effectively if they are aware of their own learning style preferences. Honey and Mumford identified four learning styles:
1. Activists – these learners are interested in novelty. They willingly become involved in new experiences and are attracted to different ideas and approaches. However, they tend to give insufficient attention to the application that attracts them.

2. Theorists – these learners are most concerned about linkages and relationships. When presented with new information, they need to fit it into their overall existing framework. They are keen to reject ambiguities.

3. Reflectors – these learners must have time to think about new experiences or ideas that confront them. They are cautious with new material and can be viewed as indecisive because of their reluctance to draw quick conclusions.

4. Pragmatists – these learners are driven by a need to ensure that any new material they encounter can be applied in practice. They need to know if new ideas can work. They want to act quickly on new ideas and material.

These preferred learning styles can be accommodated when designing training programmes, as shown below.

· **Activists** – have a practical approach to training but tend to go unprepared. They are flexible, optimistic and open minded (not sceptical) and this tends to make them enthusiastic about anything new They prefer practical problems, enjoy participation and challenge, are easily bored and have a dislike of theory. Hands-on training is most suitable.

· **Theorists** – tend to be perfectionists who do not rest easy until things are tidy and fit into a rational scheme. They require their learning to be programmed and structured; designed to allow time for analysis; and provided by people who share the same preference for ideas and analysis.

· **Reflectors** – need an observational approach to training. They need to work at their own pace - slow, cautious and non-participative – where conclusions are carefully thought out. Reflectors are thoughtful people who prefer to take back seats in meetings and discussions. They do not find learning easy – especially if rushed

· **Pragmatists** – need to see a direct value and link between training and real problems and aim to do things better. They enjoy learning new techniques and tasks and are good at finding improved ways of doing things. Pragmatists are essentially practical, down-to-earth people who like making practical decisions and solving problems. However, they get impatient if new ideas do not reflect themselves in practical applications.

△ ACTIVITY 3   △ △ △ △

Effective personal development planning depends on setting appropriate objectives. Effective objectives are:

Specific	rather than broad or general in nature
Measurable	because you will need to know what will constitute success
Achievable	because there is no point in setting unachievable objectives, although they should not be too easily achievable
Relevant	to your career and development
Timebound	so you have target dates for each step in your plan

Improve my IT skills is not a SMART objective! President JF Kennedy was about right when in 1961 he set America the ojective of getting a man on the moon: I believe that this nation should commit itself to achieving the goal, before this decade is out, of landing a man on the Moon and returning him safely to the Earth.

△ ACTIVITY 4 △△△△

The Development Cycle

· Establish the purpose – why is development required?
· Identify development needs – the development of a personal, structured and development plan (portfolio) to identify priority needs for planning of CPD. A portfolio is a collection of the employee's activities over a period of time and can be used to assess the accountant's training needs.
· Look at development opportunities – what kind of opportunites are there which might satisfy your needs?
· Formulate an action plan – plan the activity that will satisfy your needs.
· Undertake development – implementation (must be relevant and useful to the identified needs) of the plan.
· Record outcomes – what has been achieved as a result of the development activity?
· Review and evaluate – reflect on the whole process.

It is a cycle because it can now be re-entered by reflecting new learning needs. By following the Development Cycle, you will be able to identify and satisfy your own personal development objectives and at the same time maximise your contribution to your employers business objectives.

△ ACTIVITY 5 △△△△

1 Describe the problem situation – My employer just finished explaining how to operate a machine. I understand most of the details, but I am confused about one of the procedures.
2 Define the problem – I am afraid that, if I try to operate the machine, I may damage something. This could hurt my career. If I tell my employer that I don't understand all of the procedures, he may think that I am a slow learner. This could hurt my career. If I ask someone else how to operate the machine, I might get incorrect information that will damage the machine and still make people think that I am a slow learner.
3 Choose a solution – I could ignore my confusion and hope that I will 'figure it out' if I just try to operate the machinery for a while. I could try to catch another worker's attention and ask if he knows how to work this equipment properly. I could locate my employer right away and admit that I am still a little confused. Asking my employer for advice right away seems like my best solution. The employer should appreciate my honesty and I will avoid damaging equipment which is my most serious concern. It is the employer's job to explain how the equipment works.
4 Apply a solution – when I explain my confusion to my employer, I will point out that I was only unsure about one of the instructions. I will mention that I didn't want to damage any equipment. I like to work safely.
5 Evaluate the solution – I will probably know from the employer's reaction if I made the right choice, as far as he is concerned. If he seems reasonable and patient with this explanation it will tell me something. When I finally operate the machine (without incident or accident!) I will probably know I did the best thing possible.

Chapter 5
Culture and ethics

△ ACTIVITY 1   △ △ △ △

The third world country may regard poverty as its greatest social evil, and see a relatively small risk to employees as well worth taking. In this sense, it is not unethical for the technique to be used abroad, providing:

· those involved know the risks they take
· those injured are properly compensated
· the company takes every means available to reduce the risks.

The three points clearly result from decency and justice. Of course, if the host government were not concerned with the well-being of the population, such as in an occupation or military dictatorship, the ethics would be less clear cut. Even so, the company can still behave ethically if it keeps to the three points mentioned above.

The argument above does not extend as far as, say, dangerous pollution. In this case, those affected would not be those who are in a position to accept or reject the risks, and it would not be possible to apply the notions of decency and justice in any meaningful way.

Multinational ethical judgements are more problematic when considering cultural factors that do not necessarily relate to economic priority. For example, bribery, nepotism and dishonesty in tax affairs are considered normal in some cultures, but not others. As firms become more international, they are required to confront these issues. A firm ethical line on bribery is likely to lead to few orders. An honest tax return is effectively a subsidy to rival firms.

Donaldson argues that it is unethical to refuse to do business in such conditions, as this is to assert that ones own cultural norms are in some ways superior to those pertaining elsewhere. Instead, he produces two guidelines to help ethical decision-making.

1   Is it necessary to indulge in this behaviour to operate effectively?
2   Are basic human rights going to be violated?

In the first case, it may be possible to trade effectively without resorting to bribery and so on. For example, many of a global company's customers are other global companies, and it may well be the case that the local norms do not apply. However, it remains open to the global business to go along with such activities if no alternative exists.

In the second case, an affirmative answer should discourage the company from further investment and development.

△ ACTIVITY 2   △ △ △ △

In many countries, it is far from unusual for children to work, and they contribute a vital part of household income. The pressure group are anxious because it violates their own moral code, not that of the overseas country or the families of the children.

Withdrawing the business, or insisting that adult labour be used immediately may well

KAPLAN PUBLISHING

threaten the factory and local employment. It is not clear that this would be any less ethical than continuing without change.

A better approach might be to work with the factory to ensure that the children receive education, health care and conditions of service that would be rather better than they would get outside the factory, with the longer term view of replacing child labour. This compromise seems much less than ideal, but is perhaps the least unethical way forward from the present position.

△ ACTIVITY 3 △△△△

Loyalty and whistle blowing represent a classic example of competing values. Competing values are the basis for what are known as ethical dilemmas – a choice between competing 'rights' as opposed to a right versus wrong choice.

Loyalty is a strong value in our society. In the case of whistle blowing we often focus on loyalty to a fellow employee. But there is also the question of loyalty to the company – and loyalty is seen as a positive – a good thing to demonstrate.

Whistle blowing, on the other hand, has a less positive connotation in our experience. We don't have positive word images of people who engage in this activity. In fact we have very mixed messages. On one hand we demean 'rats, tattletales, snitches, informants' and the like. The other reality is that we have responsibilities to others which sometimes require us to 'tell'.

In extreme cases, it could be argued that loyalty wins out over whistle blowing and can be blamed, in part, for the debacles at Enron and WorldCom.

At a practical level, most employers have a reasonable expectation that when an employee is in possession of information about a potential threat to the well being of the organisation, its employees or interests, that employee has an affirmative responsibility to bring that information forward. This is often detailed in employee codes of conduct and supported by the creation of special helpline/hotline functions to receive such calls while protecting the identity of the caller.

One position to take is that, barring extenuating circumstances, employees have an obligation to their employers to act in ways which serve that employers' legitimate (and legal) interests – including the reporting of actions by fellow employees (up to and including the Board of Directors) which act against those interests and/or the public good. Loyalty to a friend should not come into the equation since no true 'friend' would put you in a position where you had to choose between doing what is right and protecting that same friend from the consequences of something they should not have done in the first place.

△ ACTIVITY 4 △△△△

This is a depressingly common situation. In an immoral company, the guidelines are there to defend senior managers, and the company, from blame when outsiders discover dubious activities. In truth, there is little that the young manager can do if he believes that it is ethical to stick to the guidelines.

Chapter 6
Ethics in public practice

△ ACTIVITY 1   △ △ △ △

The important information the letter evidences includes:
· Who the parties are (Jack Bloggs' partnership and Mr Client).
· What the contract is about (the provision of book-keeping services).
· What the parties' addresses are.
· The date of the contract.
· The fact it has been agreed to.
· What work is going to be done for the price (writing up the sales ledger only). It is important to make this clear as this forms one of the most common areas of dispute.
· What that price is.
· Whether that price includes VAT (if the book-keeper is VAT registered).
· What charges will apply if the client wants extra work.
· What credit will be allowed (e.g. here, Mr Client is given 28 days to pay).
· What happens if the client does not pay (e.g. if Mr Client does not pay within 28 days, interest can be charged on Jack Bloggs & Co's bill and they can stop working for Mr Client).
· How the contract will come to an end (e.g. 30 days' notice either side).

To work effectively, a letter of engagement must be drafted in clear and certain terms. It must not be open to misinterpretation.

Extra terms can be built in easily – such as exclusion clauses or choice of law clauses that records which country's law and courts govern the agreement (important where the client is foreign or overseas work is envisaged).

△ ACTIVITY 2   △ △ △ △

Self-employed practitioners can seek publicity by drawing up a leaflet and distributing it locally but Derek's leaflet needs some corrections.

His advertisement might not comply with the law nor conform with the requirements of the British Code of Advertising Practice as to legality, decency, clarity, honesty and truthfulness.

The name of his practice is misleading. It identifies with royalty but Derek has no justifiable claim to the name and cannot demonstrate expertise in that particular area. It also gives an impression to the public that the firm is multi-partnered and broadly based when in fact it is a very small firm. And a practice with a mobile phone should not describe itself as 'international' merely on the grounds that calls can be taken overseas.

His claim to be 'the biggest and best in town' is subjective and incapable of substantiation, and should be avoided.

Derek's boasting of his creative accounting skills and his ability to reduce tax bills could bring the profession into disrepute and claiming to have the cheapest fees around would be unfair to other practitioners. He should not make comparisons unless they are objective, factual and verifiable, and relate to the same services. Instead of advertising that he has 'loads' of certificates, Derek should only admit to the ones that are applicable to the bookkeeping services he is offering.

FED UP WITH THE HEADACHE OF ACCOUNTING?
VAT man causing you problems?
Let us handle everything for you.

· VAT returns	· monthly figures
· annual accounts	· bank reconciliation
· cash flow	· using your system or starting from scratch

Good rates – friendly service – fully qualified – fully insured – any size of business – special rates for start-up businesses

Derek Debit
123 Somewhere Lane
Anywhere
London
Telephone: 07822865867

ROYAL INTERNATIONAL BOOKKEEPERS – THE BIGGEST AND BEST IN TOWN

FED UP WITH THE HEADACHE OF ACCOUNTING?
VAT man causing you problems?
Let us handle everything for you...

· 'creative' accounting	· reducing your tax bill
· VAT returns	· monthly figures
· annual accounts	· bank reconciliation
· cash flow	· using your system or starting from scratch

Good rates – friendly service – fully qualified – holder of LOADS of Certificates – fully insured – any size of business – special rates for start-up businesses – discounts for introductions to friends – cheapest fees around

Derek Debit
123 Somewhere Lane
Anywhere
London
Telephone: 07822865867

△ ACTIVITY 3 △△△△

The code of ethics outlined in the Guidelines on Professional Ethics requires that members should strive for objectivity in all professional and business judgements. Objectivity is a state of mind, but in certain roles the preservation of objectivity needs to be protected and demonstrated by the maintenance of a member's independence from influences which could affect his/her objectivity.

Porter & Co – the code of ethics gives clear guidance on the risk posed to objectivity by the acceptance of goods and services from a client. The value (£3,000) of individual golf club membership would not be considered to be modest and the threat to the audit objectivity of Porter and Co (if the memberships are accepted) is compounded by the fact that the total value of offer to the firm is £15,000 (5 x £3,000). On this basis, I would be concerned that objectivity could be, or be perceived to be threatened, and would strongly recommend that the partners politely decline the offer.

In addition to the above, I would also be concerned as to the motive of the managing director in making the offer. Given the total value of the offer, the timing of it (soon after the start of audit work) and the fact that it was made solely to the partners would alert me to the possibility that in return for the free membership, the company may have unreasonable expectations as to how the audit firm may respond when coming across contentious issues in the company's financial statements – for example, the inclusion of unacceptable accounting policies.

Bosworth and Company – the Code of ethics gives clear guidance on the risk posed to objectivity as a consequence of family and other personal relationships stating that 'objectivity may be threatened or appear to be threatened as a consequence of a family or other close personal or business relationship'.

The fact that an audit manager of Bosworth and Company is married to the new financial director of one of the firm's audit clients, clearly poses a potential threat to audit objectivity. Given that the financial director is responsible for the preparation of the company's financial statements, there may well be a perception of impropriety with regard to the figures reported if her husband (as a senior member of the audit team) has a role in the audit function. To avoid such a threat I would strongly recommend that the firm ensures that the audit manager has no involvement whatsoever with that audit (or any other) assignment relating to Thomson Limited. Given the size of the firm this should not unduly affect its operational efficiency.

My concern as to the possibility of perceived impropriety with regard to the figures reported in the financial statements, would be compounded by the fact that the financial director of the company will be entitled to an annual bonus based on the reported figures. Clearly she would have a vested interest in a high reported profit. Given this situation it is important that Bosworth and Company should be seen to be totally objective in their audit approach. Such an approach involves careful selection of staff for specific assignments such that all members of the audit team are totally impartial.

Olivers – the Code of ethics gives clear guidance on the risk posed to objectivity as a consequence of undue dependence on a client or group of connected clients where the receipt of fees represents a large proportion of the total gross fees of a member or of the practice as a whole. Currently fees receivable from the two connected companies owned by Thomas Ash, represent 8.7% (£72,000/£830,000) of Olivers' gross practice income. This would not appear to represent a threat to the perceived objectivity of the firm but acceptance of the third audit appointment would mean that 16.7% (£152,000/£910,000) of the firm's gross practice income originates from the three companies owned by Thomas Ash. This could call into question the firm's objectivity with regard to all three audit assignments, and in the circumstances it may be prudent for Olivers to politely decline the further audit appointment.

KAPLAN PUBLISHING

PRACTICE SIMULATION 1
ANSWERS

Task 1 (a)

Explanation	
Confidentiality	· Members should respect the confidentiality of information acquired during the course of performing professional work. · Members should not use or disclose any such information without proper and specific authority. · or unless there is legal or professional right or duty to disclose.
Integrity	· Members should be straightforward and honest in performing professional work.
Independence and objectivity	· Members should be fair · Members should not allow prejudice or bias or the influence of others to override objectivity.
Professional and technical competence	· Members should refrain from undertaking or continuing any assignments which they are not competent to carry out unless advice and assistance is obtained to ensure that the assignment is carried out satisfactorily. · Members also have a continuing duty to maintain professional knowledge and skill at a level required to ensure that a client or employer receive the advantage of competent professional service based on up-to-date developments in practice, legislation and techniques. · Members have a duty to maintain their technical and ethical standards in areas relevant to their work through continuing professional development.
Professional behaviour	· Members should act in a manner consistent with the good reputation of the profession. · Members should refrain from any conduct which might bring discredit to the profession.
Due care	· Having accepted an assignment, a member has an obligation to carry it out with due care and reasonable dispatch having regard to the nature and scope of the assignment.

KAPLAN PUBLISHING

TASK 1
(b)
Boat builders

The relationship with the son is a threat to objectivity in these circumstances. The fact that you have a better relationship would be enough to make it a problem, but the added incentive of the future work in his new venture makes it even more likely that there will be an issue with objectivity. In order to avoid lack of independence it would be advisable for another member of the firm to act as the mediator in these circumstances so that there would be no question over the objectivity and independence of mind of the firm.

The admission of 'theft' from the company by the son and the improper payment of the employee are both reportable to SOCA (or the Money Laundering Reporting Officer in your firm).

You should discuss the matters with the son to confirm the position and to point out the importance of the situation, particularly in the light of the potential sale as this may affect the sale value of the business (beware of 'tipping off' under the Money Laundering Regulations). You should then discuss the matter with the other director again stressing the importance of giving accurate information to a potential buyer of a business.

You should also consider whether it is appropriate for you to continue to act for a client who you know to be dishonest.

The above should be discussed with your partner before any action is taken.

Care home

The matters relating to the road maintenance and the rent are only suspicions and you have no evidence to support them. Both situations could be covered by a general written assurance from the owners that only business expenses are included in the accounts and that all income has been disclosed. You could pay particular attention to the invoice for road maintenance when preparing the accounts for the care home.

Similarly the apparent expensing of the boat in the care home accounts can be investigated and dealt with so that it is not reflected in the accounts of the business, if indeed it is the boat that has been put through the business.

The fact that the husband has told the wife that the boat cost less than it actually did is not an issue for you to deal with, you cannot use the information that you gained in the course of your work in this way.

Property developer

You have inside knowledge about the urgent need for the boat builders to sell their property, however it would be unethical for you to disclose this to the property developer.

However, in order to benefit both clients without compromising your professionalism you should ask the property developer if you may disclose his name to possible buyers. You could then tell the boat builder about the property developer and introduce them if appropriate. You should write to each to advise them to take independent professional advice regarding the sale and purchase so that your firm has no conflict of interest.

If you agree a reward from either party for your part in the transaction this must be transparent to both parties.

See below for the issue of the property developer and the art gallery.

Art gallery

You cannot specifically tell the art gallery owners about the property developer's plans; however it would be possible to encourage the property developer to let the art gallery know of his plans as soon as possible. You could also encourage the art gallery to check out there legal position with regard to security of tenure before going any further with their plans and putting too much time in to it.

The selling of your friend's prints should be discussed with the client and you should attempt to persuade them to correct the situation (beware of 'tipping off' under the Money Laundering regulations). If they will refuse to correct it you should take legal advice (having discussed the matter with your partner and reported it to the Money Laundering Reporting Officer). You should not disclose the matter to your friend.

Your brother-in-law

You cannot disclose confidential information to your brother-in-law, however, the audit report is on public record at Companies House and you could encourage him to look at the accounts before he takes on the new job. You could also discuss the matter with the client as to the advisability of taking on a new employee when they are in this financial position.

If and when your brother-in-law accepts the appointment you would need to make a disclosure about the family relationship to your firm who would then have an obligation to disclose the relationship to your client.

Your house

Members of the Association of Accounting Technicians must be seen as having honesty and integrity in all areas of their life and therefore it would be inappropriate to accept the offer. As this did not arise in the course of your professional work you have no reporting responsibility.

TASK 2

The trainee's impression of accountancy is misguided. Accountants do not generally receive gifts and if any large gifts are offered they should be declined.

The issue is whether the acceptance of a gift results in an threat to objectivity, whether actual or perceived. Therefore, whilst it may be reasonable to accept a bottle of wine at Christmas, it generally would not be reasonable to accept a holiday or any gift which represents a significant financial sum.

The client pays for the service that is provided and there should be no need for additional financial recompense. To an onlooker the gifting of significant value could suggest a lack of independence and therefore it should not be accepted.

TASK 3

Confidentiality

Employees of a company have a duty of confidentiality which remains after having left the company. The trainee should not be disclosing such detailed information about the company that he used to work for.

Conflicts of loyalty

An employee owes a duty of loyalty to both their employer and their profession. In this case there is a conflict between the two.

When members become aware that their employers have committed an unlawful act which could compromise them every effort should be made to persuade the employer not to perpetuate the unlawful activity and to rectify the matter. It would be advisable to discuss the matter with the Director of Professional Development at the AAT, and to seek legal advice.

Where the matter cannot be resolved the member should consider resignation.

TASK 4

Completion of time sheets and completion of expenses claims both assume honesty and integrity. It is well known that in some organisations it is common practice for people to claim more on expenses than they are really entitled to. This amounts to fraud. It can also be a temptation to be less than accurate about how time is spent when time sheets are filled in, which may result in time being charged to the wrong client and ultimately a client being billed for work that has not been done.

In order to promote high ethical values within an organisation the example has to come from the top. If the partners in a firm are seen to have a relaxed approach towards expense claims it is likely that this will filter down through the firm. If partners are seen to have high levels of honesty and integrity, staff will know what is expected of them and are more likely to maintain high levels of honesty.

Cases where people have not been honest should be dealt with firmly to demonstrate that it will not be tolerated.

TASK 5

You need to confirm with the client that you have authority to disclose this information.

When you do send the information you need to include a disclaimer making it clear that the information:
·   is confidential
·   is for the purposes of raising this particular finance only
·   has been prepared without carrying out an audit
·   has been prepared from information, records and explanations supplied by the client.

TASK 6

Your liability as a professional can not be limited by a lack of understanding or knowledge on your part and you must take steps to ensure the client is given correct advice.

Where you are unsure of your expertise in any area you must consult with an expert to ensure you are giving appropriate advice. If a matter is highly judgmental you should take legal advice.

This situation also raises the issue of your personal Continual Professional Development. You have a responsibility to ensure that you are sufficiently up to date to do your job properly. It may be appropriate to do your own research into this area which could consist of looking at the VAT website on the internet, reading appropriate text books, referring to the legislation, seeking advice from appropriate qualified individuals.

The fact that the client does not wish to pay for the service is an issue for the terms of engagement. You have to ensure that your fees have been agreed at an appropriate level which will enable you to do the work without the quality suffering. It is not improper to incorporate the work into the overall agreed fee, however you must ensure that the quality of work will not suffer.

TASK 7

You need to consider whether you have the expertise and knowledge to be able to answer these questions.

The question regarding the sum of money amounts to investment advice and you have to be clear as to whether or not you are authorised to give this type of advice.

Since this advice has not been subject to agreement of terms in any way and is outside the normal run of professional work, the preferred course of action would be to encourage the client to make an appointment to discuss the matter fully, and not to get drawn in to a full discussion under these circumstances.

If you respond to the client's queries you must be clear that the advice is informal and that consideration in depth may lead to a revision of the advice given.

TASK 8
(a)

Client's question / comment	Your response
How much will you charge?	Explain that fees are charged on basis of time spent and work involved. It may be appropriate to quote a fee if you have sufficient knowledge of the work to be able to do so, and you have the authority within your firm. You must ensure that the fee is sufficient to enable the work to be properly performed.

KAPLAN PUBLISHING

How do I get the information from my previous accountant?	The client should inform the previous accountant, telling them the name of the new accountant. The firm should then write a 'professional clearance' letter, asking whether there are any reasons why they should not act for the client and asking for the hand over information.
A friend of mine said his accountant would not release any information once he had changed accountants.	The accountant can retain documents belonging to the client when the fees relating to those documents are outstanding as long as the documents have come into their possession by proper means (this is a right of lien). They cannot retain documents where the fees relating to the work performed on them have been paid.
I would like you to hold some money on my behalf for reasons that I would rather not discuss. Can you do this for me?	You will need to establish the reason he wishes you to hold the money for him. If he is not prepared to tell you, you should not hold the money as there is a risk that it was obtained from, or is to be used for, illegal purposes.
The sign of a good accountant is how much tax they save you, how much tax do you think you will be able to save me?	This is a matter of educating the client into understanding the service you provide for him. You should never make an assertion as to the amount of tax that will be saved.

TASK 8

(b)

Do not proceed on this basis. This suggests either that he has not paid his previous accountant's fees in which case there is a possibility he will not pay yours, or that he is concerned about what the previous accountant will say in which case he may not be an appropriate client.

You should try to persuade him that you need to obtain professional clearance before you can act, and if he continues to resist you should suggest that he seeks an alternative accountant.

TASK 9

As this is a separate engagement, the terms must be agreed before commencing work. A letter of engagement should be prepared covering:

· the nature of the assignment, the scope of the work and the format and nature of the report to be produced

- the fact that this is not investment business
- the timing of the engagement (start and completion dates)
- duration – i.e. the fact that the engagement is not recurring
  the client's responsibilities in terms of the provision of information
- the firm's responsibilities
- the basis, frequency and rate of charge for the service
- third parties – i.e. solely to be used to assist in raising finance from a specified third party, and is not to be used for any other purpose.

The letter must be signed by your firm and the client.

In these circumstances the charging of a contingency fee is acceptable.

TASK 10

Suggestion	Your comment
Point out how much lower our fees are than other local firms	Where members seek to make comparisons in their promotional material between their practices or services (including fees) and those of others, great care will be required. In particular, members should ensure that such comparisons: · are objective and not misleading · relate to the same services · are factual and verifiable
Point out that we give a better service than other local firms	· The comment above also relates to this. · Care must be taken to ensure that this sort of comparison does not discredit or denigrate the practice or services of others.
Offer a 25% discount for the first year to all new clients	· The issue here is what the 25% is on. · The firm must be very clear that it would be a 25% reduction on what would otherwise have been charged by that firm for that service. · It is not improper to charge a lower fee as long as the quality of work does not suffer.
Offer a commission to all staff for any clients introduced to the firm	· There is no problem with offering a commission to employees for introducing new staff.
When new employees join the firm from another practice, give them an extra incentive to bring clients from their old firm with them	· A member should have regard to the bad will which is likely to result from soliciting the client of an employer whose service they have recently left. · A member should act professionally and with integrity in this respect.

Offer a free initial consultation for every potential client	· There is no problem with offering a free consultation at which levels of fees are discussed.
Offer a commission to existing clients for any new clients they introduce to the firm	· A member should not give, share or offer any commission, fee or reward to a third party (other than an employee) in return for the introduction of a client unless the client is aware of the arrangements with that third party and · either the third party is a member of a body which is governed by comparable ethical standards, or · the third party complies with ethical standards comparable to AAT and the member accepts responsibility for ensuring that the introduction is carried out in accordance with such standards.

PRACTICE SIMULATION 2
ANSWERS

TASK 1

Ethical principles	I have a responsibility to:
Competence	· Maintain an appropriate level of professional competence by ongoing development of my knowledge and skills. · Perform my professional duties in accordance with relevant laws, regulations, and technical standards. · Prepare complete and clear reports and recommendations after appropriate analyses of relevant and reliable information.
Confidentiality	· Refrain from disclosing confidential information acquired in the course of my work except when authorised or unless legally bound to do so. · Inform subordinates as appropriate regarding the confidentiality of information acquired in the course of their work and monitor their activities to assure the maintenance of that confidentiality. · Refrain from using or appearing to use confidential information acquired in the course of my work for unethical or illegal advantage either personally or through third parties.
Integrity	· Avoid actual or apparent conflicts of interest and advise all appropriate parties of any potential conflict. · Refrain from engaging in any activity that would prejudice my ability to carry out my duties ethically. · Refuse any gift, favour, or hospitality that would influence or would appear to influence my actions. · Refrain from either actively or passively subverting the attainment of the organisation's legitimate and ethical objectives. · Recognise and communicate professional limitations or other constraints that would preclude responsible judgement or successful performance of an activity. · Communicate unfavourable as well as favourable information and professional judgements or opinions. · Refrain from engaging in or supporting any activity that would discredit the profession.
Objectivity	· Communicate information fairly and objectively. · Disclose fully all-relevant information that could reasonably be expected to influence an intended user's understanding of the reports, comments, and recommendations presented.

TASK 2

There are two ethical issues described in this scenario. The first concerns insider dealing (sometimes called insider trading) and the second issue is about confidentiality.

Employees – and especially accountants – have an obligation to respect the confidentiality of information about an employer's or a client's affairs acquired in the course of their work. Confidentiality is not only a matter of disclosure of information. It also requires that anyone acquiring information in the course of performing his or her work will not use that information for personal advantage or for the advantage of a third party. The duty of confidentiality continues even after the end of the relationship between the professional and the employer or client.

There are two types of insider dealing: legal and illegal. Illegal insider dealing is the buying or selling of a security of a company (eg. shares, bonds or share options) by insiders who possess or who have access to material non-public information – this is important information about a company that affects its share price or might influence investor's decisions. The act puts insiders in breach of their fiduciary duty.

The company executives obviously have material information. The senior sales person in the scenario knows how much the company has sold and whether it will meet the estimates it has provided to investors. Others within the company also have material information. The accountant who prepares the sales forecast spreadsheet and the administrative assistant who types up the press release also are insiders.

Insider dealing is a serious issue and your room mate is right to be concerned about the situation. Even though she is not a director or even in management, insider dealing laws and employer policies apply to her. They apply to all employees. It is not clear whether your room mate actually received any material information that would disqualify her from buying or selling shares in the company but she should seek advice from her manager and let her company know what she heard over lunch. After that she would be able to select the best course of action. Some companies announce times to their employees when they can safely trade without being accused of trading on inside information

As well as the issue of insider dealing, your friend should be reminded that confidential information needs to stay confidential, even if she is talking to her family or best friend. She needs to familiarise herself with her employer's confidentiality policies and any other applicable restrictive covenants.

TASK 3

Is it any of your business?
Incorrectly recording expenses and revenue to an employer's benefit for taxation purposes, even though a lot of companies may do it, still does not make it right. You should not condone the use of any statement that is misleading, false or deceptive. Financial information should clearly describe the true nature of business transactions, assets and liabilities. It should classify and record entries in a timely and proper manner. As an AAT member, you should do everything that is within your power to ensure that this is the case, and in particular that such information is in accordance with accepted accounting standards. Regardless of service or capacity, you should protect the integrity of your professional services, maintain objectivity and avoid any subordination of your judgement by others.

What should you do?
In applying the standards of ethical conduct, you may encounter problems in identifying unethical behaviour or in resolving an ethical conflict. As an employee you owe a duty of

loyalty to the employer and also to the profession. In this situation there is a conflict between the two because of the employer's actions and you should try to persuade him or her to behave lawfully. In most companies, when faced with significant ethical issues, you should follow the established policies of the organisation bearing on the resolution of such conflict.

Who should you speak with about your situation?
You should consider the following courses of action.

· Discuss the situation with your immediate superior except when it appears that he or she is involved, in which case the problem should be presented initially to the next higher managerial level. If a satisfactory resolution cannot be achieved when the problem is initially presented, submit the issues to the next higher managerial level. If the immediate superior is the chief executive officer, or equivalent, the acceptable reviewing authority may be a group such as the audit committee, executive committee, board of directors, board of trustees, or owners.

· Contact with levels above the immediate superior should be initiated only with the superior's knowledge, assuming the superior is not involved. Except where legally prescribed, communication of such problems to authorities or individuals not employed or engaged by the organisation is not considered appropriate.

· Clarify relevant ethical issues by confidential discussion with an objective advisor

What will be the likely impact on your employment?
If the ethical conflict still exists after exhausting all levels of internal review, there may be no other recourse on significant matters than to resign from the organisation and to submit an informative memorandum to an appropriate representative of the organisation. After resignation, depending on the nature of the ethical conflict, it may also be appropriate to notify other parties.

TASK 4

(a) The difference between a gift and a bribe is in the intent of the giver. If there an explicit or implied expectation of something (of value) in return and/or if a reasonable person, knowing the details of the transaction would presume such an expectation/obligation to exist, then it is a bribe.

Offering or accepting gifts, entertainment or other personal favours or benefits from customers, suppliers, contractors or competitors may present a conflict of interest. Employees should consider whether a gratuitous transaction is consistent with accepted business practices and whether, in the view of an independent observer, public disclosure of the matter would embarrass the company. It is always improper for employees and members of their immediate family to request anything that could be construed as an attempt to influence the performance of duties. Procurement decisions must be made on the basis of quality, service, price, delivery, value for money, or other similar factors. Some gifts or benefits of token or small value are acceptable; others are not. When in doubt, seek the opinion of your supervisor.

(b) Money laundering refers to introducing money from criminal sources into the legal business cycle.

To prevent involvement in transactions possibly related to money laundering, all employees should look out for any business processes that are conducive to or suggest the possibility of money laundering and document any suspicious elements.

Signs of suspicious behaviour in the case of new customers include:
· Checking their identity is proving to be difficult. The customer is reluctant to provide details
· The customer is trying to use intermediaries to protect their identity or to hide their involvement.
· There are unusual requests for delivery or collection
· The source of the funds (especially cash) may not be known or may not be reasonable.
· The customer has been introduced by an overseas bank, another client or a third party based in a country where the production of drugs, drug trafficking, terrorist or money laundering activities are prevalent or which does not have money laundering legislation or regulations or a standard equivalent to the European Union Money Laundering Directives.

In the case of regular and established clients:
· The transaction does not seem reasonable in the context of normal business.
· The size and frequency of orders is not consistent with normal activities.
· The pattern of transaction has changed since the business relationship was established
· Money is paid by a third party who does not appear to be connected with the customer

You must report as soon as practicable any suspicions you have about a business deal you are involved with. Be careful not to tip off the customer that you are suspicious as that in itself could constitute a criminal offence. You do not have to make further enquiries or investigations to support your suspicion that money laundering has or is taking place, this will be carried out by the authorities.

TASK 5

(a) **When is disclosure justifiable**?
Whistle blowing occurs when a worker raises a concern about dangerous or illegal activity that they are aware of through their work – in this case it is harassment. The justifiability of a whistle blowing act revolves around issues such as the manner of the disclosure, the reasons for it, and the motives that lie behind it. It would appear reasonable to claim that whistle blowing is only justifiable where certain minimal conditions have been met. A justifiable disclosure is arguably one which:
· does more good than harm
· serves some purpose in correcting or preventing the wrongdoing concerned
· is made in a responsible manner
· follows upon the exhaustion of internal channels of complaint and redress

(b) **Policy on harassment**
The company should support a workplace that is free from unlawful harassment and expect that all employees will treat each other with fairness and respect. Harassment on the basis of race, colour, national origin, religion, sex, disability or sexual orientation must not be tolerated as it is strictly prohibited

Harassment includes, without limitation, verbal harassment (derogatory statements, slurs, epithets), physical harassment (assault, physical interference), visual harassment (cartoons, drawings, postings, e-mail) and innuendo. Sexual harassment includes unwelcome sexual advances, requests for sexual favours or other visual, verbal or physical conduct of a sexual nature that is made a term or condition of employment or is used as the basis of employment or advancement decisions, or has the purpose or effect of unreasonably interfering with work or creating an intimidating, hostile or offensive work environment.

Any retaliation against an individual who has complained about harassment or discrimination, or against an individual for cooperating with a discrimination or harassment investigation, should also be prohibited. No person should be subject to discipline, retaliation, intimidation, or any other adverse treatment because he or she has made a complaint of discrimination or harassment in good faith.

TASK 6

(a) One of the fundamental principles in the AAT's guidelines on professional ethics – professional and technical competence – states that, in agreeing to provide professional services, a professional accountant implies that there is a level of competence necessary to perform those services and that his or her knowledge, skill and experience will be applied with reasonable care and diligence. You must therefore apologise to the customer/client and refuse to perform the valuation, as you are not competent to carry it out without appropriate advice and assistance to ensure that it is performed satisfactorily.

You should also be aware of any real or apparent conflict between your personal interests and those of the company you work for. A conflict of interest may arise if you:
· worked as a consultant in a private capacity for a supplier or trade customer;
· carried on a business in your own time of a similar nature to your work in the company;
· sought personal gain to the detriment or prejudice of the company in business or private dealings

(b) **The development cycle**
By following the development cycle, you will be able to identify and satisfy your own personal development objectives and at the same time maximise your contribuition to your employers business objectives. The stages in the cycle include:
· Establish the purpose (Why is development required?) – you have a responsibility to ensure that you are sufficiently up to date to do your job properly.
· Identify development needs (What specific developments needs do you have at this time?) – to understand business valuation you need to know about basic valuation standards of value, research techniques, analysis of financial statements and company risk factors, and the asset approach to value.
· Look at development opportunities (What kind of opportunites are there which might satisfy your needs?) – there are specialist courses, text books and qualified individuals who can give advice.
· Formulate an action plan (Plan the activity that will satisfy your needs)
· Undertake development (Undertake the selected activity)
· Record outcomes (What has been achieved as a result of the development activity)
· Review and evaluate (Reflect on the whole process)

(c) **Keeping a reflective account**
Reflection means looking back on an experience and making sense of it to identify what to do in the future. Completing a reflective account can provide you with:
· enhanced understanding of the workplace
· a deeper knowledge of the skills neccessary for work
· an ability to analyse and improve your own performance

· self knowledge of strengths and weaknesses
· knowing the effect you have on other people and how things affect you

Reflection helps you repeat what was effective, learn from mistakes, and it can build confidence. It is an effective way of identifying development needs and is an important part of the Continuing Professional Development process. It will also help you focus on the learning derived from training and development activities.

TASK 7

The requirement to compete and deal ethically is intended to convey the values of honesty, candour and integrity in business transactions. Failure to apply such values violates the Code of Conduct regardless of whether the victim is the customer or the company.

In this case, the sales manager is asking for a commitment that inflates the number of orders by 5,000 units solely to provide a price discount that would otherwise not be available. Under the circumstances nothing unethical would occur in the above transaction. The contract allows for part of the order to be cancelled and the price does not change. However, using the returns policy solely for the purpose of arriving at a lower sales price is dishonest and defeats the employer's pricing policy. It is unethical for this strategy to be proposed, and for it to be accepted, regardless of whether it is technically in compliance with the language of the contract.

Because this situation rewards dishonesty it may make the customer wary about the ethical values of the sales person, if not the entire company that he or she represents. It may make the customer question current and future dealings with the company.

TASK 8

Ownership of the computers is not the issue causing concern as no one is questioning the employer's property rights. The problem lies with the destruction of records that may be demanded as part of a legal investigation. It might be seen as an effort to cover-up.

A computer's hard drive may be viewed as a storage location for information under some circumstances. On the other hand, it would be wrong for you to create an extra back-up copy of the data since that would violate the records retention policy and potentially compromise confidentiality.

Appropriate document retention and accurate record keeping is so important in today's work environment. Companies should have clear document creation and retention policies and ensure that everyone in the organisation understands and complies with these.

A document *creation* policy should prohibit employees from generating unprofessional emails and describe other non-business documents that employees should not create or copy. A document *retention* policy is a set of guidelines that a company follows to determine how long it should keep certain records, including e-mail and web pages. It should specify, at a minimum, the following elements:
· identification of documents that should be retained;
· the period that specific types of documents should be retained;

·   the process for destroying documents; and
·   the circumstances under which document destruction should be suspended.

TASK 9

The main points to be aware of for each of the following are:
(a) **Letters of engagement**

    The purpose of the letter of engagement is to provide written confirmation of work to be undertaken and the extent of your responsibilities. It can be used to manage clients' expectations and is likely to be an important document in a dispute such as a claim for professional negligence.

    An engagement letter should set out the scope of the engagement and the terms of business, to include as a minimum:
    ·   the type of service to be provided and report to be produced;
    ·   the responsibilities of the client, including the obligation to provide full information;
    ·   quality of service and complaints procedures; and
    ·   fee arrangements including the general basis on which fees are computed and where practicable, the level of fees likely to be charged for any assignment.

(b) **Methods of charging for your consulting services**

    The ways of charging clients are numerous. There are hourly rates, by the job fixed rates, contingency, percentage or performance arrangements, flat fee plus expenses, daily fee plus expenses, and many other methods of charging for your consulting services.

    It is the usual practice to charge clients for the time spent on work done for them, so it is therefore essential to complete a weekly time sheet showing how you have used your time. The total number of hours worked should be accounted for on a daily basis, listing the hours spent on the work of named clients. Charging fees on a time basis can create transparency, which helps the client and practitioner see that value is achieved.

    Charges can be based on your annual salary, as this is a fair indication of the level of your knowledge, experience and ability. A common multiple used is 1.25% of your annual salary costs per day. For example, if you are paid £20,000 a year plus an employer's pension contribution of 5% of salary and employer's National Insurance of £2,560, your daily charge out rate is (£20,000 + £1,000 + £2,560) x 1.25 per cent = £294 per day. For a seven hour working day your hourly charge-out rate becomes £294/7 hours = £42 per hour.

    As well as being charged for the time you spend, you should also charge for expenses incurred in performing the work. These may include travel expenses where necessary, telephone calls, photocopying expenses and printing costs.

(c) **Obtaining professional work**

    You are permitted to promote and advertise your professional services, provided the methods used are consistent with the good reputation of the profession. Forms of unacceptable promotion of professional services include, but are not limited to, those that:
    ·   are false or deceptive
    ·   include the use of harassing conduct
    ·   create an unjustified expectation of favourable results; and
    ·   contain self-laudatory statements that are not verifiable.

KAPLAN PUBLISHING

Promotional material may contain any factual statement, but should not make disparaging references to, or disparaging comparisons with, the services of others.

Ways of obtaining professional work include:

- listings in trade and professional directories
- paying employees a bonus or another accountant/third party a fee for the introduction to a new client.
- approaching clients and non-clients by direct mail addressed to named individuals.
- telephone communications or personal visits
- personal introduction through the medium of a person known to both parties
- publicising your name, qualifications and other relevant information in connection with books, articles, interviews, technical releases etc.

(d) **Handling client's monies**

You must maintain one or more bank accounts for clients' monies. Such bank accounts may include a general client account into which the monies of a number of clients may be paid.

When you are entrusted with monies belonging to others you should:

- keep it separately from personal or firm monies and deposit it without delay to the credit of a client account;
- use it only for the purpose for which it is intended; and
- be ready to account for it to any persons entitled to such accounting.

If it seems likely that the client's monies will remain on client account for a significant period of time, you should, in agreement with the client, place it in an interest bearing account within a reasonable time. All interest earned on clients' monies should be credited to the client account.

You must not hold clients' monies if you know or suspect that such monies were directly or indirectly obtained from, or are to be used for, illegal activities.

INDEX

KAPLAN PUBLISHING

KAPLAN PUBLISHING